Social Development

Routledge Studies in Development and Society

Social Development

Critical Themes and Perspectives

Edited by

Manohar S. Pawar and David R. Cox

Routledge
Taylor & Francis Group
New York   London

First published 2010
by Routledge
270 Madison Avenue, New York, NY 10016

Simultaneously published in the UK
by Routledge
2 Park Square, Milton Park, Abingdon, Oxon OX14 4RN

Routledge is an imprint of the Taylor & Francis Group, an informa business

© 2010 Taylor & Francis
The rights of Manohar S. Pawar and David R. Cox to be identified as authors of this
work has been asserted by them in accordance with sections 77 and 78 of the Copy-
right, Designs and Patents Act 1988.

Typeset in Sabon by IBT Global.

Library of Congress Cataloging-in-Publication Data
   Social development : critical themes and perspectives / edited by Manohar S. Pawar
and David R. Cox.
      p. cm. — (Routledge studies in development and society)
   Includes bibliographical references and index.
   1. Community development.   2. Community development—Moral and ethical
aspects.   I. Pawar, Manohar S.   II. Cox, David R.
   HN49.C6S625 2010
   307.1'4—dc22
   2010002997

ISBN13: 978-0-415-87926-2 (hbk)
ISBN13: 978-0-203-84701-5 (ebk)

Contents

PART III
Ethical Issues in Social Development

PART IV
Future of Social Development

Figures

Tables

Acknowledgments

Successful completion of any edited book project depends mainly on several authors agreeing to contribute chapters to the book and cooperating with the editors until the end of the project. We deeply appreciate the time, effort, patience and cooperation of all contributors to this volume. Their names and details are provided under "Contributors" at the end of the book. We would also like to thank peer reviewers of the book for their valuable comments and suggestions. One of the editors (Manohar Pawar) received a Research Centre Fellowship, Institute for Land, Water and Society, Charles Sturt University (CSU) and a small publication grant from the Faculty of Arts, CSU, to work on this demanding project. Our thanks to Professor Ross Chambers, deputy vice-chancellor, academic; Professor Sue Thomas, deputy vice-chancellor, research; Professor Anthony Cahalan, dean, Faculty of Arts; and Professor Max Finlayson, director of the institute, for the fellowship and the grant. The editorial and production team at Routledge, particularly, Mr. Max Novick, Jennifer Morrow and Michael Watters greatly facilitated the publication of this book and we are grateful to them. Thanks also to Sally Goodenough for preparing the index. Most importantly, we would like to acknowledge the love and support of our families, without whose support a project like this could not be completed.

Manohar S. Pawar and David R. Cox

1 Introduction

Why a Focus on Social Development in the Twenty-First Century?

Manohar S. Pawar and David R. Cox

The main objective of this book is to discuss some critical themes and perspectives pertaining to social development and to demonstrate that a social development approach is both practical and in some ways more required in contemporary times than ever before. Indeed, we would argue that a major reason why we are today confronted with major problems at international, national and local levels is because the ideas and ideals behind comprehensive social development, as presented in this text, have never been sufficiently widely accepted and implemented.

This is why, at the end of the first decade of the twenty-first century, we see it as necessary to bring out a text on social development with an emphasis on the local level. Essentially, it is because not only have the hopes that many of us had for social development in the 1980s not been realized, but even the vision in many quarters appears to have faded. In the 1980s, we were part of a tremendously exciting and challenging enthusiasm for social development, were aware of a plethora of ideas and plans, and felt that the whole enterprise had the support of the international community, many nation-states and a flourishing non-governmental organization (NGO) sector. We were almost convinced that the goals of social development, well-being and quality of life, as commonly presented and seemingly widely espoused, would be largely met as the century drew to a close.

In many ways, this social development impetus climaxed in the World Summit for Social Development held in Copenhagen in March 1995. Much work at many levels went into preparation for this summit and into dissemination of its ten commitments (United Nations [UN] 1995, 1996). Already, of course, there had been many small-scale development projects and some notable larger-scale schemes dedicated to bringing many of these commitments closer to achievement. Yet somehow significant sustainable changes at the macro level were difficult to identify. By the end of the century, the world seemed not to have moved all that far in areas such as global poverty reduction or the provision of adequate health and education services for all. The nation-states, led by the UN, therefore seized on this change of century to enunciate and commit themselves to a set of Millennium Development Goals, most of them to be achieved if possible by 2015 (United

Nations Development Programme [UNDP] 2003). While not infrequently still referred to, another decade has passed with few indications that most of these goals will be met in global terms, despite some significant national success stories.

Two decades after the optimistic 1980s, the annual figures pertaining to poverty, infant and maternal mortality, morbidity rates and access to a variety of essential services make for dismal reading when read in the light of 1980s' expectations (see UNDP 1980–2010). Economic growth, heightened productivity and a range of technological developments have provided sections of the global population with a standard of living almost inconceivable half a century ago, yet have bypassed other sections almost completely. Inequalities within and between nations have reached staggering proportions, rightly regarded by some commentators as downright obscene.

However, it is not only that the most basic goals of social development have failed to be met in global terms, but also that the commitment to such is seemingly no longer there, or certainly not as strong. Of course there is still widespread engagement in the development field, especially at the aid level and through technology projects, but it appears largely not to be buttressed by a belief in or commitment to the goal of social development for all, despite the fact that some ministries and departments use social development in their nomenclature. Today we seem to be much more focused, and understandably so, on such matters as the potentially devastating impact of climate change; the impact of massive and largely uncontrolled global financial markets; the need to maintain or increase economic growth rates to support employment and high standards of living; a failure in many societies to act in an inclusive manner; and the migration implications of significant inequalities and, to a lesser degree, of aging populations and static or decreasing workforce numbers—all of which, of course, render the already vulnerable populations of the world even more vulnerable.

Hence the concern today in many quarters is not so much the identification of and commitment to social development processes and goals, as it was in the 1980s and 1990s, but gaining recognition for the potentially highly significant implications of climate change, uncontrolled asylum flows, unregulated global financial markets, failed states and widespread social conflict. Does this change of focus mean that social development is no longer relevant, or that it requires a new paradigm? Are we simply harking back to a past era when we bring out a book on social development in 2010?

For us, the answer to these questions is no. A social development that is truly multidimensional and multilevel is today more important than ever (see Chapter 2). We find it significant that, in the post–global financial crisis era, we hear commentators referring to the importance of resilience, self-reliance, meaningful partnerships, more inclusive societies, a better balance between market freedoms and government supervision, and a more cohesive and sustainable societal development process. There is a strong focus once again on identifying and addressing at least some of the root causes of the challenges confronting today's world, such as excessive dependency on technology and outsiders to solve problems, and on the unlimited use of increasingly scarce natural resources to meet perceived needs. It is widely seen as possible to address such root causes, at least in part, by identifying and developing the resources already inherently available at all levels, from the individual and household to national and global structures—a basic belief of social development.

In the so-called developed countries, there is, once again, widespread concern about how to achieve an adequate quality of life for all, equitable and effective education and health care services, appropriate welfare systems, sustainable employment markets, ecologically sensitive and sustainable housing and transport systems, and supportive communities in the face of, for example, high depression, drug abuse and suicide rates, alongside growing numbers of comparatively isolated elderly persons. At the same time, in a large number of developing and least developed countries, the overall quality of life for many inhabitants remains abysmally low, often in conjunction with poorly functioning governance systems. To us, these realities suggest that an appropriate approach to social development remains highly necessary across the wide diversity of countries in terms of development levels achieved to date.

Yet change is endemic, and the situation today is different in many ways from that which existed in the 1980s. First, globalization trends have continued to broaden and strengthen as global trade, the global financial industry, global communication systems, corporate activities and increasing human mobility render the globe a more interactive and interconnected unity than ever before, albeit with both positive and negative outcomes. Moreover, many contemporary challenges have necessarily presented as having global dimensions and calling for global responses. This is particularly obvious in the fields of climate change, migration movements and humanitarian aid in the face of natural disasters and postconflict reconstruction. Despite these trends, in many ways we are still in the very early stages of devising and implementing effective global systems, and ones in which a large majority of states trust and a majority of peoples have confidence.

Second, trends within many nation-states continue to signify a problematic national development level. One can point to the significant number of failed states, the high levels of corruption in probably a majority of states, inadequate levels of people's representation in governance and high levels of inequality in many states' outreach to, concern for and support of their commonly pluralistic populations and diverse local conditions. Many states have also been plagued by internal conflict and high levels of violence, and often for decades. While a number of commentators have wondered whether the nation-state is able to survive as a viable entity, there are few signs of its demise any time soon. However, national level social development has become and remains an even more important and more difficult level for achieving people's well-being than it was in the last century (see World Bank 1997).

A third difference from earlier times, at least in prevailing perceptions, concerns the local level within nation-states. Despite the fact that the local level has been, throughout post–World War II development activities, both commonly discussed and often the target level of mostly small-scale development intervention, there remained a widespread belief that the development of, and levels of well-being within, local levels were largely a consequence of developments at other levels. For example, it was assumed that adequate national economic growth levels and a reasonably effective system of governance would ensure that the local level would be at least reasonably well catered for. Increasingly, however, it has been realized that this is a false assumption. The fruits of even high levels of economic growth have often not been equitably distributed, while even relatively efficient governance systems have been frequently preoccupied with selected population groupings or geographical areas, and so engaged in a degree of biased development.

With time and after much experience, it became increasingly clear that the local level had to be seen as important in its own right, and deliberately brought into the overall social and economic development processes. Some referred to this need as localization (e.g., World Bank 2003), some as people-centered development, and many as grassroots, village/community or local development. This trend, however, occurred not only because it often seemed that many local levels were being neglected by the overall development process, but also and at least equally importantly because the local level usually contained the potential to make a significant contribution not only to its own development but also to national level development; moreover, it seemed that the national level often needed this contribution.

In addition to this change in perceptions regarding the local level, there seemed in practice to be an increased focus on the importance of specific types of activity at the local level. In many contexts, there has been significant reference to the caring community, or caring society manifested in large part at the community level and reflected, for example, by a seeming increase in local voluntary activity. There has been an increased interest in community organizing, with this activity being undertaken by a range of personnel, including the current President of the U.S., Barack Obama (Obama 2007). The community-garden movement has boomed in countries like the U.K., often using public land for shared community food production. Land care and other such movements have focused on local involvement in creating a healthy and sustainable local ecology. Community involvement in a range of service provision in areas like health, disability, education, local safety needs and accommodation has been increasingly apparent in many countries (see Stepney and Popple 2008). Self-help organizations in great variety have increased in number and coverage, and have been seemingly symptomatic of a perceived need to become more self-reliant as individuals, families, communities, and ethnic groups. Even in developed countries, but especially in developing countries, there are many good examples of local level social development, albeit often isolated ones (see Hazare 2003; Roy 1997; and Pawar 2010), suggesting the usefulness of their replication.

Do these changes at the international, national and local levels suggest that the focus today should be on issues other than social development? There are several levels to answering this question. At one level, the answer is that the focus today is, and possibly to at least some degree must be, on specific critical realities, rather than on general development trends or even root causes. For example, many saw it as necessary to take action against the realities prevailing in Saddam Hussein's Iraq and the Taliban-dominated Afghanistan, and lengthy, highly resource-intensive and very destructive wars have been undertaken. Similarly, the September 11, 2001, attack on New York's Twin Towers and other events resulted in a major focus on terrorism and its perceived sources, with major implications across a wide range of areas of international and national activity. As a final example, the widely perceived and highly significant pending consequences of climate change have brought this issue to center stage on many agendas. With these being only some of the very specific and immediate challenges of the twenty-first century, all with far-reaching implications, it is hardly surprising that social development has been pushed to much lower down on the agenda.

At a second level, the answer to our question is that particular national agendas are driven much more by party politics, with their underlying ideologies, than by visionaries, humanitarians, groups or processes preoccupied with general levels of well-being, however much societies may seem to revere the odd champion of such an approach, such as a Nelson Mandela. Political struggles in many nations have revolved not only around the preceding three crucial issues (involvement in controversial foreign wars, terrorism and climate change) but also around other very specific and usually highly politicized issues. For example, asylum-seeker situations have, across the Western nations, generated tremendous party political and often politically opportunistic heat, with usually little attention given to what these asylum flows really signify, especially at their points of origin. A second key example is the welfare field. With neither the "individual as responsible" market approach of the U.S. nor the welfare-state approach of parts of Europe, or any other approach for that matter, being a demonstrable success in terms of desired welfare outcomes or sustainable costs, political agendas continue to revolve around health, education, housing and related issues. A third important, but less dominant, example revolves around issues of pluralism and social inclusion. The many indigenous minorities, recent immigrant groups, migrant worker populations and other significant socially excluded groupings are often prominent in political agendas, as many nations supposedly seek to establish a socially inclusive society. When such issues are highly politicized, in party politics and election terms, not only are they unlikely to be satisfactorily resolved, but they also will commonly be trivialized in terms of the level at which their true nature is understood and possible intervention models are explored. Yet the very nature of political life today seems to suggest that this situation will not change, at least in the near future.

At a third level to answering our question, it is necessary that we reexamine the very concept of social development as an overarching paradigm for undertaking activities at all levels—international through local. While an eminently logical concept, as we seek to show in Chapters 2 and 3, is it still plausible to suggest that the concept of social development can ever be the key approach to all development? While economic development has tended to dominate to date, the preceding discussion suggests that it will continue to be very difficult for comprehensive social development to achieve center stage, and for additional reasons. It is natural that systems will often be swamped by pressing issues, driven in part by the fact that most people are preoccupied with pressing needs and comparatively unable to focus on what might be in their long-term best interests. It also seems highly likely that party politics will continue to dominate political life, ensuring that its agendas and the level of debate will be largely determined by party political interests. In contrast to both these trends, a social development-driven approach seeks to weigh up both short-term and long-term impacts, the interests of all parties in an inclusive sense, and the need to integrate economic, social, cultural and ecological factors when examining any situation and devising an intervention strategy. Is it then not only an implausible approach but also almost a utopian one, being a luxury not available to many social structures and situations? After all, even the nongovernment not-for-profit sector has largely failed to stay true to this social development vision, despite the confidence that many of us placed in it.

It is clear, then, that there do exist valid reasons why international and national structures will often tend to focus on short-term and somewhat politicized responses to specific issues far more than on long-term and comprehensive social development goals. Yet we would argue that to do so is always a grave mistake. We must strongly resist any tendencies for international and national agendas that seek responses to present challenges—such as failed states, terrorism and climate change—to be limited in how they address these challenges because they largely reflect prevailing power or political realities and are inclined to see these clearly important issues as able to be separated from a wide range of associated developmental factors. Only responses that are well based, in terms of a detailed understanding of any challenge in terms of its nature and root causes; comprehensive, in terms of taking into consideration the economic, social, cultural and ecological dimensions of any situation; and inclusive, in terms of engaging with any challenge at all the levels relevant and from the perspective of all peoples affected, will be sustainable and effective.

While this may seem to be an unrealistic goal in many contexts, it is possible to at least strive to operate at this level, even if complete success in many specific situations is unlikely. For example, the UN should seek to ensure that all international gatherings, such as the December 2009 conference on climate change, will be, as far as possible, influenced, or even ultimately guided, by social development considerations and goals. Similarly, both international and national bodies should seek to bring a social development dimension into all national deliberations. Both international and national decision making, on a wide range of issues, will often have implications for such basic matters as maintaining adequate food production, water availability, sustainable use of all natural resources, quality of life in rural and urban areas, and the maintenance of an ecological environment conducive to the well-being of all people. The social development dimension, if presented as suggested in these chapters, will often be ignored or overridden in specific contexts; however, it remains essential that it be presented, and in such a way that it might gradually come to be appreciated as an essential component of all decision making at international and national levels.

At the same time, however, an effective social development strategy must always contain a focus on the local level. This is partly because much international and national action will have an impact on local levels, and this impact cannot be seen as insignificant or irrelevant to all decision making because of the frequent widespread implications of this impact. As is argued in more detail in Chapter 3, this local level focus is necessary both in itself, in terms of improving living standards within local communities, and in terms of the potential impact of local level developments at the national level—both directly through such as social capital and natural resource development, and indirectly through political engagement of the local level in national developments. Whatever the extent of development progress at international and national levels, something can almost always be achieved at the local level if this level is effectively addressed by structures and professions concerned with overall social development. It is for these reasons that this book contains a strong emphasis on local social development.

Some readers will no doubt argue that a major aim of this book should have been to defend the very concept of social development in light of some significant critiques of it, emanating largely from academic circles. Without seeking to do justice to these critiques, some examples at this point may be helpful (see also Chapter 2). First, there are those who regard social development as essentially a critique of, and a preferable alternative to, economic development. With our multidimensional approach to social development, we do not see these as valid alternatives. In our view, the evidence is clearly that both are essential and interactive, with the nature and processes of economic development requiring as much adjustment to past experiences and twenty-first century conditions as any other dimension of social development. A second critique is to depict social development as communitarian in nature, while at the same time presenting a highly unrealistic or even idealistic view of the potential of most communities to engage in their own development. Our response here is that it is blatantly obvious that social development must occur at all levels, with no level being inherently more important than any other. Ours is, therefore, a multilevel depiction of social development. A related critique is that, at the ideological level, social development has been hijacked by the neoliberal camp, with social development being made to appear as placing responsibility largely on nonstate actors, thus allowing government to stand aside. In contrast to this, a key element of our approach to social development is that the state is always ideally a major player by leading in planning for social development, by creating an enabling environment within which other actors and levels can act, and by generating the resources almost invariably needed for social development, despite the focus on maximizing self-reliance. Finally, there are those who decry various common emphases in social development, such as participation, self-reliance, capacity building and partnerships. These issues are addressed in several chapters in the text. Here, let us simply say that there is a major difference between, on the one hand, seeking to maximize the undoubted benefits of a focus on such perspectives, and, on the other hand, arguing, as critics sometimes do, that such outcomes are seen as readily attainable and always effective, or that these perspectives are invariably accepted and implemented by the various approaches to social development. In our minds, they are important perspectives that should be regarded as helpful stepping-stones toward achieving sustainable development, if indeed specific situations are conducive to their promotion, which is clearly not always the case.

The preceding discussion may enable the reader to appreciate the reasons for the core focus of this book being on social development, with a specific focus on the local level. The book is organized into four parts. The first part contains a conceptual understanding of social development, presenting our conceptual understanding of both social development generally and local level social development. In the second part, "Critical Perspectives in Social Development," we have selected several critical themes that have dominated the social development literature and appear to us to be of central importance in the effective implementation of a social development approach. These are participation, self-reliance, capacity building and bottom-up approaches. These themes have been acknowledged in a wide range of contexts and a variety of ways. Therefore, we saw it as necessary to draw together this wide discussion and to present an overview of the nature and importance of each of these themes. However, it should be pointed out that the remaining two perspectives covered—namely, the partnership approach and personnel issue—are relatively much less discussed in detail in the literature, despite many references to both themes. We therefore saw it as necessary to address the partnership perspective and to present a model for developing an effective personnel strategy for implementing social development.

In the next part, Chapter 10, "The Ethics of Social Development," is a little different and is presented here as a significant contribution to this important but somewhat unexplored aspect of social development. In the last part, "The Future of Social Development," appreciating that the very idea and major features of social development have been the subject of ongoing debate in some circles, we acknowledge the need to remain open to new understandings and approaches by presenting one suggested new social development paradigm (Chapter 11). However, we do not regard the "new social development" presented in that chapter as being significantly different to the approach presented in Chapter 2. In the final chapter, drawing on the analysis in the previous chapters, we make some concluding remarks on and some suggestions regarding the future of social development.

The scope of the book is thus broad and international, while at the same time highly relevant to the local level in both developed and developing countries. It can be used as a textbook or reference source for undergraduate, postgraduate and higher degree courses, having been designed for the use mainly of newcomers to the social development field, whether these be students, development practitioners, policy personnel, or teachers, trainers, academics and researchers, particularly from within the fields of development studies, social work, social welfare, human services, and community and social development.

REFERENCES

Hazare, A. 2003. *My village—my sacred land*. Ralegan Siddhi. Ralegan Siddhi Pariwar.

Obama, B. 2007. *Dreams from my father*. Edinburgh: Canongate Books.

Pawar, M. 2010. *Community development in Asia and the Pacific*. New York: Routledge.

Roy, B. 1997. The barefoot college project, Tilonia. In *Integration of endogenous cultural dimension into development*, ed. B. Saraswati, New Delhi: IGNCA and D. K. Printworld. The book chapter may be viewed from the following website. http://www.ignca.nic.in/cd_05021.htm; the book content may be viewed from the following website. http://www.ignca.nic.in/cd_05.htm (accessed May 30, 2007).

Stepney, P., and K. Popple. 2008. *Social work and community: A critical context for practice*. London: Palgrave Macmillan.

United Nations. 1995. *World Summit for Social Development*. New York: Author.

———. 1996. Special section on World Summit for Social Development. *Social Development Issues* 18 (1): 67–84.

United Nations Development Programme (UNDP). *Human Development Reports 1980–2010*. New York: Oxford University Press.

———. 2003. *Human development report: Millennium development goals: A compact among nations to end human poverty*. New York: Oxford University Press.

World Bank. 1997. *World development report: The state in a changing world*. New York: Oxford University Press.

———. 2003. *World development report: Sustainable development in a dynamic world*. New York: Oxford University Press.

Part I

Conceptual Understanding of Social Development

2 Social Development

Manohar S. Pawar and David R. Cox

INTRODUCTION

The main argument of this chapter is that, despite conceptual ambiguity and different perceptions of it, social development as a goal, strategy, idea and ideal has remained with us. The term has passed though phases of popularity, decline and reemergence in varied manifestations. It has not been devoid of ideological orientations and has been greatly influenced by these. Despite all its ups and downs, we shall argue in this chapter that social development is practical and its goals achievable. To develop this core argument, the first section of the chapter analyzes several meanings of social development; the second traces its historical evolution and shows how social development draws strength from various theoretical/ideological traditions; and the final section discusses an emerging approach to social development. Achieving social development at all levels on a global scale is a challenging task, but we believe it is a practical and necessary task, provided people and institutions are willing to undertake it and committed to it.

WHAT IS SOCIAL DEVELOPMENT?

At the outset, it is important to raise this basic question of what is social development. Doing so reminds us of a story of the description of an elephant by visually disabled persons whose description was dependent upon the part of the elephant they touched and the way they sensed it. In response to one survey on social development content in social work education, a respondent from a developed country stated, "Anyway, at first it was difficult for me to understand the definition of so called 'social development'. In Japan we always use this term when we think of developing countries" (see Cox, Pawar and Picton 1997b, 35). When I approached a potential contributor to this volume, the reply was, "Unless the war in Iraq stops, writing about social development does not make any sense to me." We also have seen some social work educators' disinclination to consider social development. To some, it is not a clear and practical subject, and they reject it outright. Even when just the concept is used, it is often contested. Although in the current environment it is a real challenge to develop an acceptable view of social development, it is important to do so. However, we shall first look at how several scholars have conceptualized the term, and then take their thinking further with the ultimate aims of clarifying the concept and promoting its practice.

The word "social," as a prefix to development, is generic, broad and all-encompassing, and, wherever the word "social" is attached to other words in a similar way to its use in social development, the meaning gets diffused and generally creates confusion among users of this word to the extent that it is often taken lightly or casually. The root of the word social is found in Latin, where *socius* (noun) means "ally, confederate," but also, by extension, "sharer, partner and companion." Its adjective *socialis* means "of or belonging to companionship, sociable, social." Another Latin word associated with *socius* is *sociare*, which means "to join or unite together, to associate: to do or hold in common, to share with." *The Shorter Oxford English Dictionary* lists four meanings for the word "social" that emphasize, respectively, belonging, mutuality, group living, and activities to improve conditions of a society by addressing problems and issues.

Similarly, development (noun) as a suffix has different meanings and is used in a range of different fields such as biology, music, drama, sports, mining, building/housing, photography, politics and economics. Its dictionary meaning is derived from the verb "develop," which means "grow gradually; become or make more mature, advanced or organized" (Hornby 1992). Develop also means "to bring out the capabilities or possibilities of; bring to a more advanced or effective state; to cause to grow; to elaborate or expand in detail; and to bring into being or activity; generate; evolve." Thus, development connotes an act or a process: an act of improving by expanding or enlarging or refining, and a process in which something passes by degrees to a different stage, especially a more advanced or mature stage (Dictionary.com 2007).

To understand "social development" in a simplistic way, by combining the lexicon meanings of the two words, one thing is very clear, namely, that social development does not mean development of just one individual, one family, one neighborhood, one community, one corporation, one nation, one nation-state or one region. It also does not mean development of just one aspect of any entity, such as the economic or political, to the neglect of other aspects. Social development means the collective development of the whole entity, whatever that entity might be—thus growing, advancing, maturing step by step or stage by stage in an unified way, and comprehensively covering all aspects and dimensions of such entities as a society. Growth, advancement and maturity may be readily understood in a biological sense. But does this understanding apply to communities, societies and institutions? What is advancement? Is it progressing from one stage to a relatively better stage? Do well-developed countries present a matured, better stage, while many countries in Africa, Asia and Latin America present a poorer stage that needs to be changed to a "matured, advanced stage" as portrayed by developed countries? Do extreme increases in material production and wealth, to the extent of affecting the climate, violence within and between countries, and growth in the numbers of the isolated elderly, as we see in many developed countries such as the U.S. and Japan, constitute an advanced matured stage, and therefore the ultimate attainments of social development? Certainly, impressive economic growth and development, though necessary, is not social development. The world's collective growth, change, advancement, maturity and development raise fundamental questions in terms of development for what, for whom, how and for how long. Keeping these debatable questions in mind, it would be interesting to see whether these questions are addressed in the following definitions of social development.

Definitions of social development are varied and many, and they may be flexibly grouped under three categories depending upon the approach they follow. One category of definitions emphasizes, among other things, systematic planning and the link between social and economic development. A second group of definitions shows that bringing about structural change is the core element of social development. And a third focus is on realizing human potential, meeting needs and achieving a satisfactory quality of life. One of the critical issues in defining social development is its relationship with economic development. Is economic development embedded in social development, or is social development complementary to economic development? The 1995 World Summit on Social Development distinguishes the two and sees social development, without defining it, as necessary to complement economic development, and so do the UN Development Programme (UNDP) *Human Development Reports* in many ways. Some definitions seem to capture this issue by suggesting that social and economic development are different but at the same time juxtaposed.

Some definitions that focus on systematic planning and linking social and economic development are as follows:

> The concept of social development is inclusive of economic development but differs from it in the sense that it emphasises the development of the totality of society in its economic, political, social, and cultural aspects. (Gore 1973, 10)

> Social development is a process of planned social change designed to promote the well-being of the population as a whole in conjunction with the dynamic process of economic development. (Midgley 1995, 25)

> [Social development is] planned comprehensive social change designed to improve people's general welfare. The interrelatedness of major social problems requires the economic and cultural efforts of national

and international government structures and society's institutions and all its citizens. (Barker 2003, 403)

Some definitions that focus on structural change are as follows:

Social development is a comprehensive concept which implies major structural changes—political, economic and cultural, which are introduced as part of deliberate action to transform society. (Pathak 1987, 57–58)

Development should be perceived as a multidimensional process involving the re-organisation and reorientation of entire economic and social systems . . . [it] involves radical changes in institutional, social and administrative structures as well as in popular attitudes and even customs and beliefs. (Todaro 1997, 69)

Definitions that focus on realizing the human potential, needs and quality of life include:

Social development includes improvement in the quality of life of people . . . (a more) equitable distribution of resources . . . broad-based participation . . . in the process of decision making; and special measures that will enable marginal groups and communities to move into the mainstream. (Pandey 1981, 33)

Social development has two interrelated dimensions: the first is the capacity of people to work continuously for their welfare and that of society; the second is the alteration or development of a society's institutions so that human needs are met at all levels, especially at the lowest level, through a process of improving the relationships between people and social economic institutions. (Paiva 1982, 4)

Social development is the process of planned change designed to bring about a better fit between human needs and social policies and programs. (Hollister 1982, in Midgley 1993, 7)

Social development implies evolution and transformation through which people and societies maximise their opportunities, and become empowered to handle their affairs. (Mohan and Sharma 1985, 12–23)

Social development is directed towards the release of human potential in order to eliminate social inequities and problems. (Meinert, Kohn and Strickler 1984, 70)

The three basic components or core values of development are life-sustenance, self-esteem and freedom. (Denis Goulet 1971, in Thirlwall 1989, 8)

[S]ocial development is focused not only on the well-being of individuals, but more frequently than not on the achievement of the well-being and fullest possible human realisation of the potentials of individuals, groups, communities, and masses of people. (Billups 1994, in Lowe 1995, 2169)

[Social development is] a participatory process of planned social change designed to promote the well-being of the people, and which, as such, offers an effective response to the innate needs and aspirations of the whole population for the enhancement of their quality of life. (Cox, Pawar and Picton 1997a, 5)

The term social development can refer to: improvement in the welfare and quality of life of individuals; or changes in societies—in their norms and institutions—that make development more equitable and inclusive for all members of a society. (Davis 2004, iv)

A critical examination of these definitions clearly shows that the conception of social development differs from author to author. Some focus on the process, some on the outcome, and some on both. Some definitions include the meaning and purpose of social development, and what needs to be done to achieve it, whereas others cover only one aspect of it. The conceptual analysis suggests that social development is about systematically introducing a planned (sometimes radical) change process, releasing human potential, transforming people's determination, reorganizing and reorienting structures, and strengthening the capacity of people and their institutions to meet human needs. Additional goals include reducing inequalities and problems, creating opportunities and empowering people, achieving human welfare and well-being, improving relationships between people and their institutions, and, finally, ensuring economic development. Along with these concepts, it is also useful to look at the eight characteristics of social development presented by Midgley (1995, 26–28), although some of the eight may overlap with the preceding concepts as in reality they emanate from them. Four of these characteristics address the issue of process, clarifying what the process is about. These are positive change, progressive development, intervention through organized efforts and economic development. The other four characteristics refer to interdisciplinary theoretical bases, ideologically oriented strategies, an inclusive or universal scope, and the welfare goals of social development.

Although the precise nature of the concept of social development may be contested, controversial and debatable, few would disagree with its goals. Yet the social development literature offers little clarity about how these goals, values, strategies and process of social development can be implemented and achieved in the field. In other words, these concepts do not cover the "how" and "how long" of development and social development. Due to the lack of discussion on, or uncertainty regarding, the practical aspects of social development, some people may perceive it as a utopia or an ideal, and so not realistic. Thus, the greatest challenge for social development thinkers is to demonstrate that social development can be practiced and achieved in the real world. It is not a vague concept or relevant only to developing countries. Focusing on this issue of the practicality of social development, we may gain some insights from the historical origins and theoretical basis of social development.

HISTORICAL ORIGINS OF SOCIAL DEVELOPMENT

Early Civilizations

Readers of the history of social development may wonder whether it is possible to trace authentic and convincing historical origins of the term and practice of social development. The idea of change and social development, not the exact nomenclature itself, was there with the ancient Chinese, Greek and Indian civilizations. Pathak (1987) notes that social development ideas have been part of western social thought for more than 2,500 years. They were present during the Buddhist period and in the writings of Manu and Kautilya. The goal of the welfare and well-being of the whole universe was part of the Indian culture thousands of years earlier. For example, *Lokah Smastah Sukhino Bhavantu*, which means may all the beings in all the worlds become happy, is part of many Hindu people's everyday prayer. However, what causes change and development, and what kinds of change and development lead to welfare and well-being, are not conclusively revealed in human history.

Biological Change Ideas

From a biological point of view, change, development and decay are the essence of life and occur in cyclical form. There is nothing static in the universe. The application of these biological phenomena to nonbiological aspects of life, society and cultures suggests that they too undergo similar cycles, and thus the concept of a golden age arises. History shows that many civilizations have achieved a period of great advancement, reached a peak and then gradually experienced a decline. Is social development part of this cycle? Midgley (1995) contends that social development is not retrogressive, but progressive. It is an important assumption that may hinge on the precise cause of social development. In biological science, growth, change, development and decay are attributed to natural causes or forces, though some of this kind of change and development process may be facilitated or maneuvered by human intervention. Change due to natural causes is not part of social development, but conscious human efforts to deal with the consequences of natural change certainly can be. Midgley traces the theory of social change to ancient Greek thinkers, particularly Heraclitus' view that when opposite elements fuse (dialectic) and produce a new phenomenon, change occurs. He traces it also to St. Augustine's view on stages of progressive change caused by both material and spiritual forces. Finally, he refers to Ibn Khaldun's thoughts on human conflict (between nomadic tribes and settled dwellers) and change.

Social and Economic Change Ideas

During the era of the Renaissance and Enlightenment from the fifteenth century on, many thinkers rejected the traditional, dogmatic and religious explanations of social change, often formulated in terms of advancement followed by decline, and instead emphasized that social change occurs stage by stage in an ongoing progressive manner. Perhaps drawing on the work of early Greek philosophers, the cause of change and progress was attributed, on the one hand, to ideas in terms of thesis, antithesis and synthesis (see George Hegel's and his followers' thoughts) and, on the other hand, to economic and social forces in terms of materialism (see thoughts of Adam Smith, Karl Marx and Friedrich Engels). Although these two causes at that time appeared different, on reflection, one may see the link between ideas and material forces capable of impacting the other, but keeping their own entities.

Planned Social Change

It appears that these and similar thoughts laid an initial rudimentary foundation for planned human intervention that sought to bring about social change and development. Further developments, such as ideas of creating a perfect society, birth of the sociology discipline and Auguste Comte's views on the use of the scientific method to solve social problems, gradually overcame nonintervention thoughts (see Herbert Spencer's views) and influenced many Fabian socialists and sociologists who supported planned intervention for people's welfare. One such sociologist was Leonard Hobhouse (see also Dean's chapter in this volume) who coined the term "social development" to connote a process of planned social change (Midgley 1995, 29 and 45). Although in the nineteenth and twentieth centuries, the extent to which governments should and should not intervene was a controversial issue, the Industrial Revolution, growing mechanization, industrialization, migration of people from rural to urban areas and consequent urbanization together resulted in governments' planned intervention through various welfare programs and services (e.g., Bismarck's social insurance and poor laws) primarily relating to health, education and housing. But the extent of coverage, operation and delivery differed significantly from one country to another. Reaction to the impact of the great depression and World War II led to some additional and important welfare measures, such as a New Deal and the Social Security Act in the U.S. and the Beveridge report and its implementation in the U.K. and its influence beyond, and eventually evolved into the concept of the welfare state.

Colonial Period and Social and Community Development

Although Hobhouse first used the term "social development" in the U.K., it appears that European colonies provided fertile ground for practicing social development. Social development in many colonies in Africa, Asia and Latin America was either a well-planned approach of colonial administrators or it was a necessity of the time. Which is not clear. However, the process, impact and outcome of colonization and decolonization was a mixed blessing for colonies, and the whole experience was generally negative for the colonized, although colonizers may hold an entirely different view. The initial exciting entry into the new world in the name of exploration and adventure, gradually creating a place for trade and commerce. It also eventually established colonizers' rule by suppressing and subjugating people by several means including violence, resisting independent movements to the maximum, sowing the seeds of divisions and conflicts, and finally surrendering to the local people. Such developments are often narrated as colonial history that no one would recall with pleasure and pride.

However, European colonizers have also been widely acknowledged for contributing to infrastructure development, laying the foundations of educational systems, health services, postal systems, some welfare services—particularly through missionaries, prison building, tax systems and the rule of law, however self-benefiting these may have been for the colonizers. The main motivation in doing all this was really to exploit the resources of the colonies and export them to Europe, and not to promote the welfare and well-being of the people. Although such colonization practices were prevalent for a few hundred years, during the sixteenth to the eighteenth centuries, new developments in the West, particularly during the era of the Enlightenment, Industrial Revolution and industrialization, and an increase in manufacturing and production increasingly influenced colonial administrators. To colonial administrators, nineteenth- and twentieth-century colonies were not just places for exploitation but also for the consumption of goods produced in Europe through growing industrialization. To promote a market in the colonies for such products, systematic economic development measures and limited welfare services were needed and were therefore initiated. Exporting raw materials from, and importing finished products to, colonies was almost the rule of that time, and remains so for some countries even today. Thus, strategic economic development in colonies was the need at the time to strengthen the industrial base in the industrialized countries.

It is this socioeconomic situation that appears to have provided a fertile ground for practicing social development in some colonies. Midgley (1994, 1995), drawing on the colonizer-promoted mass literacy and related activities to improve conditions in Western Africa in the 1940s, suggests that the emergence of a social development perspective, one that transcended mere literacy and education to endorse community development, was a product of these times. However, we are uncertain about attributing the origin of social development to Western Africa in the 1940s. Much before that period, the British had established a relatively good educational system in India and had promoted agriculture and exported cotton from India and from many other colonies to the U.K.; and within this whole process, economic development, community development and welfare were inextricably closely connected. However, we are unsure whether colonial administrators consciously planned and combined economic and welfare activities in colonies. During those colonial times, many countries in Africa and Asia achieved neither satisfactory economic development nor adequate welfare services. Moreover, the development of welfare services often remained subsidiary to economic development in many colonies. Nonetheless, the idea and potential of combining economic and welfare development, with all its potential benefits, may be sensed from the trial-and-error economic and community development experiments that occurred in the colonies, whatever the mixture of motives.

Colonial administrators exported not only raw materials but also people. Some people were exported to other colonies to enhance agriculture and economic development activities, and some others, particularly elites, went to the U.K. for further learning and education (e.g., Mahatma Gandhi and Jawaharlal Nehru and his dynasty from India). Exposure to the West enlightened them with ideas of freedom, democracy and the rule of law. On their return as "finished products," some of them joined and led the growing independence movements in several colonies. Seeking to attain their dreams of freedom from colonizers, of independence and of nation building, their long struggle and sacrifices eventually yielded results. Many colonies became independent nations and established political and administrative systems with varied strengths.

However, the legacy of colonization and the links with colonizers continued. In the decolonized countries, social, economic and political power structures were concentrated in the hands of elites, who, drawing on their own economic and community development experiences and their exposure to Western welfare systems, initiated grand, national building projects. These elites lured the masses by promising that they would build a strong nation, achieve economic prosperity and eradicate poverty, adopt a Russian central planning model, develop welfare provisions, and employ community development as an important approach to achieve all this. Perhaps watching these promising developments in decolonized nations, as Midgley (1994) notes, in 1954 the British government formally adopted the term social development to connote the combination of traditional social welfare and community development. Midgley quotes an official British document which states that social development involves "nothing less than the whole process of change and advancement of a territory considered in terms of the progressive wellbeing of society and the individual" (United Kingdom, Colonial Office 1954, 14, in Midgley 1994, 6).

The great hopes for community development in independent India, and its spread in many countries, largely failed due to several complex factors. Power structures from village to upper levels resisted community development initiatives, and these structures siphoned off most of the benefits. It was also difficult to access the thousands of villages. Further, the lack of coordination among interministerial bureaucracies, an overemphasis on social services, centrally led bureaucratic and reporting procedures, and a lack of involvement of communities with their linkages to higher level regional units diminished the prospects of community development in India (see analysis of Korten 1980), and so may be the case in similar countries. Most importantly, influenced by Western economic development theories (e.g., see Rostow's stages of growth and the Lewis theory of development in Todaro 1997) and modernization theories, the nation-building priority was dominated by centrally led economic growth and development that offered little room for community-development practice. In the mid-1960s, most community-development programs were terminated or drastically reduced. In his analysis, Korten (1980) states, "Community development had promised much, yet delivered little." At the same time, several countries borrowed money from international agencies, such the International Monetary Fund (IMF), World Bank and aid agencies, to boost rapid economic development.

United Nations and Social Development

Although some countries achieved impressive economic prosperity, they often remained far behind Western developed countries, while such prosperity as did eventuate hardly percolated down to many local levels. Poverty, health, education and low standard of living issues did not reduce but continued unabated, while some countries were also not able to repay their debts. This kind of lopsided economic development, exacerbated in some countries by the debt crisis, was a great challenge, not only to many new nation-states, but also to the UN, which significantly changed its strategy from limited remedial welfare services to a social development strategy that emphasized social services and not just economic development. Since the 1960s, the UN has played a key role in popularizing the social development approach. It renamed one of its sections the Commission for Social Development in 1966, established the Research Institute for Social Development, organized meetings of experts and published their work on social planning, supported the International Labour Organization's adoption of a basic needs approach in 1976, convened the World Summit on Social Development in 1995, and in 2000 developed the Millennium Development Goals that clearly emphasize social development (UNDP 2003). These significant social development milestones within the UN have resulted in several notable activities, which would require another chapter to elaborate. However, such activities appear to have encouraged many organizations and countries to adopt a social development perspective in their work.

These early developments in the UN and actions by the UN have clearly influenced the World Bank. Davis (2004), in his paper "A History of the Social Development Network in the World Bank, 1973–2002," clearly shows how the Bank was initially obsessed with the effectiveness of projects, and how that obsession gradually changed in the mid 1980s to include a social development perspective in the Bank's work. It further states that the establishment of the Bank's social development network in 1997 and its work typically reflect and embody the following:

A focus on people and societies—rather than specific sectors or the economy.

In-depth country and local knowledge—permitting adaptation to diverse conditions.

A bottom up perspective—including support for participatory approaches that encourage people to solve problems and that empower the poor.

A concern with social systems, and with the economic, social and political factors that support inclusion, social integration and sustainable social development.

Support for a strong government role in reducing social barriers and making development more equitable and inclusive (vii).

Publications on Social Development

Along with the popularization of the social development concept by the UN, several scholars (e.g., Gore 1978; Midgley 1995; Cuyvers 2001; Patel 2005) and UN organizations (e.g., the Research Institute for Social Development and the Economic and Social Commission for Asia and the Pacific) have published on the social development theme. The International Consortium for Social Development (formerly known as the Inter University Consortium for International Social Development) has regularly published a *Social Development Issues* journal since the 1970s. Oxfam has published a journal entitled *Development in Practice* since the 1990s. The Asian and Pacific Association of Social Work Education has recently changed its journal name to *Asia-Pacific Journal of Social Work and Development*. Recently, in India, the Rajagiri College of Social Sciences initiated a new journal known as *Rajagiri Journal of Social Development*. In Africa, the *Journal of Social Development in Africa* has been published out of the School of Social Work in Zimbabwe since 1985. Finally, both Indian and American encyclopedias on social work have a chapter on social development.

Ideologies and Social Development

Historically, many aspects of, and the implementation of, social development may be traced to four ideologies. These are individualist or liberal, populist, collectivist and partnership/institutional (Midgley 1995, 2003). The organizations of the nation-states and societies are also influenced by these ideologies. The individualist or liberal ideology gives prime importance to individuals at the cost of neglecting or ignoring other entities in society. In its extreme form, it does not accept any form of control of the individual. As it poses practical difficulties in organizing societies and helping other individuals in a dignified way, the ideology is used with moderation—thus the emergence of neoliberals and related versions of the ideology. This neoliberal ideology emphasizes the individual's liberty, freedom, rational choice and natural rights. It is the mother of capitalism that pervades the globe today. It is a very powerful ideology and perhaps both cause and cure for a number of contemporary social problems. Those societies which follow an individualist/liberal ideology hold the individual responsible (to blame) for her or his situation and expect the individual to struggle, become self-reliant and create her or his own destiny. The social development goals of welfare and well-being are then achieved by enabling the individual to develop—that is, by developing capacities—and by developing institutions along certain lines (e.g., reflecting the free market and privatization, and ending regulatory regimes) and introducing policies and programs that uphold the individual's liberty and freedom to develop knowledge and skills, to start enterprises, to compete in the market, to exploit opportunities, to contribute to capital formation, and thereby generally to achieve one's own welfare and well-being. When all individuals do so, social development goals can be achieved. For those who are incapable of participating within these liberal societies—through, for example, some incapacity—help is provided on a charitable and remedial basis with the option of buying welfare services in the market.

By contrast, populist ideology emphasizes people and their communities at local levels. Midgley (1995) states, "Populism champions the cause of ordinary people against the establishment, seeks to serve their interests and represent the popular will" (90). Followers of this ideology follow and lead people's interests and mobilize people to organize communities and initiate change or action, sometimes by radical means. In many postcolonial, newly formed states (e.g., India), some leaders have emerged from among the ordinary people, gained power by popularizing people's interests—relating developments to their needs, issues and aspirations—and by developing and using slogans that reflect these interests. This ideology is helpful in bringing together and organizing neglected groups such as women, children and the elderly, and so focusing on their related issues. Many policies and programs have been developed to meet peoples' interests. The populist ideology lends itself to community organization, community development and social-action approaches to achieve social development goals or to improve conditions. It also operates as a bottom-up approach, and one that is effective at local levels. One of the core aspects of social development, namely, participation, stems from this ideology. Many non-governmental organizations (NGOs), community organizations and community and social development workers implicitly or explicitly use this ideology to improve the conditions of the people and communities with which they work.

Differing from the preceding two ideologies, the collectivist or socialist ideology emphasizes collectives of people, collective ownership of property and collective decision making. Labor movements, trade unions and cooperatives are partly influenced by such ideology. According to this ideology, the state is a form of collective which can effectively manage economic and social development and meet peoples' needs. It is based on the assumption that

> the state embodies the interests of society as a whole, and that it has a responsibility to promote the wellbeing of all citizens; government is collectively owned by citizens and represents their interests; the state is therefore the ultimate collective. (Midgley 1995, 125)

This ideology sounds somewhat idealistic, as there are many governments which are not accountable to citizens and in turn suppress them. However, by and large, the state as a collective, irrespective of its liberal democratic and communist form, has played a remarkable role in the economic development of countries as well as by introducing several welfare measures, though the balance between the two—economic development and welfare—significantly differs from one country to another. In fact, the general trend suggests that some states and international agencies have overemphasized economic development by neglecting social dimensions of societies and by damaging the ecology, though they appear to be moving toward correcting the imbalance. However, it may be noted that collectivist or socialist ideology is an umbrella kind of ideology that encompasses many other significant aspects. For example, there are both democratic and communist states: some follow highly centralized planning and some follow decentralized planning; some are highly authoritarian and top-down, and some encourage participation of citizens, while others do not. Yet, all of them aim to improve conditions and achieve social development.

The fourth ideology is a partnership ideology, which Midgley (1995) calls the institutional perspective. Since the term "institution" in this context may confuse readers, we have replaced it with the term "partnership ideology." All the ideologies previously presented have strengths and weaknesses, and can be found in practice in different forms and to varying degrees in all societies and communities. For heuristic purposes, they may be delineated separately, but in practice and for achieving social development goals, the best elements of all the three ideologies may be combined, or at least accepted in such a way that partnership among these ideologies may be developed to better achieve social development goals. The essence of the partnership ideology is that partnership among the ideologies, theories, nation-states, and national and international agencies needs to be nurtured to achieve social development goals. Although the state needs to steer the partnership, market, state and community have to be the main drivers. There are many examples to show how all three are needed, for emphasis on only one type of ideologically oriented development is seen to lead to distorted development. For example, in self-help groups and microfinance schemes, individuals' awareness, capacity and skills need to be developed; individuals have to come together in groups around some norms, with the group ensuring that it meets the needs and interests of the members; and the state should work to create an enabling environment so that individuals and groups can perform effectively and so meet their needs and achieve their well-being. Then, because some communities and nation-states are capable of generating their own resources and others are not, partnerships between internal and external members and agencies need to be developed. When needed, this process may include external aid and personnel that work with communities at various levels to facilitate social development. Partnership is also needed among all the sectors of development, as they are all inextricably linked, and achieving one at the neglect of the others is detrimental and will result in distorted development.

The question is, can individualist, populist and collectivist ideologies coexist in societies so as to change current conditions and achieve social development goals? The partnership ideology suggests that it is possible to plan a combination of the three ideologies and to apply them in such ways as to introduce social change and achieve social development goals.

On the whole, the historical evolution of the concept of social development suggests that, although the concept is not new, it has gradually emerged from a natural phenomenon to a planned phenomenon, with various scholars, institutions, socioeconomic and political contexts and ideologies influencing its current form and shape. Contemporarily, social development is an important agenda of many governments. For example, in the U.K., the Overseas Development Administration, now known as the Department for International Development (DFID), first appointed its social development advisers (SDA) in 1975. However, it did not employ them in great numbers, as their number grew from two in 1987 to only seven in 1991. However, by 1997, DFID was employing over forty SDAs who have been significantly contributing to DFID's policy development from a social development perspective (Eyben 2003). Many governments also have established a ministry or department of social development (e.g., New Zealand, Thailand, China and Trinidad and Tobago) to achieve the goals of social development. Although conservative governments in the 1980s, through their free market, liberalization and privatization policies, limited the application of the social development approach to some extent, such governments were also attracted to the idea of community participation and self-reliance. However, conservative governments' policies in some areas in fact led to negative social consequences in terms of growing poverty and inequality, both in developed and developing countries. This situation has been further compounded by climate change issues; yet it has again created excellent opportunities for social development thinking and practice.

EMERGENCE OF A WIDELY HELD AND IMPLEMENTED UNDERSTANDING OF SOCIAL DEVELOPMENT

Is there an appropriate theoretical basis to social development that can guide our understanding of the essential nature of and reasons for this approach? Are there any theories of social development? To these basic questions, responses would differ depending upon how one understands social development. Some may argue that social development as a field of practice draws from various disciplines, and that it does not have its own knowledge base or its own theory. Adopting a contrary view, however, some suggest that social development does have its own theoretical base. This is one of the most difficult and controversial issues in social development.

We argue here that, in a strict sense and from a positivistic framework, there is no social development theory, though some scholars have used the term "social development paradigm" (Karger 1994), which suggests that there is a grand theory of social development, but such we think is not the case. The current status of the underdevelopment or lack of social development theories does, however, provide great opportunities for building social development theories, and we believe that this can be done. Toward that end, we must consider some pre-stages of theory development that include identifying, and conceptualizing with clarity, concepts and variables, probable relationships and nonrelationships among them, and values, ideologies and goals which influence those concepts and variables and their relationships. As presented in this chapter, a brief exposition of the varied concepts, historical evolution and ideological orientations of social development may suggest that none of them is clear, convincing and conclusive. However, drawing from such an analysis, it may be possible to identify some core elements of, and an approach to, social development. Within a broad approach to social development, we locate seven composite concepts and variables as presented in Figure 2.1 and Table 2.1. These are existing conditions, goals, values, processes, strategies, levels and dimensions, and the figure shows the linkages among them.

The main purpose of the suggested approach to social development in Table 2.1 is to demonstrate that it is practical to progress social development. The approach first begins with an understanding of existing conditions and causes of such conditions, with a view to initiating social change, progress and development. First, it is clear that social development is about individuals, families (however viewed), groups, communities and societies within their environment (including the ecological environment). All these entities have a current status or condition. That condition may be delineated in terms of geographic location, history, culture, political type and level, economy, infrastructure, resources, health, education, opportunities for development and major problems. The cause of any condition needs to be critically examined. Existing conditions may also be analyzed on the basis of a wide range of variables, including peoples' standard of living; societies' and communities' experience of minimal progress or further deterioration; decline due to distorted development resulting in concentration of wealth and resources, inequality, a class-based society, stress and isolation; and lack of or inadequate access to the necessities of life such as food generally, nutritious healthy food, shelter, clothing, health and education services. Factors contributing to such conditions may then include gender-discriminatory practices, dictatorial regimes, natural or human-made calamities such as war and conflict, tsunamis, floods, earthquakes, droughts and famines, or industrial and technological accidents.

To understand current conditions, two questions may be posed: what are the current conditions, and why do such conditions exist? Addressing the first question is relatively simpler than the second. Several epistemological and theoretical orientations may be used to understand current conditions. These mainly emerge from research approaches that include quantitative research, survey analysis, use of census data, development of indicators, qualitative research, observation, ethnographic studies, case studies, participatory research, appreciative enquiry, media reports, and so on. Descriptions of the current conditions at the macro level are often readily available and can be used to develop a better understanding of current conditions. For example, the UNDP Human Development Index, which is based on several variables, classifies countries into those with low, medium and high

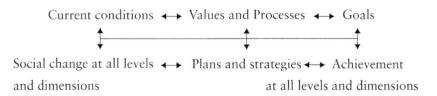

Figure 2.1 An approach to social development.

Table 2.1 An Approach to Social Development

Existing conditions
- Social change, progress/development

Goals
- Promotion of people's well-being or quality of life
- Enabling people to experience freedom to satisfy their aspirations and realize their potential

Values
- Respect for people and belief in their capacity to grow and develop
- A holistic understanding of human existence—physical to spiritual
- Acceptance of social and cultural pluralism and incorporation of the centrality of people's cultures and values
- Acknowledging the importance of ecological issues and people's link with nature and their environment
- Acknowledging that social relations are based on the right and obligation to participate, equality of opportunity, and the right of all to social justice

Processes
- A participatory process
- An empowering process

Strategies
- Capacity building of individuals, groups and communities
- Local institution building and support for people's organizations
- Fostering self- reliance
- Creating an enabling environment within which all people can develop
- Participation in the development and functioning of social institutions
- Promoting the provision of adequate resources and services accessible to all
- Promoting a pro-active role for the state in supporting participatory planning
- Engaging in the development and implementation of policies to enhance social development
- Coordinating development initiatives at all levels
- Strengthening civil society in all its various aspects

Levels
- International
- National
- Within the nation, regions
- States/provinces
- Districts
- The lowest administrative unit of governments
- Grassroots-level communities and villages

Dimensions
- Cultural
- Political
- Economic
- Ecological
- Education
- Health
- Housing
- Equity groups
- Citizens and their institutions

Source: Adapted from Cox, Pawar and Picton (1997a, 6).

levels of human development. However, this is at the societal level; at the grassroots/local community levels, such an understanding needs also to be developed because of significant diversity. There is in practice considerable debate about the way these levels are reported, measured and understood, and achievements claimed.

The perceived macro causes of current conditions that require social development have been attributed to several theories such as modernization, dependency and world systems (see So 1990). These are controversial and evolving, with supporters constantly correcting their positions as a response to critiques and new evidence. All the relevant theories may be categorized into endogenous and exogenous. Theories that attribute the current conditions to internal factors—such as culture, tradition, subsistence farming, ignorance, lack of resources, leadership, governance, the level of use of technology, lack of innovation, and so on—may be treated as endogenous theories. Modernization theories clearly fit here. Theories that attribute the current conditions to external factors—such as exploitation by industrialized countries in the West, international trade and aid regulations set by the international agencies (e.g., IMF and World Bank, World Trade Organization)—may be regarded as exogenous theories. Dependency and world systems theories clearly argue that these external factors are the cause of current and deteriorating conditions in the world. In reality, however, the causes of conditions that cry out for social development are a combination of both types of theories—clearly evident, for example, in the causes of climate change—and such conditions exist in many countries, both developed and developing, albeit to different degrees.

Second, it is important to set goals. To change conditions, systematic planned efforts need to be made to enable people to experience freedom and to realize their potential, so as to ensure their well-being and quality of life, which are important general goals of social development. Specific goals may include the welfare, well-being, standard of living, human rights, equality and equity pertaining to any or all entities—individuals, families, groups, communities and societies, along with sustaining the ecological context. Goals are the foundations of social development practice, but no goals can be discussed without their value dimensions and ideological orientations. Goals are also based on the assumption that current conditions are unsatisfactory and need to be improved, so that achieving better conditions is expressed through goals. The theory-building process calls for a clear conceptual development of goals that are tangible, practical, measurable and verifiable; yet goals of social development are often criticized as unclear and unattainable. The complexity of clearly conceptualizing these goals stems from how material goals (e.g., meeting basic needs, increasing literacy rates and education, life expectancy, etc.) and ideational goals (e.g., social justice, peace, welfare, well-being, equality, equity and empowerment) are inextricably combined in an interdependent way (see Midgley 1995). Ideational goals, such as social justice, equality and distribution, have value and ideological connotations. The literature indicates considerable debate and controversy around social development goals (see supporting and opposing arguments by Midgley 1995, 92–101), but is it now time for us to get over that debate and focus on specific goals? For example, the Millennium Development Goals, relating to poverty, health, education, discrimination, ecology, cooperation and coordination, may be viewed as social development goals. Yet, the question of who sets social development goals or agendas, and how, are vexing questions. Are they international community agencies or, at the national and local levels, a few individuals or a few elites, or all people and communities? How can people participate in setting social development goals? What are the value and ideological orientations of the goal setters? If social development goals are already set externally, how do we convince people and communities to own them? These questions have significant implications for planning and processes.

Third, the discussion of goals clearly includes values and ideologies. The set goals need to be achieved by adhering to the values of human dignity and worth, diversity, sustaining ecology, rights and obligations, and holism. Fourth, such values are closely connected to the processes of people's participation and empowerment, which are among the foundations of social development. Fifth, several strategies in the approach, which are self-explanatory, need to be implemented by following such a process. Although the overall goals may be the same—that is, the welfare and well-being of all people—specific plans, strategies and processes to achieve the goals and thereby improve conditions differ significantly, depending upon existing ideological orientations and beliefs as to the causes of existing conditions.

Sixth, such strategies need to be employed at multiple levels and in multiple sectors or dimensions (Cox and Pawar 2006). Our conceptualization of multilevel includes international, national and, within the nation, regions, states/provinces, districts, the lowest administrative unit of governments, and grassroots level communities and villages. The most important aspect of the multilevel approach currently, because of its comparative neglect to date, is the local level, which may be grassroots-level communities or villages under the lowest administrative unit of governments. While the other levels, including district, state or region and nation, are important, a short history of development has unequivocally demonstrated that development endeavors at those levels alone, undertaken in a centralized manner, have not helped social development at the local level. The majority of grassroots-level communities, villages, rural areas, and parts of urban areas have failed to receive the benefits of economic development, and so have remained far from achieving social development goals. In view of this apparent outcome, we are strongly convinced that, although social development at the national and regional levels within the nation has to be planned and promoted, the priority and focus should be the local community levels. Equally, priority also should be given to certain regions that have by and large remained underdeveloped in comparison with some other regions within a country.

Finally, social development work at multilevels should also focus on multiple dimensions or sectors that mainly include cultural, political, economic, ecological, education, health, housing, equity groups, and citizens and their institutions. Although these sectors are well planned and developed at national levels in many countries, most of the countries have overemphasized economic development, assuming that such development will percolate down, and so solve all problems and contribute to the development of the other dimensions at all levels, but such is not the case.

The cultural dimension of social development is a comprehensive, complex and controversial one, as conceptually it could include all other dimensions. However, for the purpose of delineation and discussion, we may separate out the other dimensions, though they are connected to the cultural dimension in that every aspect of society is connected to its culture. Early modernization theorists argued that, in order to become modern, to develop and to Westernize, traditional people and communities should get rid of their traditions, customs and beliefs as constituting the major hurdles in their progress. Contrary to this theory, the development of the Asian tigers and of some regions within countries showed that development and traditions can coexist. This development experience suggests that culture, customs, traditions and beliefs, and development per se can exist together. Achieving one by losing the other is no development at all. Moreover, external agents' advice to give up one's culture to develop does not appear humane, and is likely to undermine well-intended development efforts. Thus, to initiate social development, it is necessary and important for both external and internal development agents to understand people's and communities' culture, traditions, customs, and religious and spiritual practices and beliefs. How do people and communities gain strengths from their cultures and use them in all the other dimensions? Culture appears to be a foundation for all other dimensions. Understanding with sensitivity and developing people's and communities' culture in terms of religion, spirituality, the arts, customs and beliefs contribute to people's welfare and well-being, and thereby helps to achieve social development goals.

Developing the political dimension includes awareness-raising, sensitizing around issues and needs and ways of addressing them, and developing the desire and abilities to participate in affairs and decision making that affect their lives. The most important aspect of political development is leadership development at various levels and dimensions. Leadership needs to be developed in such a way that leaders are able to appreciate the importance of all dimensions and drive them. In fact, the whole development rests on the strength of the political dimension as in effect the center of "democratic" decision making, though such decision making needs to be truly participatory and people-based.

Developing the economic dimension at all levels is vital. It is important to understand and work on people's economic aspirations. What are the resources of people and communities at all levels? What are the sources of livelihood? Are communities in any ways self-sufficient in meeting their needs? How are the existing resources distributed? What are the major blocks to economic development? These blocks could be inadequate infrastructure, underdeveloped or lack of markets, and unemployment or a lack of employment opportunities. Depending upon many factors, in most cases, development of the economic dimension requires the mobilization of both internal and external resources by a range of agents, including governments, businesses, NGOs and, if necessary, international agencies. Development of primary industries, microenterprises and fair-market mechanisms are often the essence of economic development. Although it appears challenging, once economic development is generated, its rapid and unbridled growth can make or mar the social change process if it is not appropriately planned and implemented so as to enable the development of the other dimensions.

The development of long-term and sustainable economic development primarily depends upon sustainable ecological systems and human resources. Economic development that has exploited natural resources and neglected and damaged ecological systems has come under considerable criticism, and rightly so. Thus, it is important to ensure that, while pursuing economic development, ecological development is equally emphasized. It may include watershed development and management, tree planting, the growth and protection of forests, seeds and species, developing green zones, controlling and preventing pollution (CO_2 emissions), and preventing both wastage and the stagnation of natural resources such as water and soil. It is well demonstrated that good ecological development results in good economic development (e.g., see the results of watershed development projects). Recent climate change issues and actions are pertinent to this dimension.

The development of human resources calls for the development of health and educational dimensions. Good health is vital for all living beings. The development of all the other dimensions depends upon the development of healthy people and communities. To develop the health dimension, more preventive and promotive approaches need to be employed. Access to healthy nutritious food and safe drinking water, the development of healthy habits, prevention of at least the excessive consumption of alcohol, tobacco and similar other substances, and measures to reduce maternal mortality, child mortality and increase life expectancy are needed at all levels. While these are repeatedly stated in national plans and programs, they are often not translated to the local level.

Broadly and realistically, awareness is education. The education of people can readily trigger the social change process. Thus it is important to provide both formal and informal education. Primary education has been made universal and compulsory in many countries, but such quality education needs to be realized particularly at the local level. Educating people about their culture, economy, political systems, ecology, health, and how they can contribute to their development should be the goal. Developing educational infrastructure and facilitative pathways for further education need also to be given priority. The education dimension will then in turn contribute to the other dimensions.

Adequate, functional and quality housing is an important aspect of development. This dimension is closely related to health, economic and cultural dimensions. For good health and comfort, a good house and related infrastructure such as water and sanitation are essential. Millions of individuals live in mud-wall and thatched-roof houses, which are far from satisfactory. Also unsatisfactory is the situation in large urban centers where a large number of people live in slums. Poor housing certainly has implications for health. The housing development should be culturally suitable. Peoples' economic situation needs to be strengthened to the extent that they can afford their own house. Also, housing needs to be planned in such a way that it has functional sanitation arrangements. In many communities where water services are provided without sanitation, the water runs on to streets or blocks in gutters, making an excellent breeding ground for mosquitoes, which has serious health implications.

Life experiences and some current distorted development patterns clearly show that some members and groups of the community such as children, women, the elderly, the physically challenged, victims of disasters and the sick, are particularly vulnerable and often miss out on the gains of development. They may be considered as equity groups for whom necessary services need to be provided in terms of the dimensions presented here to ensure their inclusiveness in the mainstream of the society.

The development of cultural, political, economic, ecological, health, educational, housing and equity groups dimensions should be geared toward developing good citizenship and institutions at all levels. Citizenship entails rights and responsibilities and ownership of the community. Thus, the development of all these dimensions may aim to develop individual capacities, thus contributing to turning people into good citizens who constructively engage in building their communities. Similarly, the development of these dimensions needs to create good governance institutions. Each dimension should have a role in governance institutions that are effective, efficient and free from corrupt practices. The development of good citizenship and good institutions go hand in hand, and in turn should help in addressing all other dimensions. We hope that practicing social development on a global scale by following this approach at all levels, particularly in local level communities, will help to achieve universal social development.

CONCLUSION

As stated in the introduction, this chapter has looked at the concept and historical evolution of social development, and an emerging approach to social development practice. Although there are various definitions of social development, common themes may be identified in terms of goals, values, processes that may advance structural change, the juxtaposing of social with economic development, and the participation and empowerment of people and communities. The historical analysis has shown that the idea of social development has evolved over a long time. Many scholars and evolving socioeconomic and political contexts and institutions have contributed to social development, and several ideologies have embraced social development from their own perspectives. The partnership ideology appears to be the most promising as at appears to capture the best elements of all other major ideologies. Drawing from such an analysis, we have presented a social development approach that focuses on improving the existing conditions, such as distorted development, with the clear goal of enhancing human welfare and well-being. It also incorporates a value orientation and empowering and participatory processes, and suggests effective strategies for implementation at all levels and all dimensions with an emphasis on local levels. We believe that such an approach enhances the conceptual clarity of social development and affirms that social development can be practiced anywhere and its goals achieved.

REFERENCES

Barker, R. L. 2003. *The social work dictionary*. Washington, D.C.: National Association of Social Workers Press.

Billups, J. 1994. The social development model as an organising framework for social work practice. In *Issues in social work: A critical analysis*, ed. R. G. Meinert, T. Pardeck, and P. Sullivan, 21–37. Westport, CT: Auburn House.

Cox, D., and M. Pawar. 2006. *International social work: Issues, strategies and programs*. Thousand Oaks, CA: Sage.

Cox D., M. Pawar, and C. Picton. 1997a. *Introducing a social development perspective into social work curricula at all levels*. Melbourne: Regional Social Development Centre, La Trobe University.

Cox D., M. Pawar, and C. Picton. 1997b. *Social development content in social work education*. Melbourne: Regional Social Development Centre, La Trobe University.

Cuyvers, L., ed. 2001. *Globalisation and social development: European and Southeast Asian evidence*. Cheltenham, UK: Edward Elgar.

Davis, G. 2004. A history of the social development network in the World Bank, 1973–2002. http://siteresources.worldbank.org/EXTSOCIALDEVELOPMENT/Resources/244362–1164107274725/3182370–1164201144397/SocialDevelopment-History.pdf?resourceurlname=SocialDevelopment-History.pdf (accessed June 6, 2008).

Dictionary.com. 2007. Development. http://dictionary.reference.com/browse/development (accessed May 5, 2008).

Eyben, R. 2003. Mainstreaming the social dimension into the overseas development administration: A partial history. *Journal of International Development* 15:879–892.

Gore, M. 1973. *Some aspects of social development*. Hong Kong: Deptartment of Social Work, University of Hong Kong.

Goulet, D. 1971. The Cruel Choice: A New Concept in the Theory of Development. New York: Athenaeum.

Hollister, D. 1982. The knowledge and skills bases of social development. In *The developmental perspective in social work*, ed. D. S. Saunders, 31–42. Manoa: University of Hawaii Press.

Hornby, A. S. 1992. *Oxford advanced learner's dictionary*. Oxford: Oxford University Press.

Karger, H. J. 1994. Toward redefining social development in the global economy: Free markets, privatization, and the development. *Social Development Issues* 16(3): 32–44.

Korten, D. C. 1980. Community organisation and rural development: A learning process approach. *Public Administration Review* 40(5): 480–511.

Lowe, G. R. 1995. Social development. In *Encyclopaedia of social work* (19th ed.). Washington, D.C.: National Association of Social Workers Press.

Midgley, J. 1993. Ideological roots of social development strategies. *Social Development Issues* 15 (1), 1–13.

———. 1994. Defining social development: Historical trends and conceptual formulations. *Social Development Issues* 16(3): 3–19.

———. 1995. *Social development: The developmental perspective in social welfare*. London: Sage.

———. 2003. Social development: The intellectual heritage. *Journal of International Development* 15:831–844.

Meinert, R. G., Kohn, E. and Strickler, G. 1984. International survey of social development concepts. *Social Development Issues* 8 (1/2), 70–88.

Mohan, B., and P. Sharma. 1985. On human oppression and social development. *Social Development Issues* 9(1): 12–23.

Pandey, R. 1981. Strategies for social development: An international approach. In *Social development: Conceptual, methodological and policy issues*, ed. J. Jones and R. Pandey, 33–49. New York: St. Martin's Press.

Patel, L. 2005. *Social welfare and social development in South Africa*. New York: Oxford University Press.

Paiva, J. F. X. 1982. The dynamics of social development and social work. In *The developmental perspective in social work*, ed. D. S. Saunders, 1–11. Manoa: University of Hawaii Press.

Pathak, S. 1987. Social development. In *Encyclopaedia of social Work in India*, vol. 3, 53–63. New Delhi: Ministry of Social Welfare, Government of India.

So, A. Y. 1990. *Social change and development*. Thousand Oaks, CA: Sage.

Thirlwall, A. P. 1989. *Growth and development: With special reference to developing economies* (4th ed.). Basingstoke, UK: Macmillan.

Todaro, M. 1997. *Economic development*. New York: Longman.

United Nations Development Programme (UNDP). 2003. *Human development report: Millennium development goals: A compact among nations to end human poverty*. New York: Oxford University Press.

3 Local Level Social Development

Manohar S. Pawar and David R. Cox

INTRODUCTION

In Chapter 2, social development was presented in part as a multidimensional, multilevel and value-based approach to the development of a society as a whole. Social development is seen in this text as needing to encompass all dimensions of a society, including particularly the economic, political, social, cultural and ecological, within a comprehensive and integrated approach to building a society that will be inclusive and designed to give all participants the greatest opportunities possible for achieving their full potential and contributing to society. Social development needs also to be addressed at, ideally, the international, national and local levels, with a comprehensive approach adopted at each level. Finally, the goals of and approaches to social development need to be value-based, embracing values that reflect human rights and include a focus on equity and people's participation with the goal of enhancing human well-being.

In this chapter, the focus is exclusively on the local level of social development, while bearing in mind that all the levels of development are important and are ideally integrated, that development at the local level needs to be as comprehensive, in terms of the dimensions covered, as any other level, and that all local level development activities need to reflect the values on which all social development should rest. The local level of development requires specific focus in the twenty-first century because it has been the level most neglected to date, and this theme is the central purpose of this chapter. It should be noted that, while we have used the term local level social development, to fit with our multilevel understanding of social development, others have commonly referred to this level of development as grassroots development, village level development, rural development, local community development and people-centered development. For the most part, these terms can be regarded as synonymous.

NEGLECT OF THE LOCAL LEVEL OF SOCIAL DEVELOPMENT

It is certainly not the case that the local level of social development has been ignored in conceptual presentations of social development, for it is in fact quite frequently stressed. Nor is it the case that it has been completely neglected in the field, in that many, if not most, of the agencies involved at the international level have devised, encouraged, funded and participated in development programs and projects that are located, at least in part, at the local level. In our opinion, however, two tendencies have contributed to the comparative neglect of the local level. First, major development agencies at the international level tend, understandably, to place a strong emphasis on the international (i.e., relations between nations in terms of, for example, donor aid) level and on the national level. The activities they do support at the local level have tended to be those initiated by development contractors, non-governmental organizations (NGOs) and others with a concern for the local level across a specified region, but the resulting projects have been all too frequently one-dimensional and so restricted in scope, either when viewed against the concept of comprehensive social development or in terms of the extent of existing needs. Moreover, at times, some of these agencies able and willing to operate at the local level feel it necessary to select the more promising local situations located within those countries that are already making some progress. To do otherwise seems to be perceived as likely to court failure by not achieving the goals accepted by the donor, and so to experience difficulty in raising further funding. Thus, internationally initiated development work undertaken at the local level has often been criticized as being largely project based, one-dimensional, sometimes unsustainable and, even when successful, desperately requiring replication on a greatly expanded basis. Seldom does one locate a relatively comprehensive local level development program addressing any of the world's most needy areas and peoples and undertaken on an extensive basis.

Second, there appears to be a significant focus on national level development by both significant players within the international development community and by national governments themselves. This approach is consistent with the strong focus throughout the post–World War II period on macro economic development. National governments were seen as needing to modernize, largely through focusing on urbanization, industrialization and associated infrastructure development, and essentially to undertake all steps seen as necessary to grow their economy. Players at the international level were keen to support such developments through promoting global trade, especially on a free trade basis, grants for large-scale development projects, and expanding global investment markets. For some time, major donors encouraged large-scale infrastructure and other developments along with macro fiscal, educational and health initiatives that would initially favor the better-off members of elite or majority groups within the country. If and when the local level was considered, it was commonly assumed that the flow-on effects of macro economic growth-oriented development would ultimately benefit all levels, dimensions of development and all peoples, but that this first step of economic growth was critical if any significant progress was to be made.

There is, however, ample evidence suggesting that the assumed trickle-down or flow-on effects of macro economic development often did not occur, largely because the theory implied certain prerequisites that were often not present. It implied a cohesive country and population where those in power would exhibit a national and inclusive concern, whereas in reality many elite or upwardly mobile groups who gained power had little or no sympathy with other sections of the population or country. It implied also a stable, noncorrupt and efficient system of governance, which in reality did not prevail in many countries. Hence, many governments essentially failed to tax growth and to redistribute the fruits of growth through social services, income support and other programs. Instead, many countries became increasingly unequal and often politically unstable as a result. Finally, the theory implied a receptive local level, whereas in fact many local levels were suffering from such entrenched poverty and the absence of capacity-building opportunities that their ability to participate in whatever national level development occurred was extremely limited, even if they were able to migrate to the urban centers of growth, as many were inclined to do.

In recent times, the international community has increasingly recognized the importance both of enhancing good governance and of addressing local level poverty alleviation, and so on, as part of all national level economic and other development initiatives. This is particularly the case with the World Bank and International Monetary Fund following now strongly along the more balanced path long emphasized by the United Nations Development Programme (UNDP) and others (United Nations 1995; UNDP 2003), and these emphases have also increasingly become a focus of the overseas aid programs of Western governments. What is now in fact the widely accepted approach to social development is that development work should ideally be a combination of complementary top-down and bottom-up approaches to development.

LINKAGES BETWEEN NATIONAL LEVEL AND LOCAL LEVEL SOCIAL DEVELOPMENT

This focus on a combination of top-down and bottom-up development initiatives raises the question of whether a significant degree of local level social development, or bottom-up development as this in effect is, is feasible if national level development is virtually nonexistent, at a very low level, or the victim of corrupt and biased development processes. In other words, is it inevitable that a degree of national level development, and especially of national level economic development, is a prerequisite for a reasonable level of local level development to be achieved? If this proposition is correct, then one might well conclude that there is little point in addressing local level social development, especially within the numerically significant number in total of least developed countries, failed states and states generally suffering from poor governance. The question is thus an extremely important one regarding the global scope for local level social development in its own right.

This question of whether significant national level development is a prerequisite for local level social development cannot be answered in the abstract with any degree of certainty or generality, and the following attempt at an answer represents largely our own opinions, being based on little strong evidence. However, it should be noted that the United Nations' 1995 Summit on Social Development emphasized, as its first commitment, the creation of "an economic, political, social, cultural and legal environment that will enable people to achieve social development"—the so-called "enabling environment" (11). We would stress, first, that it needs to be made clear that a significant level of appropriate national level social development will almost certainly increase the chances of successful work at the local level. This will be especially true if that national level development has been comprehensive in nature, with at least political and social development taking their place alongside economic developments, although cultural and ecological development could also be critical. Our concern here, however, is how far local level development can progress without significant national level development. Our second point is that the precise nature of the link between national level development and the local level will be extremely important, and several possible scenarios are evident. Some local levels are simply neglected by other levels of development; other local levels and their development are viewed antagonistically by central governments, usually for cultural, ethnic or political reasons; while other local levels again are victims of national level instability, civil war or a central inability to respond effectively to natural disasters. The precise circumstances surrounding a failure of national level development to translate into progress at local levels will vary, but it will be these precise circumstances that will become an important factor in determining the outcomes of efforts to achieve local level social development.

Both of these points will affect local level social development at every step. We would argue, however, that whatever the extent and nature of national level social development, and whatever the precise nature of the relationship between a local level and its national level, some local level social development will always be possible if the necessary resources are available, and action to bring it about will always be worthwhile. Even among extreme local situations—such as gatherings of displaced persons, marginalized indigenous minority populations or communities, populations in extremely remote areas, and communities with very high levels of poverty—something can be achieved if the will is there at some level and if personnel is available to implement a program (see Chapter 8). These are crucial prerequisites. Ideally, some resources beyond personnel will be helpful, but even that is not crucial, especially if the available personnel are well trained and able to identify and draw on existing local resources.

It should always be possible, for example, for workers to enable the local people themselves to operate a basic literacy course, basic primary health care facilities, basic primary schools or income generation schemes that draw initially almost entirely on local resources. Any such measures will be beneficial to local level social development to some degree, however minimally, and can be implemented with no significant external resources and no dependence on national level developments. However, clearly, both some external resources and some ability to link up with national level developments will enhance the potential success of even these basic programs.

In considering the significance of the nature of the linkages between national level and local level development, we would further argue that any success achieved at the local level will carry with it the potential of either contributing indirectly to, or of increasing the pressures for, national level social development. Local level social development inevitably enhances capacities among individuals, families, communities and local organizations, strengthens social capital and begins the important process of building civil society. Each of these developments will, within a cumulative and interactive process, build national resources and result in some degree of pressure for national level development in terms of good governance, the equitable redistribution of the nation's wealth, the expansion of the nation's infrastructure and the extension of the nation's social services provision. As we argue later, local level social development constitutes an essential building block in national development. Indeed, it can be argued that developments at the local level constitute the only foundations on which a strong and secure nation as a total and unified entity can ultimately be built.

THE CONCEPT OF LOCAL LEVEL

The word "local" in local level social development does not carry any one specific connotation. Uphoff (1986, 11) saw it as signifying any or all of the following: locality (a set of interrelated communities); community (a relatively self-contained socioeconomic-residential unit); or group (a self-identified set of persons with a common interest). Alternatively, we could conceptualize local in terms of individuals, families, groups and communities, given the importance of all these types of units to engagement in the majority of situations covered under local level social development. In addition to their significance as local units or entities, in our 2006 text (Cox and Pawar 2006, 132–4), we regard individuals, families and communities as one sector of society alongside three others—namely, the marketplace or economic sector, the governance of the state or institutional sector, and the civil society sector—and we go on to argue that this individuals-families-communities sector and its development constitute the foundation of any society. The following is a summary of our argument:

If we wish to be more specific, we can discuss several ways in which important aspects of society depend on the foundations established at the local level. One argument is that ultimately it is people who constitute a society's most important resource, but like all other resources people require development, and this development begins at the local level. A crucial aspect of this is capacity building at the individual, family and community levels. A second argument is that important societal qualities, such as social capital and social integration, cannot ultimately be imposed from above but rely on local level developments [World Bank 2000/2001, 2001]. A third argument is that macroeconomic development is, to a significant degree, dependent on economic developments at the local level, such as the household economy, the community economy, and the informal economy, while other levels of economic development require that the local level functions effectively as producers and consumers within the economic system. (133)

In social development terms, it is important to see the development of the local level as not only the development of the very foundations of a society but also as building at the local level a receptivity to national development initiatives. There is thus a two-way process. On the one hand, national level development creates opportunities that then exist for individuals and groups to take advantage of. These may be capacity-building opportunities, as through accessing education and training systems; income-earning opportunities, as through engaging in the emerging employment market; or the pursuance of personal and group interests through the opportunities made available by national level development, such as those that urbanization and international links offer. On the other hand, effective national level development also reaches out to localities through the provision of services and opportunities; however, the ability of the local level to be receptive to these will depend in large part on the extent of existing local capacity building and local organizational development. That is to say, a locality needs to be prepared for participation in mainstream national development. Hence, the role of local level social development is to achieve both of these goals, namely, the preparation of localities for full and effective participation in whatever national level development offers and preparation of the entities that constitute locality to enable them to reach out and take advantage of emerging opportunities beyond the local level. Where, however, national level social development either is virtually nonexistent or exists but excludes certain population groupings, then the focus of local level social development will be significantly on self-reliant development.

RATIONALE AND GOALS OF LOCAL LEVEL SOCIAL DEVELOPMENT

In general terms, local level social development is development that takes place at the local level and is ideally initiated by the local level. It is not essentially or ideally action that occurs at the local level as a result or flow on of central level planning and decision making (UN Centre for Regional Development 1988, 14). As Midgley (1992) puts it, in what he refers to as the populist understanding of social development, "[Local level] social development is said to occur when local people collaborate to strengthen community bonds and take concerted action to improve their social and economic conditions" (4). We would argue that the philosophical base of local level social development is that local people, through their community structures, are enabled to assume responsibility for their own development.

Rationale

The rationale for focusing directly on local level social development, as set out in the preceding discussion, is threefold. Development at this level is designed essentially for three purposes:

1. To address years of neglect of development at the local level, usually reflected in extreme poverty and deprivation;
2. To compensate for failures in development at the national level; and
3. To prepare the local level for participation in further national level development, and especially in terms of being able to take advantage of opportunities that are opening up.

It is not unusual for local level development to have all three purposes in mind; however, differentiation between local level situations in terms of which of these purposes is predominant is also important. Undoubtedly the most difficult situation is reflected in the first purpose, in that initiatives to overcome years of development neglect will invariably be confronted with the realities of extreme poverty, low levels of personal self-esteem and confidence, and very little local organizational development. The second most difficult situation will tend to be where there is minimal national level development of which the local level can take advantage, restricting local development to those areas for which local resources are relatively adequate, with perhaps minimal levels of essential external assistance in the form of aid of some kind. This situation is rendered much worse if the national level in effect circumscribes or opposes local level development in significant ways, essentially by presenting barriers to it—which it may do if, for example, it perceives local development as a threat to its dominance. The third situation put forward, namely, that of enabling a local level to take appropriate and significant advantage of potentially beneficial national level developments, is the easiest situation to which to respond, especially if it is possible to work simultaneously at the national level to ensure that it does understand and respond appropriately to local level development needs. In some situations, all three purposes are relevant reasons for engaging in local level social development, and these are often both complex and extremely difficult situations for intervention.

Goals

As we see it, there are three broad goals behind local level social development initiatives, the specific relevance of each being determined by the prevailing circumstances. These three goals are as follows:

1. To assist individuals and other social entities at the local level to overcome significant problems that represent a specific barrier to these individuals' or entities' social functioning and further development;
2. To strengthen the local level as a whole by strengthening individuals, families, specific population groupings and local organizations wherever possible and appropriate; and
3. To promote local level social development within all dimensions where further development is clearly both essential to achieving overall local level social development and feasible.

All these goals are potentially important. The first goal will commonly involve a degree of remedial intervention, which is why social development commonly requires a casework component. The focus may be, for example, on those who have been victims of conflict, those who possess long-term disabilities, those who are effectively marginalized in their context, those who in desperation have turned to substance abuse, those who are culturally marginalized or those who are deeply entrenched in persistent poverty, and so on. Whatever the nature of the problem confronted, it will be important that these individuals are targeted directly by highly specific and appropriate remedial-cum-developmental intervention strategies, not only for their own immediate benefit but also in order to enable them to participate to the maximum of their capacity in ongoing development. The UN in at least the Asia/ Pacific region continues, in most of its social development reports, to place a strong emphasis on specific categories of people—children, youth, women, the disabled and the elderly—and on those within each category who are particularly in need and severely disadvantaged. While this appears to have become a common UN's response to social development, it seems to us to be a limited, but understandable, approach to social development at whatever level. The second goal places the focus of local level social development clearly on capacity building, which is really what strengthening signifies. There is a related emphasis on empowerment, while a degree of awareness-raising may also be involved, but ultimately the focus is on enhancing capacities that are central to engagement in social development at whatever level. While the first two goals are, to a significant degree, establishing the preconditions for engagement in local, and ultimately national, level social development, the third goal is concerned with this engagement more directly by promoting one or more aspects of social development in the context. Implementing this focus on these social development initiatives will depend on prior analysis of any local level social development undertaken to date, ideally with this analysis being implemented on a fully participatory basis.

APPROACHES TO LOCAL LEVEL SOCIAL DEVELOPMENT

There are various choices available in determining the approach adopted within local level social development, although the choice will often be significantly limited by prevailing circumstances. One choice is between a piecemeal or project-based approach and a comprehensive, integrated approach. The latter is clearly ideal in that it tackles simultaneously all necessary dimensions of local level social development and enables integration to be achieved between the various dimensions. By contrast, the project approach to development may constitute, for example, an exclusive focus on the enhancement of some aspect of economic opportunities, infrastructure development, capacity building within a local sector such as local government structures or a local community-based social services initiative. Provided that these specific projects adopt an appropriate process, consistent with certain principles, they may in themselves be highly beneficial. At the same time, however, each can have only a limited impact on overall local level social development because they are tackling but one dimension of the local reality and therefore will exert only a limited, although often significant, impact on the prevailing situation. They may even ultimately fail because they are not integrated within the prevailing local situation—a not uncommon outcome.

A second area of choice is between an approach that potentially embraces and involves the entire local community or a locality (in practice, of course, only those who choose to be involved) and an approach that targets a specific population within a locality or community. For example, the focus may be on women or female-headed households, or on a particular ethnic or racial group, or on those falling below a predefined poverty line. The targeted approach is often a critical one, especially when the prevailing goal or rationale is the first of those outlined in the previous section. Circumstances may necessitate targeting a specific population on the basis of the first-listed rationale behind local level social development. However, the former approach—that is, involving the total community—is the preferred one if this approach is possible. There are several reasons for this. For example, targeting a specific population may result in further stigmatizing that population, especially, of course, if nothing is done to influence positively the general community's attitudes regarding the targeted group. A second reason is that the total community approach may be an essential foundation for further local level social development, which will be for the benefit of all participants, rather than restricting development to what is possible within and for a limited population.

Some readers may also see a choice between the so-called remedial and the developmental approaches. We do not regard that choice as a realistic one, in that the approach to local level social development can never be exclusively, or even essentially, remedial. While it is frequently the case that the first step will need to contain a significant emphasis on the remedial, this can only be the first step within what must ultimately be a developmental approach.

The Local Level Social Development Process
and the Principles it Reflects

There is today virtually universal agreement, at least in principle, among those concerned with local level social development, as to the process that it should adopt. The process is in effect the application of an agreed set of principles to the development process. The five key elements of the process discussed here are that it be (1) participatory, (2) empowering, (3) equitable, (4) human rights-based and (5) sustainable, or ecologically sensitive and sound. (These five principles do not represent an exclusive list, while some of those listed may be seen as embracing others, such as self-reliance.) Taken together, these five aspects of the development process are very far-reaching and in practice quite difficult to implement, which explains why much local level social development in practice fails to live up to these ideals. It is much easier to do things to and for people than with them participating; empowering people can backfire and see some people making inappropriate or difficult demands on other levels, such as the nation, to such an extent that some people are wary of an empowering approach; rationalizing the long-term benefits for everyone of favoring an elite within development processes is often much easier than adopting an equitable approach from the beginning within an already unequal situation; recognizing all people's human rights can be profoundly unpopular politically, especially if seen as likely to undermine an elite or majority group's power base or standard of living; while ecological sustainability can readily be presented as either unnecessary or a highly contentious and dangerous approach, making it easier to constantly defer the difficult ecological decisions. Although we have reasonable consensus globally on all of these principles as such, the problem lies, albeit understandably, in procrastination regarding their application in the field, certainly by governments but even at times by NGOs and people's organizations. We have a great ability as human beings to rationalize and skirt around principles, even those that we readily endorse "in principle," when we find them difficult or costly to implement. This is why all the elements of this process must be strongly emphasized in all local level social development education, training and practice.

KEY STRATEGIES AND PROGRAMS FOR
LOCAL LEVEL SOCIAL DEVELOPMENT

The two most basic requirements for local level social development are, first, the building, where necessary, of self-confidence and self-esteem, and, second, capacity building with individuals, families, local organizations and communities—and the balance and interaction between these in intervention at the local level is crucial. In those situations where self-confidence and self-esteem are at a low level, it is imperative to address this need. At the same time, it may be difficult to address it directly and in isolation from other needs, largely because the need may not be even recognized by many people. Indeed, building self-confidence may sometimes best be addressed indirectly by, for example, focusing on capacity building while carefully building self-confidence in the process. In any event, it is imperative that workers do not overlook the importance of building self-confidence, however they choose to tackle it.

In one program involving female-headed households in Bangladesh, workers recognized the need to work with very small groups of women, who already knew each other, over periods of several months if necessary. The overt initial aim was to encourage the women to discuss their lives and family situations, needs and aspirations; to identify areas ideally requiring change; and, where possible, to engage in some very basic capacity building within identified areas of life. However, given the extent to which these women had been shunned by society over a long period and made to feel that they were worthless, the crucial indirect aim was to slowly build self-confidence and a healthier self-image. Workers often said that it could take months before some women reached the point of being even able to speak about their situations, let alone begin to see that they might be able to initiate action to change them. It was in some cases only after several months that specific programs of capacity building could be undertaken.

In this program of local level social development in Bangladesh, it is clear that the workers-enablers had no specific agendas other than those referred to previously. The aim was to encourage the women to identify those aspects of their lives that they found most unacceptable and then to encourage them to consider whether these situations could be modified or changed. Within this process, all possibilities or suggestions regarding capacity building that were identified as needed, or regarding external resources seen as required, or any feasible suggestions regarding changes that might be undertaken, were pursued by the enabler working in conjunction with the women. His or her task included ensuring that the women knew what relevant changes were occurring elsewhere in Bangladesh, understood what changes could be attempted and at least began to develop those capacities that were indispensable to implementing changes. Finally, his or her task was to support the women at every step.

Certain planning for and undertaking of change occurred within the small groups, along with any capacity building regarded as necessary and possible. For other projects, however, workers would encourage a few of the groups to combine, thus in effect giving rise to fledgling people's organizations composed exclusively of female-headed households. These local organizations might seek to obtain from government or elsewhere the external resources required for certain tasks, might together undertake further training, and would collaborate in furthering specific agreed-upon projects, while invariably supporting each other. The agency also operated some large income-generation programs, and any woman or group of women who showed interest could participate in such programs; and for many, this was the final major step out of poverty and isolation.

Within a more unified community, the initial approach would usually not be the small cell of targeted individuals used in the program in Bangladesh, but a local community. It might also be somewhat more proactive. For example, in a large-scale program in Sri Lanka, communities were encouraged to consider undertaking, with the agency's assistance, the establishment of a child care center that focused on some services the community deemed important. Many womenfolk would invariably participate in, or congregate around, the center, enabling the worker to talk informally with them about other changes or developments desired by the community. Similarly, as many men gathered to assist with the construction of the center, opportunities for the worker to talk along similar lines with them would inevitably arise and be taken advantage of. In this manner, a variety of local level social development projects would be initiated over an extended period. Consequently, the directions the development took in any specific community following the establishment of the child care center varied, but again, the agency involved was always ready to facilitate a community's participation in any existing program or to develop a new one. The process was always a highly participatory one in which directions, rate of progress and specific approaches were determined by community members, but with the local level enabler always present to support and facilitate the process.

Some local level social development programs have stressed awareness-raising and empowerment, particularly in situations where oppression has commonly been experienced over a long period. Some communities can become so accustomed to oppression that they accept it in a fatalistic way and see no point in striving against it. In such situations, a perceived critical initial strategy is to seek to change the situation by challenging people's basic perception and acceptance of reality. This needs to be done with great care so that it does not further endanger people or leave them with only a heightened level of frustration. The approach adopted by the worker must be undertaken with sensitivity and in a manner that offers constantly available and ongoing support. The two strategies most commonly adopted are awareness-raising through dialogue taking place in informal settings, and social learning—that is, posing problems and seeking their resolution through action. The assumption in such situations, and there are in effect a wide variety of such, is that "[a]n awareness of reality is an essential prerequisite to people participating fully in their own development process, in that awareness will frequently lead to a determination to initiate changes and efforts to do just that" (Cox and Pawar 2006, 147). We can, in effect, divide local level social development programs into several categories. To this point, we have focused on the often very necessary preliminary initiatives of raising self-confidence and self-esteem and of awareness-raising, both of which can be regarded as the first, and often necessary, steps in empowerment.

A second category of programs consists of those directed essentially at capacity building. Such programs may target individuals, families, small groups, local organizations or other entities, which will result in significant variation at the program level. They will also, for this and other reasons, range from the very informal approach to the reasonably formal one. For example, in the small cell formations in the outreach program to female-headed households in Bangladesh discussed previously, significant capacity building took place in the weekly or so group meetings. The topics might include basic literacy or numeracy, how to approach government agencies to present a request, household sanitation and hygiene, or small-plot food production. At the reasonably formal level, examples include the establishment of basic primary schools, health clinics and adult education centers, and all that goes on within these. And if a food-for-work approach was adopted in the construction of such centers, which has often been the case in the Philippines and elsewhere, capacity building would include instruction in handling timber, cement, and so on, within a basic construction context. In other words, capacity building in a particular situation might be the objective of a program or it might occur spontaneously and incidentally within the course of implementing another program.

A third category of local level social development programs revolve around income generation, including such programs as local credit schemes, local people's banks and local microenterprise developments. There are many examples of all these in many parts of the world, and their importance is self-evident. People require capital, no matter how small the sum, to undertake projects or make changes that will enable them to move ahead; and often they will also require access to already established broader microenterprise programs in which they can participate. This type of program may be initiated by the local people within a locality with a small grant of capital and some external training but without external personnel other than a middle-level facilitator. Alternatively, the program may be initiated by a national level agency, involving thousands of participants at many local levels and perhaps hundreds of workers (for examples, see Cox and Pawar 2006, 150–151, 206–207).

A fourth and final group of programs could be categorized as community development programs. This category includes schemes that are designed to bring about leadership development, local organizational development or strengthening, and the linking of local organizations with external sources of support, together with more comprehensive community development programs. In social development terms, the ideal situation is where the key objective is the last, namely, a comprehensive approach, with all of the other schemes mentioned above finding their place as common strategies. Indeed, the ideal community development or, more appropriately, social development comprehensive program would encompass also our first three categories of programs, with the emphases of course being dependent on local circumstances and other prevailing factors. A good example of such a program, located in the Philippines, is set out in our text on international social work (Cox and Pawar 2006, 156–159). Unfortunately, such comprehensive social development programs, though ideal, seem to be exceedingly rare.

A reasonably full list of key strategies and programs[1] for local level development, with brief explanations of each, can be found also in the aforementioned text (Cox and Pawar 2006, 142–156). However, there can be no complete list of such programs, for workers who exercise their imaginations intelligently are likely to discover a range of additional ways of achieving local level development. What we can say is that the strategies and programs referred to here have all been well tested in a variety of contexts, so that their potential usefulness is indisputable.

THE IMPORTANCE OF LOCAL LEVEL SOCIAL DEVELOPMENT

It has already been implied that local level social development is important in its own right for a range of reasons, but let us be more explicit in this regard.

The Place of the Local Level in Social Development

The basic understanding of social development as it has emerged in recent decades is that the three levels of global, national and local are each key levels of development in their own right. There is no intrinsic logic as to why any benefits of previous global or national level development should invariably trickle down to each and every local level, partly because of the inherent nature of the global and national levels and their development emphases. Local levels will often require direct targeting if they are to be receptive to developments at other levels. Despite a degree of outreach, global and especially national level developments create opportunities of which the constituent elements of a society need to take advantage, usually by themselves taking the initiative, if they are to share in the benefits. Hence, even when outreach does occur, the process must be reciprocal, with the local level being also able and ready to reach out through the process of bottom-up development.

The Significance of Pluralism in Society

The modern society is almost invariably pluralistic in a range of ways, and it is very common for political and economic developments, plus the ability to benefit from them, to follow the particular social patterns in a society resulting from its pluralistic nature. Almost invariably some categories or groups of people are effectively excluded from some developments or significantly discriminated against, and while this state of affairs can be tackled through antidiscrimination measures at the national level, these will not always work unless, at the same time, disadvantaged groups are appropriately strengthened to take their rightful place within society. Local level social development will therefore often be very important in addressing inequalities and imbalances within pluralistic societies.

The Existence of Remote Communities

Many nations possess areas that are remote or cut off in ways that render participation in national level development, as contributors or beneficiaries, a difficult process. These may be island communities separated from mainland or national centers, mountain communities cut off by rugged terrain and often heavy winters, remote areas in far-flung corners of the nation or poverty entrenched areas whose very poverty isolates them from developments elsewhere. While modern nations may develop appropriate responses to all kinds of barriers, areas can still be forgotten or overlooked when their remoteness coincides with other characteristics, such as the possession of a particular tribal, ethnic, racial or religious characteristic that sets them apart and even renders them unpopular. In most such situations, local level social development will need to focus on achieving a high degree of self-reliant development as the basis initially of survival but ultimately of significant progress.

The Importance of Building Social Capital and Civil Society at the Local level

Putnam refers to social capital as social bonding at the local level (in Korten 1995, 279), being essentially the bonding together of local organizations concerned with the overall development of their communities and societies. Hoff (1998) sees social capital as measured by "the density and intensity of social relationships within a community." The World Bank (1999/2000, 18) sees social capital reflected at the local level in, for example, citizen and parental involvement in education, health and local credit schemes, and so on, and manifested in a high level of "participation in village level social organizations" (World Bank 1997, 115). The important point here, however, is that these and other writers see social capital as a crucial ingredient in social development. In another publication, Cox (2006) has written,

> At the civil society level, social capital is again not the level of capacity building and so on that has occurred within the many social organizations but that which binds these organizations together in terms of how they network with each other, trust each other, relate to each other and ultimately how they work together within social processes. Moreover, social capital will result in certain types of social organizations that might not otherwise emerge: that is to say, organizations that reflect a community-based or community-wide approach, whether political,

economic, social, cultural or welfare in nature, will emerge in societies with strong social capital. Midgley (1995, 160) refers to such developments as social capital stock. (14–15)

The importance of social capital bonds and the foundations of civil society are crucial to both the local level and ultimately the society as a whole, and it is through local level social development essentially that these two characteristics of a healthy society are built and strengthened.

The Ongoing Reality of Vulnerable and Impoverished Populations

The final reason for the importance of local level social development must be the continuing existence in the world of some one billion poverty-stricken and vulnerable people who are unable to secure an acceptable standard of living or realize their full potential. In a world as developed and wealthy as the present one, this is unacceptable. However, given all the resources that have gone into development to date, we can only conclude that this unacceptable situation will be rectified only when there exist serious direct attempts to alleviate poverty, reduce insecurity, raise standards of living and expand the range of available opportunities at all those local levels where there is a need of such.

CONCLUSIONS

Local level social development is an important level of development and the one to which comparatively little attention has been devoted by comparison with the scale on which action is called for. Part of the reason for this has been an unwillingness to allocate the resources to this level that are clearly required, and part has also been the absence of adequate numbers of appropriately trained personnel able and willing to work at this often difficult level as enablers of development. This lack of personnel is itself in part an outcome of the fact that no profession has accepted this area of activity as part of its mandate (see Chapter 8). This last situation is beginning to change as social work in some countries begins to turn its attention to this level of social development, while the increasing reference to the importance of the local level in many quarters, especially internationally, augurs well for a growing focus on this level in the future. It is our hope that these two developments will expand and work together. If the social work profession would, at least in the so-called developing countries, take local level social development seriously, and if those agencies that endorse local level social development in principle become more committed to facilitating more action at this level, then we might expect to see a great improvement in what has for too long been a completely unacceptable situation. We should acknowledge here the boost to local organizing and development provided by the work of the current president of the U.S., Barack Obama, as a community organizer in Chicago (Obama 2007).

NOTES

1. In another publication (Cox and Pawar 2006, 143), we have listed and briefly described those strategies and programs that we regard as key ones within local level social development. That list is as follows: (a) basic literacy courses; (b) primary school education; (c) basic health care; (d) adult education, basic training, and people's capacity building; (e) awareness-raising and empowerment; (f) local income-generation programs (includes microenterprise schemes); (g) credit schemes and people's banks; (h) community-based welfare programs; (i) self-help groups and promotion of self-reliance; (j) collective responses to specific situations; (k) leadership development; (l) local organization and institution promotion and capacity building; (m) linking local organizations to government agencies and international structures; (n) comprehensive community development programs.

REFERENCES

Cox, D. R. 2006. Building resilient families and caring communities in a troubled world: The importance of strengthening social capital. In *Facing up to global challenges: Proceedings of APFAM International Conference*, ed. J. Ariffin, 9–23. Kuala Lumpur: Asia Pacific Forum on Families.

Cox, D. R., and Pawar, M. 2006. *International social work: Issues, strategies, and programs*. Thousand Oaks, CA: Sage.

Hoff, M. D., ed. 1998. *Sustainable community development: Studies in economic, environmental and cultural revitalization*. Boca Baton, FL: Lewis.

Korten, D. C. 1995. *When corporations rule the world*. London: Earthscan.

Midgley, J. 1992. Development theory, the state and social development in Asia. In *Social Development Issues* 14(1): 22–36.

———. 1995. *Social development: The developmental perspective in social welfare*. Thousand Oaks, CA: Sage.

United Nations Centre for Regional Development. 1988. *Explorations in local social development planning: 1988 synthesis report*. Nagoya: Author.

Uphoff, N. 1986. *Local institutional development: An analytical sourcebook with cases*. West Hartford, CT: Kumarian.

World Bank. 1997. *World development reports: The state in a changing world*. New York: Oxford University Press.

———. 1999/2000. *World development reports: Entering the 21st century*. New York: Oxford University Press.

———. 2000/2001. *World development reports: Attacking poverty*. New York: Oxford University Press.

———. 2001. *Understanding and measuring social capital*. Washington, D.C.: Author.

Part II

Critical Perspectives in Social Development

4 Participatory Development

Kwaku Osei-Hwedie and Bertha Z. Osei-Hwedie

INTRODUCTION

Participation has been pushed to the center of the development agenda in the face of enormous challenges confronting the globe. Since the 1990s, we have witnessed a search for development strategies that go beyond beneficiary participation to inclusive, deepened participation, together with an increasing emphasis on good governance. This does not suggest that participatory development in itself is a new phenomenon. It is as old as human society and is common to all political systems, both democratic and nondemocratic, with the former providing a more conducive environment for its practice. Even colonial governments used participatory development in the form of community development as a means to reduce costs through involvement of people in their own development.

People's participation continued to be the norm in the postcolonial era. In the 1960s, newly independent governments in developing countries relied on participatory development to mobilize the populace for national development as part of the reconstruction of the colonial past (Roodt 2001; Mayoux 2007). In the 1970s and 1980s, participatory development was also emphasized for several reasons, namely, the dismal performance of a state-led development strategy; disappointing outcomes of foreign aid; the adoption of the neoliberal/conservative ideological approach to development that necessitated a minimal role for the state; the increased reliance on civil society, primarily communities and non-governmental organizations (NGOs) as agents of development; and the trend toward a people-centered development strategy.

All the global players, ranging from the state, aid donors, NGOs or civil society organizations (CSOs) to local communities, subscribe to the promotion of participatory development as they grapple with the challenges of social and economic development. Bilateral and multilateral donors have made participatory development and good governance preconditions for aid, and their basis of development strategy and cooperation with developing countries (Japan International Cooperation Agency [JICA] 2007). However, in spite of the much-touted positive elements associated with it, questions have been raised about the efficacy, benefits and contributions to development of participation.

This chapter explores the concept of participatory development with a view to clarifying its meaning and exploring the different interpretations associated with it, its justification and the mechanisms for its implementation. Second, the chapter analyzes the hindrances to the acceptance and implementation of participatory development. Third, the discussion focuses on the sustainability of participatory development as a community-led project to gauge the feasibility of its self-reliant nature and to assess whether it has the capability of standing on its own without external assistance. This is pertinent in view of the shortcomings of local communities and prevailing conditions at grassroots or local levels in the developing countries. Fourth, the chapter puts forward suggestions as to how good governance is positively linked with participatory development, especially when good governance embraces a democratic local government system.

THEORETICAL AND CONCEPTUAL ISSUES

Participatory Development Clarified

Scholars from a range of disciplines interested in development have provided an array of definitions that focus largely on the goals to be attained through participation. One thing they agree on is that participatory development is critical to social and economic development, especially for the amelioration and eventual elimination of poverty as well as the empowerment of the powerless in society. Central to the conceptualization of participatory development are the following questions: who is participating and who should be participating? When or at what level do they participate? How do they participate or what is the nature of their engagement? Who are the beneficiaries of the process? Why is participatory development advocated? (Cornwall 2000, in Mayoux 2007).

Approaches to Participatory Development

Several development approaches or paradigms have provided definitions of participatory development that have evolved over time from a conservative to a radical to a more substantive conception of the term.

Conservative Approaches: Community and Humanist

The community development approach to participation was conservative. It was employed by colonial and postcolonial governments as part of modernization. They viewed it as mere consultation of people to legitimize development decisions taken by governments on behalf of the people. Other conservative approaches include the humanist approach adopted by some development sociologists, which defines participation as actions and interactions among people and the meanings accorded to them by those involved with the aim of avoiding the dehumanization and alienation of people. The instrumental view of participation sees it as a tool for improving the livelihood of beneficiaries (Roodt 2001). For example, Chopra, Kadekodi and Murty (1990) view participatory development as a new socioeconomic force or social institution that is nonconventional and aimed at achieving sustained development at the village level by identifying links between resources, people and government.

Radical/People-Centered Approach

The radical approach to participatory development envisages participation as transformation, empowerment and self-actualization aiming to restructure class and power relations in society (Roodt 2001). The most recent radical approach is people-centered development (PCD), which includes participation as defined by Roodt (2001), and dates from the June 1989 Manila Declaration on People's Participation and Sustainable Development put forward by thirty one NGO leaders and carried forward by the World Bank. PCD conceptualizes participation as development engaged in by the majority of the population, especially those excluded from, or marginalized within, the process of development, including women and youth. Participation of such groups is considered critical to the successful implementation of projects (Roodt 2001).

Since the late 1990s, the World Bank has made PCD the cornerstone of its development philosophy in the fight against poverty which, it emphasizes, should be people-owned to ensure realization of the first goal of the Millennium Development Goals (MDGs) worldwide, that of reducing by half the number of people living in poverty by 2015. This is most relevant to poverty-ridden Sub-Saharan Africa (SSA).

DEFINITIONAL ISSUES

The World Bank defines *participatory development* as a process through which disadvantaged people influence policy formulation, design alternatives and investment choices, and manage and monitor development interventions in their communities. The term *disadvantaged people* here refers to women, indigenous groups and the very poor. However, other stakeholders, including governments, project managers, donors and CSOs, are not necessarily excluded. Nevertheless, communities and not other stakeholders are expected to be the drivers of development processes (Bhatnagar and Williams 1992, 2).

To the World Bank, participatory development is both a means and an end. It is an avenue for participatory contribution to development policies, so that people are not only targets or recipients of development initiatives but also initiators as well as guarantors of realistic policies that meet the needs of communities and ensure ownership by people of the development process. It is an end in the sense that participation builds skills, enhances people's capacity for action, and enriches and fulfils their lives (Bhatnagar and Williams 1992).

In a 1994 publication, the World Bank defines participatory development as a "process through which stakeholders influence and share control over development initiatives and the decisions and resources which affect them" (cited in Cornwall 2000, 8). Viewed in this way, participatory development is people-oriented development that focuses on certain goals, including raising the quality of participation by local societies, allowing for self-reliant and sustainable growth without foreign assistance, fostering environmental conservation and providing equal opportunities for participation in development to reduce income inequalities, regional disparities and gender imbalances, thereby achieving social justice (JICA 2007). Bhatnagar and Williams (1992) concur that participation entails people being responsible for their own development and is geared toward improving economic and social conditions, successfully implementing development, reducing costs and guaranteeing sustainable development. Toward these ends, these authors conceptualize participation as people taking part in decision making, implementation and evaluation of development policy.

Cornwall (2000) and Roodt (2001) present a more radical conception of participatory development than the World Bank, one that is transformative and empowering. To Cornwall (2000), participatory development has three important dimensions. These are (1) representative in terms of people having an equal voice and choice in shaping their development; (2) instrumental with respect to input by the community rather than governments or donors for the sake of lessening costs; and (3) transformative in terms of empowering the powerless through developing their human, organizational and management capacity to solve problems. Cornwall's (2000) definition highlights issues of democratic representation, power and agency. Therefore, it goes beyond a beneficiary and project focus to include issues of citizenship and voice as a means of deepening and broadening the scope of participation.

Roodt's (2001) conception of participation is more radical than both the World Bank's and Cornwall's (2000). His definition includes elements of transformation, consciousness-raising, self-actualization and empowerment. Thus, Roodt sees participation as active involvement by people in civic associations and activities, community developmental organizations, political parties and local governments to influence and have a say in decisions that impact on their lives. Roodt is essentially concerned with local level decision making in both formal and nonformal structures, including organized pressure groups as part of CSOs.

This emphasis on people's active involvement and enhancement of their capacity makes participatory development a people-driven, pro-poor, pro-vulnerable and pro-marginalized (group) strategy of development that seeks to enable people to play an active role in their society's development. The need to involve people signifies that participatory development should take the form of a bottom-up, as opposed to top-down, approach to development to allow for the input of local groups and communities in their societies' development. This explains the importance attached to the qualitative enhancement of participation of local societies, including rural groups or communities, and local administrative and developmental units. In this respect, participatory development is participatory decision making with direct involvement of the population in public policy making and the implementation of policies that affect them.

Participatory development is seen as community driven. This is because it gets people involved in the decision making and the implementation of projects. Therefore, it is seen as instrumental in poverty alleviation and empowerment of the poor. In this light, it is also viewed as an effective tool in building democracy and accountability, and for achieving inclusive and sustainable socioeconomic change (Platteau 2007).

Participatory development is based on the assumption that communities have better knowledge of their local conditions and problems, and of the form of social capital available locally. For these reasons, communities are supposed to be better resourced than central governments and external bodies to determine priorities, identify beneficiaries, develop and implement projects, and enforce rules and verify actions (Platteau 2007; Platteau and Abraham 2002; Conning and Keavan 2002).

Common to all definitions is that participatory development is both a tool and goal of development (JICA 2007). In this case, people participate as agents and beneficiaries of development processes. What are contentious are the issues relating to the scope of participation that should be sought and the methods to be used to achieve this goal. Differences in opinion seem to reflect differing intellectual orientations. For example, the World Bank has been criticized for championing the instrumental approach to participation by putting greater emphasis on influencing and sharing, as opposed to increasing control, and on development initiatives instead of resources and regulative institutions (Cornwall 2000). Cornwall, in her approach to participation, opts for a focus on human rights and on people being heard and not just represented. The cost-benefit approach used by Chopra, Kadekodi and Murty (1990) is seen to have limitations because of its preoccupation with beneficiary participation, as opposed to a broader definition that embraces people's control over decisions and resources that impact on their lives.

LEVEL OF, AND JUSTIFICATION FOR, PARTICIPATORY DEVELOPMENT

People's participation is at different levels—national, regional and local—in different contexts, such as town and rural, and with different scopes of intensity. It can be either direct or indirect, with the preference being for the former as it gives people a voice in their own affairs. For example, participatory rural appraisals (PRA) are seen as one of the most important mechanisms through which communities can be actively involved in development processes (Osei-Hwedie and Osei-Hwedie 2001; Cornwall 2002). The PRA allows people, especially the poor and women, to take part in planning. It empowers communities for self-development and empowers governments, donors and NGOs to initiate and facilitate the participatory process (Osei-Hwedie and Osei-Hwedie 2001).

A number of justifications of participatory development are given, chief among them being the benefits accruing to beneficiaries as well as to governments. From the discussion, it is clear that participatory development can be justified on three utilitarian and substantive grounds. The human rights viewpoint supports participation of the poorest of the poor and vulnerable people as part of their right to determine their destiny, pave the way for pro-poor development strategies and as a means for their empowerment. The effectiveness argument favors participation of all people for the sake of sourcing accurate information for policy making and implementation, and for designing relevant projects and programs that are suited to the realities or needs of the people (Mayoux 2007).

Sharma (2007, 223) sees participation as a means of obtaining information about local conditions, needs and attitudes, without which development programs and projects could fail. It is also accepted for cost efficiency reasons, by virtue of the fact that engagement of stakeholders increases the chances of commitment and ownership of the development process, thereby ensuring its successful implementation, better use of resources and mobilization of local resources to supplement or replace external ones (Mayoux 2007).

People are believed to be more committed to a development project if they participate in the planning and preparation. This in turn makes them more likely to identify with a project and see it as theirs (Sharma 2007). Moreover, through participatory development, governments are able to collect information from people about their needs, priorities and capabilities, and to adapt policies, projects and programs to meet local conditions so that scarce resources are used more effectively (Bhatnagar and Williams 1992).

COMMUNICATION AND PARTICIPATORY DEVELOPMENT

In all conceptualizations, participation is seen as the interaction between and among community members, their environment and all stakeholders in order to improve the collective welfare of the community. Communication is the facilitator of the development process and hence the essence of participation. The participatory process is based on the acceptance of the notion that people's involvement is essential to their development. Bessette (2004) asserts that development is about people and "putting people first" (6). However, key issues revolve around the following questions: how to achieve this in the context of poverty and natural resource development; and how to promote community self-organization and self-management, especially when the state does not have the necessary means to undertake its responsibilities to satisfy basic human needs and promote socioeconomic development. Thus, participation means facilitating the active involvement of community groups, together with other stakeholders (7).

The fundamental basis of participatory development, therefore, is a meaningful communication between communities, development practitioners, extension workers and researchers in order to tackle development problems appropriately and implement the required solutions. The communication, a two-way horizontal process, must bring together all stakeholders—community members, experts, extension workers, NGOs, technical services and policy makers, among others, in a dialogue to facilitate the exchange of ideas on needs, setting of objectives and determining actions and processes (Bessette 2004).

Participation, therefore, should not refer to a one-way flow of information and ideas, giving instructions and directions to people and communities, or motivating people to participate in activities in which they have had no input. Rather, it is an interactional process that establishes a dialogue among community members, community groups and other stakeholders on development issues. Participatory development is a change from the old paradigm where development practitioners adopted a vertical approach in which a problem was identified in a given community and a solution provided with the collaboration of the local people. In this respect, people were informed of the dimensions of the problem and the solutions offered. They were then mobilized to take action (Bessette 2004).

NEW PERSPECTIVE ON PARTICIPATORY DEVELOPMENT

The new perspective on participatory development is based on a change of attitudes, where practitioners perceive communities not only as beneficiaries but also as stakeholders, owners and controllers of the development process. This requires a context where development practitioners establish partnerships and synergies with other actors in the community. In this manner, development becomes interactive. Participatory processes aim at helping people to know and accept that they can solve their problems by taking action themselves, or by being the key participants instead of passive and helpless onlookers. It also helps people to realize that development cannot happen or be sustained without their active involvement (Bessette 2004).

Development is conceptualized as a universal process for which communities are responsible. Thus, it must not be controlled from outside. Rather, societies should define their own models and processes of development in relation to their specific context, culture, values and resources. It is emphasized that development is not just an issue of material welfare, but it also embodies notions of freedom, democracy, equity, social justice, political openness and upholding of human rights (Bessette 2004). Through participation in the decision-making process by ordinary people, socioeconomic development is expected to enhance a sense of community, strengthen community bonds, promote peace and social justice, and satisfy basic needs (Midgley 1995; Osei-Hwedie 2007).

It is clear, therefore, that participation is more than consultation. Participation is also not the same as mobilization, which is merely to harness community support for projects and activities determined by outsiders such as governments, NGOs and donors.

Participation, therefore, involves the following: dialogue and exchange of ideas among different groups and individuals; focusing on local development issues, problems and possible solutions; the identification of necessary actions, awareness building, motivating and implementing action; the effective circulation of information among various community groups and stakeholders; consensus building and development of local collaboration; and monitoring and evaluating the development process (Bessette 2004).

Participatory local development emphasizes that planners, practitioners and researchers must give up their assumed fundamental power to define problems and to solve them for the people. The focus on grassroots participation is based on the perception that, for a project to be sustainable, it must address issues identified by the people themselves, and with a management structure which they understand, identify with and control (Osei-Hwedie and Osei-Hwedie 2001). Participation assumes that people have a fundamental right and duty to engage fully in decisions that affect them at all levels and at all times (Osman 1997; Makumbe 1996; Mikkelsen 1995).

CHALLENGES TO PARTICIPATORY DEVELOPMENT

Community Factors/Characteristics

Despite the promise of participatory development, there are certain factors and conditions that act as barriers to this. Some of these barriers are discussed in this section. Cleaver (2001) notes that there is a myth that a community is capable of doing anything. This is based on the erroneous assumption that they are natural social entities with solidarity relations that only require mobilization of their latent capacities. In this regard, Platteau (2007) emphasizes that, for example, rural communities differ in several fundamental dimensions from urban communities, and that in this context the participatory approach is more complex than is normally imagined.

Platteau (2007) and Bjorkman and Svensson (2006) also indicate that, despite the fact that communities may have better knowledge and understanding, this may not be enough for effective participation. This is because communities must be able to use the information and knowledge in a way that creates effective action. This requires coming together, sharing, discussing and acting cooperatively, and this may be difficult, for example, in a divided community.

Feasibility/Implementation Factors

Theoretically, participatory development seems feasible. However, the challenge lies with its practicability. In practice, it is often an elusive goal due to factors endogenous and exogenous to the process (Osei-Hwedie and Osei-Hwedie 2001). The biggest hindrance is the fact that, by its very nature, it is revolutionary and entails transformation of the way things are done by donors, governments and people. It can, in practice, result in changing the nature of power relationships. Moreover, its implementation and sustainability are dependent on governments. Unfortunately, changing the status quo tends to attract resistance and fear on the part of those in power.

Operational, Structural, Social Values and Practice, and Costs Factors

Other factors that prevent participatory development from being realized may be categorized as operational, structural, social values and practices, and costs.

Operational Factors

Operational obstacles relate to internal operational procedures at donor, government or CSO levels that do not lend themselves to participation by ordinary people. Consequently, changing the nature of interaction has proved difficult, as the emphasis on "experts"—be they project designers and managers (primarily donor personnel), government officials (borrowers or hosts of funded projects) or NGOs (mobilizers of grassroots populations)—is the strongly prevailing one. Often the experts do not believe that the poor, illiterate and disadvantaged can make important contributions to their own development in terms of providing good ideas for development activities, projects and programs, management capacity, monitoring and evaluation for successful outcomes, and sustainability. For example, it has been noted that the World Bank needs to accept, genuinely and fully, that the poor have intellectual and social skills critical to project design and implementation (Bhatnagar and Williams 1992; Uphoff 1992), and move away from an overreliance on technical experts at its headquarters or in the field.

In relation to governments, there is an overcentralization of power by central governments at the expense of local bodies. There is also resistance by governments at national, regional and local levels to including people, especially the poor and marginalized, in all levels of decision making. This is done through a monopoly over power and development resources by elites at central, regional and local levels. This, together with elites' fear of and hostility to people's participation, leaves no room for their involvement in development processes. In SSA, for example, elites combine power positions, based on such factors as class, race, gender, age, education and traditional culture, to prevent meaningful participation taking place (Roodt 2001). In poor and rural societies, chiefs, traditional leaders and other notables may oppose any outside intervention that may threaten their socioeconomic position and privileged status (Platteau 2007).

In addition, the limited capacity of state institutions and lack of structures through which people can participate hinder its practice. Furthermore, in SSA, state structures are weak, and there is a lack of or inadequate democratic local governance structures. These conditions, together with the relatively new democratic culture and structures, prevent promotion of participation. The majority of countries in SSA are "third wave democracies" having transited to democracy in the 1990s. Hence, many people have neither grasped the essence of participation nor appreciated their own potential role. NGOs are no better placed to champion participation as they are at times unrepresentative, donor-dependent or captured by state machineries as in Zimbabwe and Botswana (Roodt 2001). In a nutshell, the operational environment at times does not support participation of the local level.

Structural Factors

The relationship between mass participation and development is a complex one. For example, successful efforts at development have not always been through democratic processes. At the same time, grassroots' cooperation with governments has not always led to development. The key seems to be how to enhance development while at the same time promoting democracy, political participation and freedom (Osei-Hwedie and Osei-Hwedie 1999).

Another issue appears to be that the politicization of grassroots organizations has negatively affected their ability to provide for mass participation in development activities. In many instances, as in the case of Botswana with the Village Development Committees, participatory structures have been transformed into forums where politicians and civil servants persuade the people to accept decisions made by the central and district government authorities (Osei-Hwedie and Osei-Hwedie 2001).

The challenge is to address what Midgley (1987) refers to as the "realities of statism" (6). This relates to the dilemma of participation in the context of state-sponsored development. It is assumed that the state will transfer control of resources to the grassroots and enable the people to determine the process and outcome of development. In reality, however, the state plays a key and ongoing role in determining policies, providing resources, creating infrastructure and delivering social services (Osei-Hwedie and Osei-Hwedie 2001). Thus, where the interests of the state and that of the masses conflict, the state takes precedence and the wishes of the masses are ignored (Osei-Hwedie 2007).

Structural hindrances include socioeconomic conditions of inequality and poverty that prevent the poor from participating and being sufficiently aware to seize the opportunity to change their situation vis-à-vis the better-off people and an unaccountable government. The poor, especially in Africa, are dependent on elites who control production assets such as land and capital, and hence are really not in a position to bite the hand that feeds them.

Social Values and Practices

Social values and practices refer to prohibitive practices that are biased against women, hierarchical norms that discriminate against the young and females, and patronage-based norms that militate against equal participation of the poor, females, youth and some ethnic groups, especially minorities. Such values can operate as barriers against participation.

For example, the heterogeneity of communities in SSA's villages along gender, age, lineage and other lines compounds the problem of communication and information dissemination, especially when the focus is on the empowerment of the poor and other deprived members of the community. Conflict might arise with the local elites who tend to promote their own interests and often do not have the same understanding of external assistance. Despite this, external donors and development practitioners often believe that the elite are motivated to promote the collective good, and so they work through them (Tembo 2003; Harrison 2002). Mehta (2000) argues that, in many instances, the resources provided and institutions created do not empower the poor, but rather enable the more powerful to control the resources and "co-opt the poor to serve their interest" (16).

Exclusionary tendencies also exist in communities and act as a barrier to participation. This is because the need to preserve a sense of inclusion for a majority can lead to the exclusion of certain segments of the population such as ethnic minorities, nomadic people and recent immigrants (Platteau 2007; Conning and Keavan 2002). In such instances, participatory development becomes participation by the powerful at the expense of the poor. At times this translates to people not feeling concerned about the "well-being of others unless they belong to the same ethnic group" (Platteau 2007, 19).

Traditional practices are compounded by structural economic and social inequalities that make it impossible for the marginalized to have a voice in decision making affecting their lives. Added to this is the common belief among the disadvantaged people that there is nothing they can do to improve their existing situation, and that they have no right to participate in decisions that impact on them. This is because they believe that their traditional and elected leaders must decide on their behalf (Roodt 2001).

Cost Factors

The costs to donors, governments and local communities of promoting and sustaining participation can also discourage its adoption and practice. Costs involved include those for designing and starting up participation, as people have to be organized into groups, their capacity has to be built through education and training, and information made available to them. These are seen as time-consuming processes and likely to delay program implementation, thereby raising costs (Bhatnagar and Williams 1992; Bhatnagar 1992).

In some situations, communities are aware of agency preferences. Thus, in their relations with these agencies, they may feel compelled to decide on development activities closer to those preferred by these external bodies, in order to ensure that the necessary resources are provided. In such situations, communities depart from their own true priorities because of the need to conform to donors' wishes and to accept whatever they provide and desire (Platteau 2007). Platteau cites Gueneau and Lecomte (1998), who use a proverb by a village chief in Burkina Faso to demonstrate this: if I give you a hen free, you won't start examining the ass to determine whether it is fat or thin—you just accept it. This situation also has the effect of giving donors the confidence and belief that their approaches are valid (Platteau 2007, 8).

In many instances, agencies such as NGOs prefer collective over individual welfare, while community members look for opportunities to improve their individual situations. Moreover, community groups often see the existence of NGOs as there to facilitate the flow of aid. Thus, when some NGOs, established for specific development activities, disappear as soon as the activities and external funding come to an end, the communities become puzzled or upset. Tembo (2003) confirms that, in a case in Malawi, when a new NGO appeared on the scene, the local people did not even mention the previous NGOs and their activities, and new committees were set up to meet the demands of the new NGO. Thus, communities may see participation as only necessary to meet part of development costs, or to access whatever aid-funded development is available (Platteau 2007).

At times, key informants and prime movers of community projects, such as village headmen, teachers and other village elites, may decide on projects with funding agencies long before community members are informed of the choice. Thus, community interests come to be represented by those of the elite and external funding bodies. In this respect, people's interests are presented in such a way as to be acceptable to the donor agency as well as to suit the interests of village elites (Platteau 2007; Tembo 2007).

In many instances, the availability of external resources in a community attracts both the locally based and traditional elites to get involved in the participatory development process. In addition, in situations where community empowerment is low or lacking, the more educated and other elite groups take leadership positions, due to the attractiveness of external resources, and in order to source funding channeled through participatory development groups (Platteau 2007; Agrawal and Gupta 2005; Oyono 2004). It has also become fashionable for political entrepreneurs and the elite to establish NGOs and to act as development brokers as a way of attracting funding from the international community. This phenomenon has led to the mushrooming of NGOs in the developing world in response to the availability of aid money (Platteau 2007; Lund 2006).

Knowledge, Choices and Technical Factors

Platteau (2007), citing Khwaja (2004), stresses that community participation might not always be desirable. This is because of associated limitations that are often ignored. Some choices made by communities, especially of a technical nature, may be inappropriate, particularly because of a lack of knowledge and proper understanding of the wider context but also because of the general conditions in which projects are undertaken, such as the interconnectedness of local and external services, resources and infrastructure. In this regard, Platteau (2007) contends,

> In addition to the knowledge problem, some local services spillover benefits, and higher level rules on such services or conditional transfer to meet these needs are perfectly legitimate. To take another example, community participation might identify health services as the top priority, but the replacement of a contaminated water supply that citizens are not aware of . . . could be a more important factor in promoting improved community health than a new health centre. (36)

This explanation of those barriers often perceived as standing in the way of adopting a participatory approach is important in its own right but also as a further illustration of the complexity of participatory development.

Sustainability of Participatory Development and Promotion of Good Governance

Toward Participatory Development/Prospects of Participatory Development

Participatory development is only possible, effective and sustainable if certain preconditions are fulfilled and sustained over time. Indeed, the practice and sustainability of participation is only possible with government's commitment and political will to let the masses be part of the decision-making process. A community's capacities, in terms of skills and resources, are equally important. What is needed is a proper balance between citizen participation and external assistance of governments, donors and NGOs, in order to capture both local inputs and strategic planning expertise critical to successful development outcomes. This is where good governance is a necessary precondition of, and intricately intertwined with, participatory development.

Participatory development defined as a bottom-up, community-led or people-driven approach to development allows people to take control of their lives through the formulation, implementation and evaluation of development policies. It does not exclude the involvement of governments (top-down). Instead, it tries to minimize and overcome the shortcomings of the state-led approach to development, while appreciating the importance of national level economic planning and coordination of development planning (JICA 2007).

Role of Government

The government's role is critical to providing the conditions necessary for participatory development. Participatory development is, in essence, participatory decision making, as it entails people's ownership and control of, commitment to, and (popular) support for the development process, all elements of developmental democracy and good governance. Therefore, good governance is the foundation of participatory development, as it provides the government functions needed to promote participation and create an environment within which participatory processes take place (JICA 2007). For participatory development to occur and be maintained, first, governments have to promote democratic local governance through the devolution and decentralization of power, authority and resources to local authorities, providing them with adequate functions, power and resources to make and implement policies and decisions. Second, effective participatory structures—that is the environment for, and avenues through which, people can participate in development—must be created. These could take the form of town meetings for small communities, and organs of civil society or NGOs for large communities.

Third, people must be empowered through building their skills and capacities, and through providing them with the powers, authority and resources to enable their full participation in public policy-making and implementation. In essence, participatory development and good governance mutually reinforce each other, as the former provides conditions conducive to people's participation and the latter contributes to efficient and effective delivery of services by the government. This in turn will give rise to people's trust in their government, thereby contributing to the enhancement of the process of democratization.

Underdevelopment in SSA puts pressure on the sustainability of participatory development when this is conceived as people's self-reliance without external involvement. Due to underdevelopment, poverty and incapacity, local communities often lack adequate resources and skills. They must, therefore, depend on governments, donors and NGOs for the necessary inputs.

The Community in Participatory Development

The concept of community must be understood as a contextual, contested and endogenous construct rather than a fixed state ready for the attachment of participatory mechanisms. Due to this, the participation process cannot be a "one size fits all" process. Rather, proper and sustainable participatory approaches must be based on detailed and specific knowledge of the characteristics of targeted communities and their environments (Platteau 2007).

Participatory development, when conceived as a bottom-up approach, is often implemented to adapt to a top-down reality for several reasons. These include the nature and sources of resources needed, and the role of powerful external agents, including central government bodies, NGOs and development experts. This means that local development planning must be flexible. Chinsinga (2003, 140) notes that

> flexible local planning is essential because the results of participatory planning exercise are never comprehensive: they change over time, with techniques used, the level of organization, the personalities of the participants, the socioeconomic situations, and so on.

It must be recognized that there are limitations in the abilities of communities. Local people can do certain things with their own skills and resources. However, there are situations where others must help them to strengthen their resolve and capacity to take action through systematic analysis and implementation of appropriate solutions. The way forward, therefore, is to formulate a theory of development that accepts the local and the external levels as equally important.

Reconceptualization of Participatory Development

Often, participation is wrongly viewed as a neutral process implemented in the context in which both experts and communities can put their views, beliefs, convictions, attitudes and perspectives on hold when they engage with each other. However, this is far from reality. Stakeholders need to see participation as "an untruncated process of negotiation" that requires changes in the attitudes and perspectives of stakeholders. Participation, in other words, requires "meaningful reforms" of power relations between local people and planners (Chinsinga 2003, 12). Participation must be seen as a negotiation process in which all actors communicate and interact, hoping to eventually make insightful and sustainable decisions. However, in practice, the planning team almost always influences, animates, induces, manipulates and controls the negotiation process. Authentic local participatory development can only be achieved through negotiation processes between planners and the local people being structured in a manner that accepts all participants as equal partners. The spirit of give and take must prevail among all the stakeholders in grassroots development (Platteau 2007).

If participation is taken as a negotiation process, then local needs, opinions, knowledge and expertise will be accepted as legitimate and flexible, which development plans must respect (Clark 1991; Goudsmit and Blackburn 2001). Development practitioners must have an open mind as well as knowledge and experience as to what is feasible and acceptable in communities. Local people's participation is influenced by the level of their understanding of the forces militating against their welfare. Without a comprehensive appreciation of the causes of their conditions, people may resist participation. The lack of knowledge by poor people of their own status may be due to the impact of poverty, which forces them to be concerned with survival rather than anything else (Clark 1991; Makumbe 1996; Ubgomeh 2001; Chinsinga 2003). Chinsinga (2003) quotes Ubgomeh's (2001) point that "in regions (and countries) of extreme poverty participation can become a luxury not all can afford" (141). Thus, the livelihood of the poor must be improved and guaranteed for them to participate fully and effectively in development. The poor need assistance to develop and manage their own organizations through which they can realize their collective strengths and rights, and negotiate constructively and effectively for their own development (Chinsinga 2003; Oyugi 2003).

CONCLUSION

Participation by the masses is very critical to the development process, to democratization, and, most important, to giving voice to and empowering the poor, marginalized and vulnerable groups in society. It is also an imperative to harnessing people's commitment to and ownership of, as well as the successful implementation of, development projects. However, authentic participatory development is rare and difficult to achieve because of the inherent shortcomings of communities, governments, donors and NGOs. On one hand, communities might lack the will, capacity and resources. On the other hand, centralized authority of government structures, and donors' and NGOs' modes of operation and expertise, might be too overbearing and inflexible to permit the opening up of avenues for people's say in decision making, planning or implementation.

Development programs cannot succeed unless the people accept, own and participate in them. The participatory process, therefore, confirms the sovereignty of the people. It is both about meeting people's needs and creating an environment through which people can address their needs. Therefore the promotion of participatory development is based on the acceptance of self-determination.

In reality, what is needed for meaningful and successful development to take place is a balanced partnership between people's engagement and strategic planning and expert skills. This, in essence, requires the existence and sustenance of good governance, especially local democratic governance in which governments, donors and NGOs allow for greater participation, and that people in practice take responsibility for their own livelihoods with the support of the former. Thus, ideally, there is a need to develop participatory processes that recognize the legitimacy, desirability and benefits of outside involvement, while at the same time appreciating a locality's need for some autonomy.

REFERENCES

Agrawal, A., and Gupta, K. 2005. Decentralization and participation: The governance of common pool resources in Nepal's Terai. *World Development* 33(7): 1101–1114.

Bessette, G. 2004. *Involving the community: A guide to participatory development communication.* Penang: Southbound; Ottawa: International Development Research Centre.

Bhatnagar, B. 1992. Participatory development and the World Bank: Opportunities and concerns. In *Participatory Development and the World Bank*, ed. B. Bhatnagar and A. Williams, 13–30. Washington, D.C.: International Bank for Reconstruction and Development/World Bank.

Bhatnagar, B., and Williams, A. 1992. Introduction to *Participatory Development and the World Bank*, ed. B. Bhatnagar and A. Williams, 1–10. Washington, D.C.: International Bank for Reconstruction and Development/World Bank.

Bjorkman, M. and Svensson, J. 2006. *Power to the people: Evidence from randomized experiment of a community based monitoring project in Uganda.* Stockholm: Stockholm University.

Chinsinga, B. 2003. The participatory development approach under a microscope: The case of the poverty alleviation programme in Malawi. *Journal of Social Development in Africa* 18(1): 129–144.

Chopra, K., Kadekodi, G., and Murty, M. 1990. *Participatory development.* New Delhi: Sage Publications.

Clark, J. 1991. *Democratizing development: The role of voluntary organizations.* London: Earthscan Publications.

Cleaver, F. 2001. Institutions, agency and the limitations of participatory approaches to development. In *Participation: The New Tyranny?* ed. B. Cooke and U. Kothari, 35–55. London: Zed Books.

Conning, J., and Keavan, M. 2002. Community based targeting mechanisms for social safety nets: A critical review. *World Development* 30(3): 375–394.

Cornwall, A. 2000. *Making a difference? Gender and participatory development.* Sussex: Institute of Development Studies, University of Sussex.

Gudsmit, I., and Blackburn, J. 2001. Participatory municipal planning in Bolivia: An ambiguous experience. *Development in Practice* 3(5): 587–595.

Harrison, E. 2002. The problem with the locals: Partnership and participation in Ethiopia. *Development and Change* 33(4): 587–610.

Japan International Cooperation Agency (JICA). 2007. Participatory development and good governance. Available from the Global Development Research Center Web site: http://www.gdrc.org/u-gov/doc-jica_gg.html (accessed October 23, 2007).

Lund, C. 2006. Twilight institutions: An introduction. *Development and Change* 37(4): 685–705.

Makumbe, J. 1996. *Participatory development: The case of Zimbabwe*. Harare: University of Zimbabwe Publications.

Mayoux, L. 2007. The rise of participatory development. http://www.lindaswebs. org.uk/Pagel_Development/Participation/Participation.htm (accessed October 23, 2007).

Mehta, A. 2000. The micro politics of participatory projects: An anatomy of change in two villages. In *Development encounters—sites of participation and knowledge*, ed. P. E. Peters, 15–28. Cambridge, MA: Harvard University Press.

Midgley, J. 1995. *Social development*. London: Sage Publishers.

———. 1987. Popular participation, statism and development. *Journal of Social Development in Africa* 2(1): 5–15.

Mikkelsen, B. 1995. *Methods for development work and research: A guide for practitioners*. New Delhi: Sage Publications.

Osei-Hwedie, K. 2007. Implementing the "social" in "development": The challenge of social development in Sub Saharan Africa (SSA). Paper presented at the 15th Symposium of the International Consortium for Social Development, on the theme "Seeking Harmony and Promoting Social Development in a World of Conflict," Hong Kong, July 16–20, 2007.

Osei-Hwedie, K., and Osei-Hwedie, B. Z. 1999. Social development and cooperative governance: Incorporating the marginalized. *Social Development Issues* 21(3): 60–65.

———. 2001. Grassroots participation: The challenge of social development in Botswana. In *Social Development in Africa*, ed. A. Kidanu and A. Kumssa, 47–60. Nairobi: United Nations Centre for Regional Development, Africa Office.

Osman, S. 1997. Participatory governance, people's empowerment and poverty reduction. http://www.undp.org/seped/publications/conf pub.htm (accessed September 29, 2007).

Oyono, P. R. 2004. One step forward, two steps back? Paradoxes of natural resources management decentralization in Cameroon. *Journal of Modern African Studies* 42(1): 91–111.

Oyugi, W. 2000. Decentralization for good governance and development. *Regional Development Dialogue* 21(1): 3–20.

Platteau, J. P. 2007. Pitfalls of participatory development. Paper prepared for the United Nations. http://www.fundp.ac.be/pdf/publications/61702.pdf (accessed December 10, 2007).

Platteau, J. P., and Abraham, A. 2002. Participatory development in the presence of endogenous community *imperfections. Journal of Development Studies* 31(10): 1687–1703.

Roodt, M. 2001. Participation, civil society, and development. In *Development: Theory, policy and practice*, ed. J. Coetzee, J. Graaff, F. Hendricks and G. Wood, 469–481. Oxford: Oxford University Press.

Sharma, K. 2007. Towards good governance in Africa: Critical dimensions and the experience of Botswana. In *Governing development across cultures: Challenges and dilemmas of an emerging sub-discipline in political science*, ed. R. B. Jain, 215–238. Opladen, Germany: Barbara Budrich Publishers.

Tembo, F. 2003. *Participation, negotiation and poverty alleviation: Encouraging the power of images*. Adelshot: Ashgate.Ubgomeh, G. 2001. Empowering women in agriculture education. *Community Development Journal* 36(4): 289–302.

Uphoff, N. 1992. Monitoring and evaluating popular participation in World Bank-assisted projects. In *Participatory development and the World Bank*, ed. B. Bhatnagar and A. Williams, 135–153. Washington, D.C.: International Bank for Reconstruction and Development/World Bank.

5 Self-Reliant Development

Madhavappallil Thomas and Manohar S. Pawar

INTRODUCTION

Self-reliance has reemerged as an important theme in local level development and social development discussions generally. While there is a large body of literature focusing on the various aspects of local level development and social development, there is very little that explores the concept of self-reliance as it relates to social development. An extensive search of various databases yielded very few articles that focused on self-reliance in the context of social development. This chapter, therefore, is an attempt to bridge this gap. It explores the concept of self-reliance as used and referred to in various contexts, including development discussions, and goes on to examine some of the essential characteristics of self-reliant individuals, families, communities and societies as perceived by various writers. Additionally, it examines policies and programs that are oriented toward fostering self-reliance and the economic and social independence of people and communities. There is also a brief discussion of some proposed strategies that promote self-reliant growth and development. However, it is recognized that there are various local, national and global level forces that pose significant challenges to local development generally and to self-reliant social development in particular; hence the impact of globalization challenges and of the global economy on people, communities and nations are explored. Finally, we discuss some of the internal and external threats to development that are structural and functional in nature, and which in turn impact on self-reliance and local development endeavors at the local and national levels.

SELF-RELIANCE AND LOCAL SOCIAL DEVELOPMENT

The meaning of self-reliance given in dictionaries is the capacity or ability to rely on one's own capabilities (power, resources, judgment or ability to generate an outcome) and manage one's own affairs. In this sense, self-reliance implies autonomy and independence in the existence of human beings. These basic notions of autonomy, independence and reliance on one's own capabilities, powers and resources have, however, been expanded beyond this simple definition to apply in a variety of contexts and situations. For example, self-reliance is often discussed in association with survival needs, commonly focusing on increasing the likelihood of one's viability in the face of adverse situations. Based on this notion, it follows that self-reliant individuals, families and communities are those that have taken the necessary steps to lessen their dependence upon society for aid in meeting their livelihood needs. Self-reliant people and communities do this by proactively expanding knowledge and building capabilities in order to achieve the basic needs and necessities of life. More specifically, for example, these individuals and communities learn to build and maintain their own homes, make their own clothes, create local water supply systems, and establish and maintain their communication and transportation systems.

This expanded notion of self-reliance has been used in association not only with development generally, but also with several specific concepts referred to in the context of development discussions and debate. For example, one can clearly relate self-reliance to the achievement of human needs and can even extend this notion to human rights and the resulting rights-based strategies advocated by several scholars (Ife 2001; Reihert 2006) for achieving human needs and social needs. As discussed earlier, since self-reliance implies meeting survival needs in the face of adversities, as well as generally, the literature tends to refer to this trait or characteristic of individuals, families and communities as resilience. This relationship between self-reliant survival and resilience has given rise to such expressions as resilient individuals, resilient families and resilient communities. Resilient economies and resilient nations (or national resilience) are also expressions implying that these too have certain inherent capabilities that can be mobilized for continued survival when confronted by natural calamities, such as Hurricane Katrina or the Indian Ocean Tsunami, or economic downturns, such as the global recession that began in 2006–2007. In this sense, the concept of resilience may be considered as a hallmark or a characteristic trait of self-reliance for attaining livelihood means. The resilience dimension as a trait for self-reliant survival has neither been explored in the literature nor found a meaningful place in discussions concerning self-reliant development. Yet such an exploration can only enrich our understanding of self-reliance in the context of development generally.

Similarly, self-reliance for continued survival under adverse circumstances also implies that individuals, families and communities have the capabilities to mobilize resources from within and use these resources as an investment for continued and sustainable future survival, growth and development. Therefore, resource mobilization necessarily assumes a pointed significance not only as a means to the attainment and realization of survival needs but also as an effort to invest the mobilized resources for continued and sustainable self-reliant growth. Mobilized resources may include human resources, social capital, social assets, land, and economic, political and cultural resources generally. In this sense, one can argue that building people's capacities and social capital are both associated with continued and sustainable self-reliant development.

A resource-based initiative for self-reliance necessarily requires participation of people and communities at the grassroots level. Self-reliance assumes that there is no significant or at least unnecessary dependence on external sources or aid for earning a livelihood or for sustaining the ability to earn a livelihood. Thus, self-reliance refocuses the responsibility on to people and communities, and the development of their strengths, capabilities and potentialities. In other words, the active participation of people and communities is vital to sustainable self-reliance and growth. Moreover, people and communities are more likely to feel empowered when they realize that the solutions for attaining their livelihood means and maximizing their potentialities are inherent within themselves and their communities, rather than searching outside for solutions or depending largely on outside aid for local level development.

From an ideological and value-oriented perspective, self-reliance has certain philosophical overtones. In this sense, it may be argued that every individual has the inherent ability (Pawar 2010) to be largely autonomous and independent in attaining their survival and existential needs. Since it is an innate or inherent quality in every individual, it can be seen to be the responsibility of every individual to lead a self-reliant and independent life as far as this is possible. From these premises, it can be said that not realizing the innate and inherent abilities of individuals is irresponsible, unacceptable and even immoral. In this view, for whatever structural and functional reasons, people who depend on external sources for their livelihood means are sometimes blamed for their failures. These assumptions and interpretations pose the inevitable value-oriented moral question: should individuals be made responsible for realizing their innate and inherent abilities and so meeting their survival and livelihood needs? Or should external entities, such as governments or the public sector, assume responsibility for those individuals who are seemingly unable to realize their innate and inherent capabilities in meeting their survival and livelihood needs? It is evident from the preceding discussion that self-reliance is a value-oriented principle as well as a way of life with certain philosophical corollaries of individualism.

From an individualistic standpoint, the articulation of self-reliance is often associated with conservative ideology that stresses that human needs can be best understood as individual needs, and therefore achieving survival and livelihood needs is solely the responsibility of individuals and families. In contrast, liberal ideology emphasizes the importance of creating and providing opportunities for employment, which in turn will build self-reliance and growth. In this context, the society also assumes certain responsibility for creating and providing access to various services and gainful employment. Thus, in this perspective there is an element of interdependence between individuals and society in meeting human needs.

As mentioned earlier, self-reliance is often mentioned in the context of social development, economic development, regional development, community development and locality development, but without elaboration. We therefore see it as important and appropriate to conceptualize self-reliance in the broad context of development—self-reliant development. However, the application of self-reliance to the development context has a much wider meaning than the philosophical overtones of individualism. To take one example of the very specific application of self-reliance, the UN High Commissioner for Refugees (UNHCR 2005), in its publication "Handbook for Self-reliance," defines self-reliance in the refugee context as follows:

> Self-reliance is the social and economic ability of an individual, a household or a community to meet essential needs (including protection, food, water, shelter, personal safety, health and education) in a sustainable manner and with dignity. Self-reliance, as a programme approach, refers to developing and strengthening livelihoods of persons of concern, and reducing their vulnerability and long-term reliance on humanitarian/external assistance.

In this quotation, the UNHCR addresses not only survival needs but also the health, education and other ongoing concerns of vulnerable populations such as refugees. Thus, self-reliance as it relates to development has potentially a broad significance. Of course, there is often necessarily an element of interdependence and external intervention in creating opportunities for a self-reliant approach to meeting the livelihood means of people and communities. In the context of refugees again, the UNHCR (2005) further notes,

> Self-reliance helps people to claim their rights and provide a basis for equality, equity, empowerment and participation. It promotes collaboration, trust, and social and economic interaction between communities, and strengthens coexistence. It can prevent human suffering and social unrest. It can motivate and attract governments, NGOs [non-governmental organizations] and donors to provide support and strengthen their partnership. It can reduce dependency, offset demand for handouts and subsidised services and reduce the impact of budget constraints.

Here the UNHCR highlights the issues related to human rights, equity and fairness. These conceptualizations of self-reliance, when applied to development more generally, seem to suggest that public sector entities such as governments, not-for-profit organizations and other external agencies may be involved in helping individuals, families and communities to achieve self-reliance in meeting all types of human and social needs. All such help and support, however, is seen as temporary, with the assumption that people and communities, if helped appropriately in terms of their needs, may become self-reliant in the long run. One way of depicting this is to see it as important for external resource entities to adopt a self-reliance entry mode, or partnership entry mode, in providing aid, help or support, so as to facilitate local level and general social development (Li and Qian 2008). Although these terms are borrowed from economics and business, the ideas as applied to self-reliance and development call for joint ventures, joint resource and service distribution networks (partnership entry mode) and internalization as manifested in the form of ownership of assets, capital and resources (self-reliance entry mode). Thus, it can be said that, in self-reliant development, the involvement of external entities needs to be based on a partnership entry mode and/or a self-reliance entry mode.

HUMAN NEEDS, HUMAN RIGHTS AND SELF-RELIANCE

An exploration of the links between human needs and human rights is likely to provide a deeper and wider understanding of self-reliance in the context of development. At the outset, it may be argued that, on the one hand, the attainment of various human needs such as survival needs, social needs, economic needs, and political, cultural and spiritual needs enables people and communities to become self-reliant. Conversely, on the other hand, self-reliance empowers individuals, families, localities and communities to realize these various needs and capabilities to their maximum potential. In this sense, self-reliance goes far beyond the articulation of survival needs and embraces social, political, cultural and spiritual needs. Thus, a self-reliant community or locality is committed to empowering those individuals who are unable to meet these various needs by themselves, in order that they might become largely self-sufficient.

In the literature generally, and within the social work profession, human needs are articulated in several ways. For example, the National Association of Social Workers defines human needs as (a) need for physical and mental well-being; (b) need to know; (c) need for justice; (d) need for economic security; and (e) need for self-realization, intimacy and relationship. Another well-known conceptualization of human need at the individual level has been offered by the famous psychologist, Abraham Maslow. Maslow's hierarchy of human needs include (a) psychological survival needs (nourishment, rest, sex, warmth); (b) safety needs (preservation of life and sense of security): (c) belongingness needs (to be part of a group, to love and to be loved); (d) esteem needs (approval, respect, acceptance, appreciation, etc.); and (e) self-actualization needs (to be able to fulfill our potential). It is, however, possible to view human needs within the framework of human rights, as the UN, through various proclamations and conventions, has done. According to the UN (1992),

Human rights could be generally defined as those rights which are inherent in our nature and without which we cannot live as human beings. Human rights and fundamental freedoms allow us to fully develop and use our human qualities, our intelligence, our talents and our conscience and satisfy our spiritual and other needs. They are basic for mankind's increasing demand for a life in which the inherent dignity and worth of each human being will receive respect and protection.

The main international source of basic human rights is the UN Universal Declaration of Human Rights (UDHR), though further elaboration and extension can be found in various other conventions, covenants, and declarations.

Human rights have been categorized into three types: (1) civil and political rights; (2) economic, social and cultural rights; and (3) collective rights. They are also referred to respectively as first-, second- and third-generation rights. Ordering them as first- to third-generation rights has been sometimes interpreted as reflecting high to low importance, with some scholars even doubting whether the third-generation rights are human rights (see Ife 2001; Uvin 2004).

The first set of human rights, civil and political rights (Articles 2–21 of the UDHR) are known as "negative rights" because they tend to restrict the role of government. These include the right to life, liberty and security of the person and their derivates. These first-generation rights are individually based and mostly legalistic, and it is assumed that every individual possesses these rights and needs to be protected against their violation or abuse. Thus, these are called negative rights. The second set of human rights, namely, economic, social and cultural rights (Articles 22–27 of the UDHR), are treated as "positive rights." These include: the right to adequate food and clothing, the right to housing, the right to education, the right to employment, the right to an adequate wage, the right to adequate health care, the right to social security, the right to be treated with dignity in old age and the right to rest and leisure from work. Although these second-generation rights do not have universal acceptance, they suggest active roles and responsibilities for governments in achieving these rights. These are positive rights in that they require governments, other agencies and individuals to take action to preserve or satisfy these rights (Reichert 2006). The main aims of the second generation rights are social justice, freedom from want, and participation in the social, economic and cultural aspects of life (see UN 1992; Ife 2001). Ife's (2001) analysis suggests that "these are rights of the individual or group to receive various forms of social provision or services in order to realize their full potential as human beings" (26).

The third set of human rights is known as "collective rights," which states that "everyone is entitled to a social and international order in which the rights and freedoms set forth in this declaration can be fully realized."

Ife (2001) observes that the third type of human rights—such as the right to economic development, the right to benefit from world trade and economic growth, the right to live in a cohesive and harmonious society, the right to breathe unpolluted air, the right to clean water and the right to experience "nature"—"belong to a community, population, society or nation, rather than being readily applicable to an individual, though individuals can clearly benefit from their realization" (27).

These articulations of human needs within the framework of human rights add another level of meaning to the concept of self-reliance, in that self-reliance may be expanded to include the realization of human rights and so may include a rights-based approach to developing the capabilities of individuals, families and communities in the realization of various human needs and human rights.

"COLLECTIVE RELIANCE" VERSUS SELF-RELIANCE

As brought out in the preceding discussion, self-reliance in local level social development must imply a commitment on the part of individuals, families and communities to share the available resources with those who are unable to meet their various human needs and human rights. Self-reliance, therefore, does not mean mere individualism or the self-centered understanding of individualism. This commitment to share resources and capabilities adds another dimension to the concept of self-reliance in the context of sustainable local development, that may be referred to as "collective reliance"—a term coined by the authors to explore the realization of collective needs and collective rights within the social development framework. Collective reliance recognizes the opportunity for individuals to benefit from the sustainable self-reliant growth and development of localities and communities. It stresses the need for collective action and the active participation of people in the process of achieving self-reliance or collective reliance. It recognizes the ability of individuals, families and communities to act collectively and to mobilize resources together in resolving problems at the local level. The importance of collective reliance in the development of poor communities primarily rests on the availability of basic infrastructure and services, such as housing, sanitation, water and transportation, as well as access to health care, education and employment. The availability of these provisions and services not only benefit the poor and the disadvantaged in meeting their various needs, but potentially all community members. However, often such services and provisions are inadequate, due perhaps to a lack of resources within local government to supply and maintain such services in the face of increasing demands from people and communities. In many communities, such inadequate services can result in marginalized people in particular being unable to meet their needs. It is also observed that, in many of these localities and communities, there is inadequate collective action, organized advocacy and lobbying aimed at obtaining the required services. Collective reliance requires that people and communities act collectively and promote mass participation in the process.

Collective reliance or shared reliance calls for a commitment to a participatory approach in the development process. A participatory approach aims to promote people-centered local development, thus enhancing self-reliant and sustainable growth without external dependence. It fosters equal opportunities and reduces inequalities in the distribution of goods and services. Participation also calls for people to be responsible for their own development by actively taking part in the decision-making process and the implementation and evaluation of policies and programs geared toward sustainable and self-reliant development (Bhatnagar and Williams 1992). Collective reliance thus focuses on collective action of people by promoting their participation in achieving various human needs in the development process.

RESILIENCE AND SELF-RELIANCE

Resilience is an important characteristic or trait of self-reliant individuals, families and communities. Such individuals and communities will demonstrate resilient traits when confronted with adverse situations and calamities that challenge their ability to survive. A resilience-informed approach thus promotes self-reliant growth and development that is sustainable. Resilience as a concept emerged in the 1970s, representing a paradigm shift from psychopathology to the identification of protective and risk factors that differentiate resilient individuals from non-resilient individuals (Anthony 1987). Generally defined, resilience refers to "manifested competence in the context of significant challenges to adaptation" (Masten and Coatsworth 1998, 206). It has been viewed as interactional in nature and defined as a "dynamic process encompassing positive adaptation within the context of significant adversity" (Luthar, Cicchetti and Baker 2000, 543). In contrast, others consider resilience to be the "ability to maintain adaptive functioning or to regain functioning in the presence of one or more risk factors without experiencing one or more serious long term harmful outcomes" (Nash and Bowen 1999). Most researchers seem to examine two important concepts as intrinsically present in any understanding of resilience: "risk factors" and "protective factors." While risk factors refer to conditions that increase the likelihood of developing a problem, protective factors imply conditions that buffer, interrupt or prevent problems from occurring (Greene 2002; Greene and Conrad 2002).

For example, risk factors that are found within the child's family include the poverty level of the family of origin, the types of problems in the family of origin, and the presence of only one parent. Jones (1998) found that inadequate housing, including homelessness, significantly correlated with higher levels of foster care reentry. Patterson (2002) has identified a number of characteristics of families that show resilience in the face of great adversity. These include family cohesiveness, family flexibility and family communication. A focus on these individual, familial and environmental protective factors, and their potential to empower people and communities when faced with challenges to their livelihood means, offers greater insight into programs and services that promote self-reliance and local level development. Such protective factor-oriented initiatives are particularly likely to promote self-reliance among vulnerable populations.

Resilience can also be found in the environment. Jones (1998) noted that children who reside in neighborhoods characterized by a high prevalence of weapons and substance abuse are at higher risk for re-referral and reentry into out-of-home care. Similarly, early education programs are found to provide children with protective factors that counteract the chaos and instability of homelessness (Douglass 1996). Rutter and others (1979) noted that children from schools that promote high self-esteem and scholastic success have a lower frequency of emotional and behavioral problems, both of which Jones (1998) found were significantly correlated with re-referrals to Child Protective Services after children had been reunited with their families. A stable school environment, access to health care, access to security services, access to social services, affiliation with a religious organization, emotional support outside the family, and so on, are also examples of protective factors within one's environment. In the context of local level development, it is of paramount importance to build community resources that can maximize the capabilities of vulnerable children and families.

Resilience and strengths perspectives are closely related and are often used interchangeably by scholars. The strengths perspective emphasizes the resources, assets, potentials and capabilities of individuals, groups, families, and communities (Greene 2002; Saleebey 1997). This approach also marks a paradigmatic break from the typical human service perspective, which has for far too long focused on pathology and deficits. Traditionally, professionals were asking what was wrong with people and communities; by contrast, the strengths perspective asks what is right. People and communities are seen as having strengths, possibilities and solutions with which to build their own futures, instead of focusing on problems, liabilities, and pathologies (Brueggemann 2002). This perspective upholds the belief that people have untapped, undetermined reservoirs of mental, physical, emotional, social, and spiritual abilities that can be realized to maximize their potential (Weick et al. 1989). Such an approach undoubtedly goes a long way in promoting self-reliant development in localities and communities.

RESOURCE MOBILIZATION AND SELF-RELIANCE

Involvement with local development activities shows that every community has an inventory of assets and resources upon which to build its own future. Community-asset maps usually bring out a vast array of individual talents, capabilities, productive skills and institutional resources that are often not mobilized for building communities and developing localities (Kretzmann and McKnight 1993). Mobilizing the internal and external resources of individuals, families and communities is very important in achieving self-reliance and collective reliance.

A resource-based approach is likely to provide an effective strategy for mobilizing assets and resources for self-reliance and local level development. A resource-based view, as originally associated with industry and business, was used to determine the strategic resources available to a business firm. Barney (1991) argued that a sustainable competitive advantage derives from the resources and capabilities a firm controls that are valuable, rare and not substitutable. These resources may be categorized as tangible and intangible assets, such as a firm's management skills, its organizational processes and routines, and the information and knowledge it controls (Barney, Wright and Ketchen 2001).

The application of a resource-based approach offers great scope and opens newer avenues toward achieving self-reliant local development. A resource-based view would mean that every community is seen to possess a sustainable competitive advantage that is generated by the unique collection of resources and assets within each community. In other words, this perspective describes how communities can build their own businesses for generating employment and income opportunities, for developing goods and services, and for mobilizing and using their own capacities, assets and capabilities. In terms of self-reliance, the ability to build resources and capabilities also means building capacities. In development endeavors it is essential and crucial to build capacities not only of the poor and other vulnerable populations, but also of governmental institutions at all levels, and especially the local where local development is concerned. Such organized and collective action can go a long way in ensuring self-reliance and collective reliance.

Capacity building is often viewed as a catalyst for economic growth that in turn promotes sustainable survival and self-reliance. It is oriented toward developing human resources, enhancing organizational capabilities and bringing about institutional change. For example, investments in expanding educational avenues and providing access to financial and technological resources for the residents of a community not only provide employment opportunities but also generate income for sustainable self-reliant growth and development (UN Development Programme [UNDP] 1997). Development of such resources and capacities are necessary preconditions for developing the self-reliance of individuals, families and communities. The UNDP (1997) defines capacity building as a process by which "individuals, organizations, institutions and societies develop abilities (individually and collectively) to perform functions, solve problems and set and achieve objectives" (3). Clearly, enhancing human resources and improving institutional and organizational effectiveness would improve productivity and growth among people and communities, which in turn supports their continued self-reliance. To recapitulate, a resource-based strategy to mobilize resources and to build assets and capacities of people and communities can form the foundation for sustainable and self-reliant local development.

SELF-RELIANCE AND SOCIAL DEVELOPMENT

In the foregoing sections, we have explored the concepts of self-reliance and collective reliance/shared reliance as referred to in discussions and writings related to social development endeavors. Several essential features and interlinked notions of self-reliance—such as human need, human rights, resilience, resource mobilization and people's participation—were also discussed. Let us now explore further the following questions: how does self-reliance fit with the conceptual framework of social development? What are the kinds of policies and programs that promote self-reliant social development? What are the strategies for achieving self-reliant development?

Although an extensive discussion of social development is not the purpose of this chapter, it is, however, pertinent to briefly describe the social development framework as it relates to self-reliance. Social development has been defined and conceptualized by scholars in various ways (see Chapter 2). In this book, Pawar and Cox analyze the main elements in the definitions of social development. These are social development as a process of systematically introducing planned change, releasing human potential, transforming people's determination, reorganizing and reorienting structures, and strengthening the capacity of people and their institutions to meet human needs. The goals of social development include the reduction of inequalities and social problems, the creation of opportunities and the empowerment of people to achieve human welfare and well-being to improve relationships between people and their institutions and to ensure economic development. They also present an approach to social development consisting of the analysis and changing of existing conditions by following clear goals, values, processes and strategies at all levels and in all dimensions of society (see Figure 2.1 and Table 2.1).

Self-reliance as articulated earlier implies a certain level of social development, and therefore self-reliance may be considered as one of the hallmarks of social development endeavors. In view of this, self-reliant social development may be conceptualized as the fostering of continued and sustainable capabilities of individuals, families, communities and societies in order to meet their livelihood means and existential needs. It is achieved through meeting human needs and social needs, developing the inherent resilient traits of people and communities, mobilizing internal resources and external resources (human resources and social capital and assets, economic resources, political, cultural and spiritual resources), promoting the participation of people and communities, and adopting an ideology that is appropriate for the promotion of sustainable self-reliance and growth.

POLICIES AND PROGRAMS AND SELF-RELIANT DEVELOPMENT

Before identifying policies and programs for self-reliant development, it may be helpful, as an example of what is meant, to examine the efforts made over several decades in the U.S. to transfer people from dependency to autonomy and self-reliance. Research suggests that neither the organized charity efforts of the early community organization societies (COS) nor the publicly funded efforts found in more recent programs such as Aid to Families of Dependent Children (AFDC) and Temporary Assistance for Needy Families (TANF) have, for the most part, been successful in building self-reliance and empowering program recipients to become independent. For example, Ziliak (2004) analyzed data (from January 1881 to February 1883) from caseworker manuscripts of the Indianapolis Charity Organization Society. Using a hazard regression model, he hypothesized that the data should exhibit a higher rate of exit as time spent with COS accumulated. Instead Ziliak found that the probability of exit was 19% for households receiving relief up to two months. The probability then fell to 10% for households receiving relief between two and six months, further dropped to 3.5% between six to twelve months, and flattening out to low rates as time spent with COS increased. The findings were similar for both genders. The researcher then compared exit rates for female households with the results of the study conducted by Blank (cited in Ziliak 2004) on single mothers receiving AFDC in Seattle and Denver from 1971 to 1976. Blank found that, for AFDC recipients, the probability of exit was 7.3% in the first two months of the program, much less than the 20% found for women in the COS program. The exit rate for AFDC recipients between the third and sixth month was 6%, falling to 4% and then to about 2% through spells of length between twelve and twenty-four months. These results were also consistent with the findings of the study conducted by Fitzgerald (cited in Ziliak 2004) on women receiving AFDC in the mid-1980s. Ziliak therefore concludes that the work of at least one COS and two recent programs did not lead to the poor moving significantly toward self-sufficiency or self-reliance. Rather, this analysis of the data from the nineteenth-century COS and the twentieth-century AFDC shows that transition to higher income earning and self-reliance was lower than the expected outcome of the program, and that the pattern was similar for COS and AFDC recipients.

In the American context, public assistance programs have been conceptualized as a last resort safety net so that public assistance recipients do not fall below a certain poverty level. The assumed goal of these programs is not moving people to self-reliance but merely providing them with a temporary safety net. Karger and Stoez (2006) identified the following assumptions behind public assistance programs in the U.S.: (a) generous benefits create a disincentive to work, and therefore recipients must always receive less income benefits than the minimum wage; (b) welfare recipients need prodding to work because they lack internal motivation; (c) work is the best antipoverty program; (d) public assistance programs must be highly stigmatized lest people will turn to them too readily; (e) women receiving public assistance should work, and poor children should not have the luxury of being raised by a full-time homemaker. Clearly, such assumptions behind programs aiming to transfer people from dependency to autonomy are most unlikely to produce the desired results of independence and self-reliance.

From a self-reliant development perspective, it is important to identify policies and programs that are likely to promote sustainable self-reliance. In a case study (Midmore and Thomas 2006) undertaken for Pembrokshire Local Action Network for Enterprise Development, the researchers outlined a strategic framework that identified collaboration between various economic stakeholders and supported by institutional actors, and provided an assessment of increased self-reliance. Based on the analysis of the data, they identified tourism development as the leading potential sector in the local economy. The other major areas warranting an emphasis were education, human capital development, increased local sector purchasing, development of renewable energy sources, the contribution of inward investment and local leadership, and general participation. The researchers concluded that the anticipated economic outcome of their plan would be to increase the self-reliance of Pembrokshire. This is an example of how local and regional resources can be harnessed in order to promote sustainable self-reliance at the local level. Such an approach also implies a certain level of decentralization in government and political power structure.

At the individual and family level, social insurance policies and programs may be considered as promoting self-reliance to a great extent. It is a system in which people are compelled through payroll or other taxes to insure themselves against the possibility of their own indigence resulting from retirement, loss of a job, death of a family member or physical disability. The primary goal of such social insurance is to help individuals and families to maintain a portion of lost earnings (Karger and Stoez 2006). The major social insurance programs in the U.S. include Old Age Survivors and Disability Insurance, Unemployment Insurance and Workers' Compensation. Similarly, tax deductible retirement programs such as 401(k) and 403(b) in the U.S. are also based on the notion of saving for the future. As an example from elsewhere, in India, the National Rural Employment Guarantee Act 2005 appears to have potential for encouraging self-reliance, if implemented properly (Hirway 2006). In terms of their conceptualization and implementation, these policies and programs come close to the notion of self-reliance.

As another example, the microcredit financial innovation that originated with the Grameen Bank in Bangladesh underscores the importance of fostering economic independence and self-reliance through generating self-employment and income generation. Under this scheme, small loans (microcredits) and some training are provided to women who initiate self-employment activities that generate income for their livelihood. It emphasizes building the capabilities and capacities of a microentrepreneur, generating gainful employment and providing support in implementing the microprojects. In spite of the criticisms (Rankin 2002), the microcredit projects are successful programmatic efforts in the direction of promoting self-reliance and local level development.

Savings-led microfinancing schemes have gained currency in helping poor families achieve economic independence and self-reliance through low cost financial services. For example, in India, the National Bank of Agriculture and Rural Development finances more than five hundred banks that lend funds to self-help groups of approximately twenty members, of whom the majority are women from low socioeconomic backgrounds. Members save small amounts of money (as little as a few rupees a month) in a group fund. Members are allowed to borrow money from the group fund for any number of activities. As self-help groups prove capable of managing their funds effectively, they can borrow from a local bank to invest in small businesses or farm activities, with the banks lending up to four times the amount of money available in group funds. According to estimates, nearly 1.4 million self-help groups, comprising approximately 20 million women, borrow from banks under this scheme, which makes this self-help financing scheme the largest micro finance scheme in the world. Policies and programs as discussed above seem to foster self-reliance through income generating activities that promote economic independence and autonomy.

STRATEGIES FOR SELF-RELIANT SOCIAL DEVELOPMENT

The discussion on self-reliance and social development, whether it be at the global, national or locality level, often remains at the abstract level without exploring specific strategies to promote self-reliance and development. Based on the development strategies India followed after achieving independence, Singh (1986) identified the following strategies as important: a *growth-oriented strategy* aiming at building infrastructure in rural areas for the promotion of rapid economic growth; a *welfare-oriented strategy* promoting the well-being of the rural population in general and the rural poor in particular; a *responsive strategy* for helping rural people to help themselves through their own organizations and support systems; and *an integrated or holistic strategy* combining all positive features of the above strategies and designed to achieve growth, welfare, equity and community participation.

Pandey (1981), in an old but still relevant publication, discusses four social strategies required to bring about social development. The first is *distributive strategy*. This is geared toward achieving social equity in the process of national development. It includes the equitable distribution of resources and wealth. It requires changes in the distribution pattern of income and wealth. It probes such questions as, who pays? Who distributes? On what conditions? And in what ways? The second is *participative strategy*. This aims at promoting the involvement of all sections of the population in the development process. Mass sharing of the benefits, mass contribution and mass involvement are the three distinct but related aspects of this strategy. It poses questions like, who participates ? Why? Through what channels? And in what kind of programs? The third is *human development strategy*. This stresses the enhancement of productivity and the income generating capacity of the labor force. People play the role of agents and beneficiaries, rather than being merely resources. This has led to the redefining of social development as an investment in people aimed at improving the condition and quality of human life. Finally, the fourth is *social integration strategy*. This is characterized by an integrative approach aimed at bringing isolated and peripheral groups, communities and regions into the mainstream of development. It tries to reduce the disparities between different regions, social groups and communities.

Based on this exploration of self-reliant development, we propose the following strategies for achieving social development: First, *a rights-based strategy*: this is aimed at ensuring and empowering individuals, families and communities to meet their various needs—such as economic, social, political and cultural needs—to the fullest possible extent. It assumes a certain level of state intervention to create access to resources and provide opportunities for people and communities to engage in activities that foster self-reliance. Second, *a resilience-informed strategy*: this focuses on strengths, resilient capabilities and protective factors that empower people and communities to overcome adverse situations by harnessing and releasing the energies and resources available within themselves and their communities. Such an approach builds on protective factors that have the ability to buffer risk factors surrounding people and communities in times of adversities. Third, *a resource mobilization strategy*: this focuses on mobilizing internal and external resources in order to achieve social, economic, political, cultural and spiritual needs of people and communities which in turn have the potential to promote self-reliance. Finally, *a participatory strategy*: this aims at promoting collective action and building partnerships between people and community institutions in order to achieve self-reliance, individually and collectively.

CHALLENGES TO SELF-RELIANCE AND SOCIAL DEVELOPMENT

Like any other development initiatives, self-reliance and local level social development, as discussed previously, inevitably encounter a range of potential internal and external challenges and threats. Development alternatives, policies and programs, however well conceived, are not free from structural, functional and operational problems related to both internal and external environments. While the individuals, communities and nations may have relatively more control over internal, local and national level challenges, they seldom have power and control over external and global level forces that impact indigenous self-reliant efforts. Such external threats stemming from globalization have been more pronounced in recent years than during other times in history.

Local and National Level Challenges

At the local and national levels, policies and programs attempting to promote self-reliant growth and development often fail to achieve the desired results. In many cases, the assumptions behind conceptualizing such policies and programs are not fully based on transferring a program's aid recipients from being beneficiaries to becoming self-reliant. For example, the assumption behind AFDC was that a casework approach would help program recipients to move from welfare to income-generating activities. This assumes that obstacles to self-reliance are primarily rooted in individual deficiencies and not in adverse social, economic and structural factors.

Ideological positions and conflicts espoused by major political parties seem to pose challenges in adopting policies and programs that truly promote self-reliance through an adequate investment in human capital. While formulating policies and programs, political parties tend to insert their own agendas into the policy initiatives, which results in ideological conflicts. For example, during the welfare reform initiatives in the mid-1990s in the U.S., the conservatives fought to build the theme of personal responsibility into the Welfare Bill, underscoring their ideology that human needs must be understood as individual needs, and therefore meeting those needs must be the responsibility of individuals. The liberals, on the other hand, emphasized their theme of creating and providing opportunities to engage in gainful employment activities, emphasizing their ideology of providing access to work opportunities. The Welfare Bill that emerged from the reconciliation of these conflicting positions is known as "Personal Responsibility and Work Opportunity Reconciliation Act." So, understandably, rather than creating policies that build skills and capacities of aid recipients and empower them to become self-reliant, the policy was based on reconciling two competing political ideologies.

Another challenge arises from the lack of political will and commitment in adopting a pro-poor approach based on the principles of social justice and equity in the distribution of resources. In capitalist economies, while political and religious rights are guaranteed, economic rights are not guaranteed. As a result, the importance of empowering the marginalized poor to become self-reliant has not been moved to the mainstream of development conversations or policies and programs.

Active people's participation is very important for self-reliance policies and programs to take root at the local and national levels. Such collective action by the people may be radical and may entail transformation of the status quo. In many cases, collective action undertaken by people and communities may take the form of challenging the existing notions of power relationships, which in turn can create tensions and conflicts between the power structure and the masses. However, in many localities and communities around the world, people have often tended to be indifferent, inactive and unmotivated to engage in collective action to achieve goals of self-reliant growth and development.

Also, many localities and communities encounter resource constraints in supporting and funding development activities that are oriented toward self-reliance. The current economic recession has forced individuals, families, communities and nations to tighten their belts and even to cut back much needed services and programs. An aggressive reduction in funds, the elimination of programs, and massive layoffs in the workforce engaged in implementing development programs are challenges that are difficult to surmount in the current economic environment. Another important impact of the recent economic downturn is the enormous funding drain experienced by the NGOs that are involved in myriad development projects around the globe. Holloway (cited in Keith and Kulugina 2009) points out that Southern CSOs (self-organized citizen NGOs for public purposes) that are funded by foreign donors, and particularly those dependent on Northern donors, are thereby limited in achieving their core principles of effectiveness and self-reliance. Holloway argues that Northern resources, which come mostly in the form of time-limited projects, do not contribute to long-term financial sustainability, as the recipient organizations are unable to continue with the projects once these projects are concluded. At the same time, however, this dependence on foreign funds has not usually motivated these NGOs to develop and draw on the resources from within the communities, a process that has the potential to further self-reliant sustainable growth.

Another internal, structural and operational challenge arises from the fact that many of these development policies and programs originate at top levels and may have a different relevance to the grassroots. Policies and programs, however well conceived at the top level, may lose their intrinsic value by the time they reach the lower levels of the administrative structure. For example, the personnel responsible for the implementation of development projects may overstress the economic aspects of the program while ignoring those social aspects that may be much more important for the community. On similar lines, some of these programs may not even address the needs of the people and communities for whom these very policies and programs have been designed. This results in incongruence between a community's needs and externally conceived policies and programs (Thomas 1990).

Globalization Challenges

Globalization is a relatively new trend that poses external challenges to the self-reliant growth and development of many localities, communities and nations. In the context of self-reliant growth and development, scholars are divided on the merits and demerits of globalization and its impact on people, communities and nations (Payne and Askeland 2008; Midmore and Thomas 2006; Hewison 2000; Prigoof 2000). In spite of these differences in opinion, there seems to be a general consensus among writers that events, incidents and changes that occur in certain distant parts of the globe can impact, positively or negatively, the lives and livelihood means of people, communities and nations located in other parts of the world. For example, the recent economic downturn originated in the U.S., due primarily to the crash in the housing and financial sectors, has resulted in a significant global recession that in turn has posed substantial challenges to the growth and development of communities and nations around the world. Prigoff (2000) argues that the social consequences of economic globalization have been destructive to human communities, particularly in the context of world hunger. For example, "policies of the International Monetary Fund and the World Bank promoted a shift in the use of land from production for the local consumption to production for export" (Progoff 2000, 196–197). Prigoff argues that famine in the age of globalization is man-made and is the product of a faulty economic system. Hines (cited in Midmore and Thomas 2006) points out that an increasing emphasis on localization in recent years is a process that reverses the trend of globalization in favor of localization and decentralization. However, Hines cautions that localization should not limit the flow of information, technology, trade and investment. While appropriate technology transfer and inward investment can facilitate and support localization efforts, an overreliance on inward investment in an increasingly globalized world may erode the economic base of communities and result in economic vulnerabilities. From a self-reliance standpoint, these arguments seem to suggest that, while it is important for localities and communities to be locally grounded in terms of sustainable growth, it may be equally valuable for them to be globally oriented to at least some extent.

While globalization clearly has its benefits, it has negatively impacted various communities and nations. The economic crisis of Thailand during the 1980s and 1990s is a case in point. Hewison (2000) examined the economic crisis that erupted in 1997 in Thailand following the boom from 1987 to 1997 and found that it was due in part to the enormous foreign investment and the resulting globalization process. During the boom time, Thailand experienced some of the highest growth rates in the world with real increases in per capita GDP indicating massive industrial transformation of the society. The boom, however, did not last long and eventually ended in an economic crisis. Then, in response to this crisis, the

International Monetary Fund drafted a recovery plan with tighter monetary policy, increased financial liberalization and greater economic openness to foreign investment. This was more in line with globalization policies and the focus on external investment. The nationalist response that emerged against this backdrop focused more on localism and building a self-reliant economy free from foreign control. It advocated rural self-sufficiency in basic needs such as food, healthcare, housing and clothing. This notion was rooted in the premise that a "self reliant nation does not need the outside world and may choose its international links rather than being forced into international market and free trade" (Hewison 2000, 285). For example, the "sufficiency economy" policy of Thailand's king, His Majesty King Bhumibol Adulyadej—which emphasizes moderation, reasonableness, prudence/self-immunity (ability to cope with shocks from internal and external changes) and knowledge, morality and ethics at all levels (individuals and families and communities)—is a case in point (Piboolsravut 2004; Curry and Sura 2007; Kantabutra 2008). The Thai response was based on the idea that self-sufficiency leads to self-reliance, which in turn can build strong communities with the confidence to resist external pressures. Thus self-reliance empowers a community to take control of its destiny by making decisions about its own future. The Thai experience clearly suggests that an overreliance on external resources and foreign investment and globalization can bring about strong challenges to people and communities around the globe.

Similarly, questions are being raised as to whether China is abandoning its long-cherished principles of self-reliant growth and development in favor of the recent change in approach that is centered on globalization (Kerr 2007). Kerr concludes that globalization initiatives and interdependence do not mean that "China cedes responsibility and initiative to external actors; but on the contrary must continuously look to its own capabilities to ensure that gains of global integration are maximized." The researcher further notes that this "global interdependence does not relieve the need for regeneration by one's own efforts but enhances it" (102). Chinese developments suggest that it is adopting an approach that integrates localization efforts and globalization initiatives. Although the verdict is still not clear regarding the impact of globalization on self-reliance and local development, the preceding discussion clearly suggests the importance of locally grounded development endeavors that promote self-reliance while being globally oriented.

CONCLUSION

To recapitulate, this chapter explores the concept of self-reliance as used and discussed in various contexts. In particular, it examines the notion of self-reliance in local level development and in the context of social development discussions. Furthermore, self-reliance is examined in relation to human need, human rights, "collective reliance" and people's participation, resilience and resource mobilization. Based on this exploration, we have offered a conceptual framework for self-reliance. In terms of policies and programs, social insurance and income-generating initiatives, for example, seem to have the potential to move people from program benefits to economic independence and self-reliance. Our analysis of local, national and global challenges shows that an approach rooted in localized development endeavors that incorporates a global orientation may prove to be more resilient in withstanding the internal and external threats to self-reliant development. It is our hope that this chapter provides an enhanced understanding of self-reliance in relation to local development and social development more generally.

REFERENCES

Anthony, J. 1987. Risk, vulnerability, and resilience: An overview. In *The invulnerable child*, ed. E. J. Anthony and B. Cohler, 3–48. New York: Guilford Press.

Barker, R. L. 2003. *The social work dictionary*. Washington, D.C.: National Association of Social Workers Press.

Barney, J. B. 1991. Firm resources and sustained competitive advantage. *Journal of Management* 17:99–120.

Barney, J. B., Wright, M., and Ketchen, D. 2001. The resource-based view of the firm: Ten years after 1991. *Journal of management* 27:625–641.

Bhatnagar, B., and Williams, A. 1992. Introduction to *Participatory Development and the World Bank*, ed. B. Bhatnagar and A. Williams, 1–10. Washington, D.C.: International Bank for Reconstruction and Development/World Bank.

Brueggemann, W. G. 2002. *The practice of macro social work*. Belmont, CA: Brooks/Cole.

Curry, R. L., and Sura, K. 2007. Human resource development (HRD) theory and Thailand's sufficiency economy concept and its "OTOP" program. *Journal of Third World Studies* 24(2): 85–94.

Douglass, A. 1996. Rethinking the effects of homelessness on children: Resiliency and competency. *Child Welfare* 75(6): 741–752.

Gore, M. 1973. *Some aspects of social development*. Hong Kong: Department of Social Work, University of Hong Kong.

Greene, R. R. 2002. Human behavior theory: A resilience orientation. In *Resiliency: An integrated approach to practice, policy and research*, ed. R. R. Greene, 1–27. Washington, D.C.: National Association of Social Workers Press.

Greene, R. R., and Conrad, A. P. 2002. Basic assumptions and terms. In *Resiliency: An integrated approach to practice, policy and research*, ed. R. R. Greene, 29–63. Washington, D.C.: National Association of Social Workers Press.

Hewison, K. 2000. Resisting globalization: A study of localism in Thailand. *The Pacific Review* 13(2): 279–296.

Hirway, I. 2006. *Livelihood security through the National Employment Guarantee Act: Toward effective implementation of the act*. Levy Economics Institute Working Paper No. 437. http://papers.ssrn.com/sol3/papers.cfm?abstract_id=878146 (accessed December 3, 2009).

Ife, J. 2001. *Human rights and social work: Towards rights-based practice*. Melbourne: Cambridge University Press.

Jones, J. F., and Pandey, R. S. 1981. Social development: Conceptual, methodological and policy issues. New Delhi: MacMillan.

Jones, L. 1998. The social and family correlates of successful reunification of children in foster care. *Children and Youth Services Review* 20(4): 305–323.

Kantabutra, S. 2008. *Development of the* sufficiency economy *philosophy in the Thai business sector: Evidence, future research & policy implications.* http://www.sufficiencyeconomy.org/old/en/files/26.pdf (accessed December 2, 2009).

Karger, H. J., and Stoez, D. 2006. *American social welfare policy: A pluralist approach.* Boston: Pearson.

Keith, S., and Kulugina, E. 2009. Review of *Towards financial self-reliance: A handbook of resource mobilization for civil society organizations in the south* by R. Holloway. *Nonprofit Management & Leadership* 13(3): 283–287.

Kerr, D. 2007. Has China abandoned self reliance? *Review of International Political Economy* 14(1): 77–104.

Khan, M. Z., and Thomas, M. E. 1998. Administrative support to rural development programs. A paper presented at the national seminar on action sociology and dynamics of rural development. Jabalpur, India, February 5–7, 1998.

Kretzmann, J. P., and McKnight, J. L. 1993. *Building communities from the inside out: A path toward finding and mobilizing a community's assets.* Chicago: Institute for policy research: North Western University.

Kulkarni, P. D. 1979. *Social policy and social development in India.* Madras: Association of schools of social work in India.

Li, L., and Qian, G. 2008. Partnership or self-reliance entry modes: Large and small technology-based enterprises' strategies in overseas markets. *Journal of International Entrepreneurship* 6:188–208. DOI 10.1007/s10843–008–0029–3.

Luthar, S. S., Cicchetti, D., and Becker, B. 2000. The construct of resilience: A critical evaluation and guidelines for future work. *Child Development* 71(3): 543–562.

Masten, A. S., and Coatsworth, J. D. 1998. The development in competence in favorable and unfavorable environments. *American Psychologist* 3:205–220.

Midgley, J. 1995. *Social development: The developmental perspective in social welfare.* London: Sage.

Midmore, P., and Thomas, D. 2006. Regional self reliance and economic development: The Pembrokeshire case. *Local Economy* 21(4): 391–408.

Nash, J. K., and Bowen, G. L. 1999. Perceived crime and informal social control in the neighborhood as a context for adolescent behavior: A risk and resilience perspective. *Social Work Research* 23(3): 171–187.

Pandey, R. 1981. Strategies for social development: An international approach. In *Social development: Conceptual, methodological and policy issues,* ed. J. Jones and R. Pandey, 33–49. New York: St. Martin's Press.

Patterson, J. M. 2002. Understanding family resilience. *Journal of Clinical Psychology* 58(3): 233–246.

Pawar, M. 2010. *Community development in Asia and the Pacific.* New York: Routledge.

Payne, M., and Askeland, G. A. 2008. *Globalization and international social work: Post modern change and challenge.* Burlington, VT: Ashgate Publishing.

Piboolsravut, P. 2004. Sufficiency economy. *ASEAN Economic Bulletin* 21(1): 127– 134.

Prigoff, A. 2000. *Economic for social workers.* Brooks/Cole: Belomont, California, U.S.A.

Rankin, K. N. 2002. Social capital, microfinance, and the politics of development. *Feminist Economics* 8(1): 1–24.

Rees, W. E. 2006. Globalization, trade and migration: Undermining sustainability, *Ecological Economics* 59(2): 220–225.

Reichert, E. 2006. Understanding human rights: An exercise book. Thousand Oaks, CA: Sage.

Rutter, M., Maugham, B., Mortimore, P., and Ouston, J. 1979. *Fifteen thousand hours*. Cambridge, MA: Harvard University Press.

Saleebey, H. 1997. The strength perspective possibilities and problems. In *The strengths perspective in social work*, ed. D. Saleebey, 233–244. New York: Longman.

Singh, R. S. 1986. *Changing occupational structure of scheduled tribes*. New Delhi: Inter-India publications.

Thomas, M. E. 1990. *Dynamics of rural development: A critical study of two development blocks in Kerala*. Doctoral thesis submitted to the Department of social work, Jamia Millia Islmia, New Delhi, India.

United Nations. 1992. *Teaching and learning about human rights: A manual for schools of social work and the social work profession*. Geneva: The UN Centre for Human Rights.

United Nations Development Programme (UNDP). 1997. *Capacity development*. New York: Management and Development and Governance Division, UNDP.

United Nations High Commissioner for Refugees (UNHCR). 2005. *Handbook for self-reliance*. http://www.unhcr.org/pubs/self_reliance/handbook_for_self_reliance. pdf (accessed February 20, 2009).

Uvin, P. 2004. *Human rights and development*. Bloomfield, CT: Kumarian Press.

Weick, A., Rapp, C., Sullivan, W. P., and Kisthardt, W. 1989. A strength perspective for social work practice. *Social Work* 34:350–354.

Ziliak, S. T. 2004. Self reliance before the welfare state: Evidence from the charity organization movement in the United States. *Journal of Economic History* 64(2): 433–461.

6 Capacity Building for Local Development
An Overview

Gautam N. Yadama and Marsela Dauti

WHAT IS THE CAPACITY-BUILDING APPROACH?

Capacity building is ubiquitous in social development discussions. Every development endeavor aspires to build capacity of the poor, non-governmental organizations (NGOs), local governments, national ministries or other entities. What does it mean to build capacity? The answer to this question is varied and diverse. In this paper, we briefly review the various discussions of capacity building in the development literature, and reflect on what it means to engage in capacity building for local development.

Local level capacity building is often a pathway for reaching better development outcomes in marginal communities that have been previously excluded from the development process. At the core of local level capacity building lies the drive toward inclusive development anchored in social, political and economic change. Capacity building at the local level should address issues of poverty, inequality, social exclusion and poor governance. The capacity-building approach has informed programs on institutional reform, community action and postconflict reconstruction. From 1980 to 1995, the UN spent over $150 million on programs and projects that focused exclusively on capacity building in Zimbabwe (Maconick and Morgan 1999). A plethora of definitions refer to capacity building as a process, a means and an end to development. Here we identify three variations on the definition of capacity building—capacity building as a pathway to economic growth, capacity building as a pro-poor approach and capacity building as a community-driven approach.

A Pathway to Economic Growth

One of the early articulations of capacity building is to view it as a mechanism or catalyst for economic growth. From this perspective, capacity building is oriented toward investments that seek to develop human resources, enhance organizational capacities and foster institutional change. Examples of such investments would be expanding educational opportunities and increasing access to financial resources, information and technology

(Gunnarsson 2001; UN Development Programme [UNDP] 1997). These investments are seen as preconditions to economic growth and sustainable development. For example, Gunnarsson (2001) refers to capacity building as "efforts to help in building various forms of productive capacities that are assumed to become powerful vehicles of development in the recipient countries" (9). The UNDP (1997) defines capacity building as "the process by which individuals, organizations, institutions and societies develop abilities (individually and collectively) to perform functions, solve problems and set and achieve objectives" (3). Capacity building is also defined as "the search for improvements in the ability of institutions, individuals, or groups to efficiently and effectively fulfill their responsibilities" (Hussein 2006, 374). The assumption is that enhancing human resources and improving institutional performance would improve domestic capacities and increase efficiency and productivity in the long run. Another assumption is that economic growth will trickle down to the local level and the overall well-being of communities will be enhanced. This perspective emerged in the 1950s (Maconick and Morgan, 1999). Maconick and Morgan trace back the work of the UN on capacity building, shedding light on how the process has evolved throughout decades. In the earliest times, it indicated training of individuals. By the 1970s, the capacity building work of UN focused on providing support around human-resource development and institutional development in the areas of health, communication, agriculture, education and science. The capacity-building approach emphasized the role of training and technical assistance in international development.

The approach that defines capacity building as a pathway to economic growth falls short in two respects. First, it assumes that national capacity building to promote economic growth is sufficient for local development. The assumption is that enhancing a society's productive capacities in the aggregate will lead to economic growth, which in turn will trickle down to the local level. National economic growth is crucial to local development, but there is no guarantee that it will reach the poorest of the poor. Indeed, evidence indicates that economic growth might reinforce disparities between both the rich and the poor and rural and urban areas (Keng 2006). As is made evident in the 2005 Human Development Report, technology improvement, export growth and import liberalization in many countries have not improved human conditions. The impact of growth on poverty depends on how equally the benefits are distributed across the population, which is influenced by the existing distribution of income and productive assets, as well as the policies used to achieve growth (Waddington 2004). Growth is three times more effective in reducing the incidence of poverty in low-inequality countries than in high-inequality countries (Waddington 2004). A by-product of uneven development is not simply increased income disparities, but rather reinforcement of inequalities that trap households in cycles of poverty (Sumner 2005). Second, a capacity-building approach to economic growth overlooks the role that local communities are able to play in capacity-building initiatives. Communities are defined as "aid recipients" without any ownership in the development process. A top-down approach to local development that assumes communities to be disempowered and ignorant fails to achieve sustainable development in the interests of the very poor. A review of the work of the UN across the world going back to the 1970s reveals that defining capacity building merely as technical assistance, without regard to local needs and perceptions, has yielded mixed results at best (Maconick and Morgan, 1999).

Pro-poor Approach

While capacity building is at times discussed at the macro level on how it matters to development outcomes, experience from the field indicates that perceiving the poor as ignorant and powerless undermines social development (Borren 2003). From this perspective, capacity-building efforts focus exclusively on the poor because they are the least likely to benefit from development. Eade (2007) argues that "if capacity building means anything, it is surely about enabling those out on the margins to represent and defend their interests more effectively, not only within their own immediate contexts but also globally" (630). Such an emphasis on representation is of a more recent vintage in the capacity-building literature. Capacity building to enhance representation holds great promise. A more general articulation of capacity building, that underscores the agency of the poor in development, views it as "assisting the marginalized and oppressed in society to take ownership and control of their development" (Turay 2001, 171). A pro-poor approach to capacity building emphasizes the importance of motivating the poor to transform their environments, to take control of their lives by building self-confidence, thus enabling the poor to participate in local decision making and assisting them to take ownership of the development process and develop leadership. This perspective emphasizes both inclusion and empowerment, and calls for a bottom-up approach to local development. For example, Eade (1997) contends that development and relief programs are ineffective if they fail to recognize that the poor might be empowered by their own efforts and not by what others do for them. A pro-poor capacity-building approach emphasizes that the poor rather than outsiders should drive local development. The assumption is that the poor "are invaluable partners for development, since they are the most motivated to move out of poverty" (Narayan 2006, 3).

The pro-poor approach has the merit of being cognizant of who is likely to be left out of capacity-building initiatives, emphasizing the argument that the poor should be partners in development and participate in local decision-making structures. However, the process through which the poor can become partners in development is not clear. The focus of this approach is the outcome (pro-poor development) rather than the mechanisms through which this outcome can be achieved. Empowerment and capacity building are often used interchangeably to emphasize the argument that empowering the poor is essential to inclusive and sustainable development. While this approach has much value, it often comes with the assumption that the poor are "oppressed," "marginalized," lacking "self-confidence" and "self-respect," failing to take into consideration their own knowledge, strength and aspirations. Also, this approach fails to look at poverty beyond the household level to address factors which perpetuate poverty but are entrenched in institutional structures and communities where the poor live. This approach to capacity building that is pro-poor can be defined as inclusive but at times individualistic and merely focused on the household level.

Community-Driven Approach

This approach emphasizes the role that local communities must play in capacity-building initiatives. The focus is on increasing communities' access to financial services, providing opportunities for local organizations to establish networks, building partnerships between local communities and donors, and mobilizing community capacities. According to Laverack (2005, 2006), capacity building at the community level should focus on the following domains: participation, local leadership, problem-assessment capacities, critical assessment, organizational structures, resource mobilization, external linkages, agency and project management. The key question for development practitioners should be, "How has the programme, from its planning through its implementation, through its evaluation, intentionally sought to enhance community empowerment through each domain?" (Laverack 2006, 6). Eade (2007) emphasizes that "solidarity-based partnerships" between communities and donors, which are driven by accountability, can foster better development outcomes (637). Capacity building is one of the five cornerstones of the community-driven development approach of the World Bank. Evidence from the World Bank (2006) shows that community-driven approaches can improve the sustainability of development efforts in communities recovering from conflict, in particular through a process of building trust and promoting dialogue. Communities' involvement in rehabilitating water supply and sewerage, building nutrition programs for mothers and infants, and building schools can increase accountability and lead to better outcomes in the long term.

The community-driven approach is comprehensive in that it recognizes the role that communities should have in capacity-building initiatives. However, there are two aspects that merit great scrutiny. First, even though conceptually this approach seems comprehensive, in practice, there are numerous challenges that inhibit the intended results. Capacity needs to be built at several different levels, issues of inequality have to be addressed and these new capabilities should be meaningful and attainable by local populations. Addressing communities' needs comprehensively, as well as in a sustainable and context-aware manner, is essential even as it is challenging. Second, the community-driven approach centers on the need to increase capacities at the community level, but often the capacity-building approach is seen as the only way of approaching communities without recognizing the role that other approaches can play in strengthening communities and fostering better development outcomes at the local level. Monolithic approaches to local development do not foster long-term sustainable development; an array of interventions is required to enhance the capabilities of the poor.

Capacity building, as we mention at the introduction of this chapter, is about promoting positive change. However, our understanding of the processes that can lead to positive change that is sustainable and meaningful for the poor is incomplete. Each perspective that we presented previously sets its own priorities, envisioning communities as asset-rich and empowered in the future. For some, it is the capacities of the poor that should be built; for others, it is the economy of a given country. Despite the enthusiasm of each perspective, they are far from addressing challenges to development at the local level in a comprehensive way. Capacity building is often introduced as the single "solution" to local development challenges. Many development practitioners embrace the capacity-building approach as the magic bullet without recognizing the extent to which it can in practice address the challenges met at the local level. Perhaps there is merit in weaving together a variety of approaches that ensure sustainable development at the local level. Local development is not about a single approach and surely can benefit from an amalgam of approaches.

In the next section, we examine how capacity building can better address challenges at the local level, especially when it is pursued to strengthen participation, empowerment, collective action and sustainability. Capacity building should be in the service of enhancing the quality of participation, and thereby empowering people and fostering greater levels of collective action to realize sustainable development.

ASPECTS OF THE CAPACITY-BUILDING APPROACH

Participation

It is often argued in the capacity-building literature that local development initiatives should be formulated at the local level and the poor should participate in the assessment, monitoring and evaluation of projects and programs (Hohe 2005; Rahnema 1992; UNDP 1997). In practice, different scenarios emerge: the poor fail to participate, the poor and socially excluded are left out or active participation by the community fades away after project funding ends. Local participation might emerge when foreign aid lands in poor communities, but there is no guarantee that it will facilitate community engagement and sustainable outcomes over the long haul. Capacity-building initiatives often fail to consider local needs, priorities, incentives and disincentives, perceptions and knowledge.

Local Needs and Priorities

There is abundant evidence demonstrating that often donors' assistance overlooks local perceptions of the problem and felt needs (Borren 2003; Eade 1997; Mangones 2001; Parakrama 2001; Smillie 2001). In 1986, Lecomte raised the concern about the *dialectic between grassroots efforts and the input of outside assistance.* While communities expect solutions to daily problems, such as improving access to education and health-care services, donors are more concerned about the logistics. Only after projects are funded are contacts with communities established. Projects that are implemented in this way not only often fail to meet local needs, but can also engender distrust and insecurity. In spite of decades of development experience, the sharp distinction continues between outsiders with plans and communities with complex needs and dynamics that are unarticulated to the outsiders. Eade (2007) argues that "the currency of aid remains the Project" (632), rather than the understanding of the local dynamics. Aid agencies refer to "target groups" and "aid recipients," failing to recognize the "less visible processes that will undermine the impact of their projects" (633). An international agency that aims at building capacities of local communities while being blind to local circumstances might "instill priorities and ideas that are in line with its own funding and programming mandates" (Smillie, 2001). Therefore, local development initiatives fulfill the ideas of community development by the outsiders, rather than communities themselves:

> The sad reality is that most development aid has precious little to do with building the capacities of 'The Poor' to transform their societies. Not even the best-intentioned NGOs are exempt from the tendency of the Development Industry to ignore, misinterpret, displace, supplant, or undermine the capacities that people already have. (Eade 2007, 633)

Local Perceptions and Knowledge

Participation is not only about understanding local needs and identifying priorities, but also about being receptive to local perceptions and knowledge. The distinction that Girgis (2007) makes between local capacity and local knowledge is helpful in reminding us that to ensure capacity building at the local level, we must also ensure that it is done on the basis of local knowledge. Understanding what communities need does not equal understanding what communities know. We need to capture both aspects in order to ensure that we do not do a disservice to local communities:

> Practitioners identify local capacity, and many prioritise assessing existing capacity as part of their work. However, when participants discuss capacity building, they rarely raise the issue of local knowledge. The outsiders' perception of local knowledge is centred on the practitioners' needs, which are to know what local capacity is present in order to do capacity-building work, rather than what local knowledge exists. (355)

Capacity building at the local level has to be predicated on local knowledge, otherwise capacity building is not sustained over time. Capacity building is not simply about assisting the poor. For capacity-building efforts to be successful, we should recognize local processes that have the potential to undermine or sustain the intended results. For example, Van der Plaat and Barrett (2006) discuss the importance of recognizing informal governance processes at the local level. It is imperative "to understand the non-project realities" (Eade 2007, 633). They will inform interventions that are more responsive to local processes.

Empowerment

The concept of empowerment is not new to capacity building. Indeed, these two discussions of empowerment and capacity building overlap with one another. Laverack (2005), however, differentiates capacity building from empowerment in the following way:

> The difference between capacity building and empowerment approaches lies in the agenda and purpose of the process. Empowerment approaches have an explicit purpose to bring about social and political changes and this is embodied in their sense of action and emancipation, whereas capacity building has the purpose of the development of skills and abilities that enable others to take decisions and actions for themselves but does not explicitly include political activism. (267–268)

Having a good understanding of power dynamics is essential to local development. Power asymmetry can have a debilitating effect on development outcomes because of the way resources are distributed. However, the capacity-building literature does not address the multitude of power asymmetries, whether regional or local. The capacity-building approach is right to emphasize the necessity of empowering people, "to realize their potential and better use their capabilities" (UNDP 1997, 12), but the approach does not fully recognize the root causes of powerlessness and why people, after all, lack agency and ways to redress such powerlessness. Merely acknowledging that the poor need to be empowered is insufficient. Here we discuss a few sources of power asymmetry that are likely to hinder capacity-building initiatives.

North–South Inequalities

Capacity-building outcomes are conditioned by how donors and outsiders ("the North") perceive recipients and local communities ("the South") and the way that local communities themselves perceive the outsiders. In many ways, differential financial resources, knowledge and experience shape the type of partnership that emerges between the two (Girgis 2007). Partnership is driven by money supply, which manipulates the quality of the relationship and sets the agendas for local NGOs. Financial dependency engenders power asymmetry and "distorts the functioning and dignity of the weaker partner, as well as fostering the hubris of the stronger one" (Eade 2007, 635). Financial dependency of Southern NGOs increases the likelihood of undermining local capacities in the long term. Smillie (2001) sheds light on how, during relief and peace building, dependence on outside resources might undermine communities' capacities. During relief and peace-building processes, resources are placed in the hands of international organizations, which are given the role of lead development agencies. The pressure to survive and tensions over access to monetary support result in an unhealthy competition among NGOs instead of collaboration to address critical relief needs. This does not simply foster dependence on foreign aid, but also undermines the quality of services that are provided to local populations. The outcome is a fragmented landscape of NGOs competing to represent the interests of the poor with donors that are resource rich and eager to aid but knowledge poor of the conditions on the ground. The result is that regional strategies where NGOs coordinate and collaborate to realize sustainable development are put aside, and donor financing is channeled into fragmented projects through an increasing number of NGOs. Many of the NGOs are working in small communities without addressing the larger regional issues, and they lack the capacity to transcend their small community to address development issues in the region.

Disparities and Inequalities

Capacity-building efforts might not reach the poor because of power inequities that have been sustained in communities from generation to generation. Understanding these power cleavages within communities is essential. An effective capacity-building approach emphasizes the importance of understanding the power dynamics in a given community before projects are designed and implemented. For example, Mason (2006) argues that development interventions affect access to resources, which might result in disempowerment of the poor due to existing power inequalities.

A capacity-building approach that is cognizant of extant inequities in power and access to resources is more likely to result in development interventions that are sensitive to the risk of leaving the poor out of new resources and deepen inequality. Rankin (2002) contends that focusing on the poor as "agents of their own survival" does not mean that problems that originate from existing political, economic, and social structures will be challenged (10). For instance, in many cases, women who participate in microfinance projects receive the credit, but it is their husbands who control the income (Rankin 2002). Moreover, because of household responsibilities, very often women are involved in small enterprises, such as sweater knitting, that do not challenge practices of subordination. Drydyk (2005) extensively outlines a perception that when participatory development initiatives undertaken in Gambia and Eastern India are not successful in reaching the poorest individuals, they tend to reinforce the existing gender hierarchies. Sexism, racism and caste systems can cause the poor to suffer to a greater extent than the non-poor. Social, cultural, political and economic inequities are a great hindrance to capacity-building efforts. Capacity building aimed at producing sustainable and equitable development must give due recognition to and address these inequalities. Otherwise, capacity-building efforts will strengthen those with resources and power, while further weakening those without.

The empowerment approach underscores the need to pay particular attention to the processes governing the interaction between the poor and more powerful actors (Narayan 2006). Abraham and Platteau (2004) suggest that "an effective and impartial state, genuinely devoted to the protection of poor" and empowerment of the poor that enables them "to obtain relevant information, influence policies and monitor the state's instructions at the local level," are precursors to achieving sustainable development (231).

Sustainability

Capacity-building discussions uniformly claim sustainable development as the end goal of capacity strengthening. A lasting development impact results from investing in basic public services that leverage the quality of life of poor communities and enable them to engage productively in the local economy. Essential to sustainability are those investments that penetrate ill health, illiteracy, water scarcity and unsanitary conditions in communities. Investments in education, health, sanitation and skills that can enable the poor to be actively involved in their communities and be a driving force for change are more likely to lead to sustainable development (Haq 1995). There is strong evidence for sustainable development that is linked to investments in education, health, and sanitation and other services that have the potential to increase economic and social gains (Baldacci et al. 2005; Hanushek 2005; World Bank 2004). Capacity-building initiatives to achieve sustainability have seldom focused on such investments.

More often, the focus of capacity building for sustainable development is on NGOs and their organizational capability. Training sessions with NGOs routinely focus on the process of strategic planning, developing mission statements or writing better proposals, and rarely do they concentrate on issues that communities are concerned about. This type of capacity building prepares NGOs to be more attuned to the organizational and managerial standards of donor organizations and in the process even dictate outsider donor demands on communities (Smillie and Todorović 2001). Even though it is widely accepted that sustainable capacity development needs time, projects that aim at building capacities at the local level are short-lived (Eade 1997; Girgis 2007; Smillie 2001). Short-lived projects not only fail to promote sustainability, but also increase insecurity in local organizations that have to struggle between designing donor-oriented projects, finding new and reliable donors, implementing existing projects and preparing reports. Sometimes, all these steps are fulfilled in six months and undertaken by overstretched personnel; instead, sustainable capacity building of local organizations should at least take ten years or more (Eade 1997, 4).

The capacity of outsiders to build capacities of local communities is another important issue addressed in the capacity-building literature. Often, development practitioners do not have sufficient knowledge about local dynamics, the ways that local organizations operate and local traditions and customs. Often, development personnel are reassigned from one place to another, so the likelihood of knowing the context in which they operate is likely to be low (Taft and Ladnier 2005). Parakrama (2001), in an examination of humanitarian assistance provided by international organizations to war victims in Sri Lanka, notes that United Nations Children's Fund (UNICEF) programs are designed and evaluated by individuals who know very little about the target communities. The UNDP measures outcomes through indicators that are quantitative in nature, missing the processes that are important to local development.

Similarly, Smillie and Todorović (2001) shed light on the by-products of a capacity-building approach in postwar Bosnia. First, international efforts aiming at building local capacity generated hostility between the government and local NGOs. Local NGOs were perceived as overfunded by governmental agencies; hence, the government withdrew from the social sector. Second, the increased number of international agencies in the postwar period led to an excessive growth of NGOs. Often, aid was delivered with no recognition of NGOs' real capacities: some NGOs were funded beyond their capacities and in practice could not meet their objectives; and much of this growth in NGOs was driven by donor supply of aid. Local NGOs were following the priorities set by international organizations, rather than addressing local community needs. By the end of 1996, donors placed more emphasis on economic growth, overlooking social and psychological aspects of the postwar period that were critical to local populations. NGOs also shifted their attention toward economic growth, even though they had no expertise in this, so that when donors withdrew from the country, several NGOs stopped functioning and were "set adrift in a sea of jargon about sustainability" (33). The end result is a weakened NGO sector, local development needs that were never met and donor efforts to build capacities a failure.

Capacity Building and Collective Action

An important aspect of capacity building is to promote collective action on the part of poor communities to realize sustained local development. Viewing capacity building as an endeavor to promote the ability of communities to act collectively is not pervasive in the development literature. Nevertheless, we see capacity building as an exercise in strengthening those qualities in communities that allow them to mobilize, coordinate and act together in addressing emerging problems at the local level.

The ability of the very poor to act collectively is important for several reasons. The crux of local development in poor communities rests on the availability of basic services and infrastructure such as health, education, sanitation, water and roads. The poor benefit from the presence and provision of such services in significant ways. A continual supply and maintenance of such services by governments, however, is inadequate due in part to insufficient demand on the part of communities. Inadequate services in communities also occur because of local governments' inability and lack of will to supply. This combination of inadequate demand on the part of communities and inadequate supply on the part of local governments results in perpetual underprovision of basic social services. Increasing the capacity of communities to act collectively to make their preferences and needs known and make demands of local governments is an important mechanism for ensuring basic services. Moreover, coordinated action by communities will also enable them to enter into coproducing arrangements with local governments and share the burden of providing critical public services.

Capacity building must ensure that both communities and local governments realize such capabilities. This would entail local governments to be open to communities and their preferences. At the same time, households in communities must overcome their temptation to focus on maximizing personal gain to realize the greater good of widely provisioned public services that benefit from contributions in the form of labor, finances and other resources. Such efforts demand self-restraint in the present, on the part of households, for a future promise of public goods available to all in a community. Capacity building must ensure that communities and local governments arrive at a point where they are routinely able to take such decisions in the interests of community and local development rather than of a free ride. NGOs have the crucial mediating role to play in enabling local governments and communities to collaborate and coordinate development efforts.

Development outcomes are shaped by people's ability to act collectively and hold each other accountable by curbing free riding, rent seeking and corruption through a set of mutually agreed upon rules and rule systems

(Ostrom, Schroeder and Wynne 1993). When these preconditions are not met, opportunistic behaviors thrive, and public goods available to all have a greater propensity to be overused, depleted and ill-managed. The dynamics that evolve around public goods, such as households' willingness to contribute time and labor, are influenced by the nature of public goods. A good or service is a public good if it is characterized by some degree of indivisibility and non-excludability. A good is characterized by perfect indivisibility if "once produced, any given unit can be made available to every member of the public, or equivalently if any individual's consumption or use of the good does not reduce the amount available to others" (Taylor 1995, 6). A good is characterized by perfect non-excludability if "it is impossible to prevent individual members of the group from consuming it or if such exclusion is 'prohibitively costly'" (6).

For some time, the predominant view had been that the indivisible and non-excludable nature of public goods, coupled with utility maximization, invariably led people to free ride and exploit public goods (Hardin 1968). The assumption has been that individuals have no incentives to contribute to public goods and are very likely to take advantage and free ride. This decision is seen as influenced by at least two reasons: (1) a cost-benefit calculation leads to the conclusion that the benefits of contribution will be very low (or free riding will lead to higher and quicker results); and (2) with or without contribution, public goods will be provided. Such reasoning leads to free riding and overuse of public goods; both views being dangerous for the supply and sustainability of public goods such as health, education, sanitation or water systems.

The assumption that communities are trapped in an unavoidable tragedy has influenced policy analysts for several decades. The argument that communities are unable to supply and maintain public goods without the imposition of external rules is contradicted by mounting evidence of the ability of communities to coordinate and act collectively (Ostrom, 2002). When communities come together, design rules to protect public goods, and act collectively, the tragedy is not only avoided but public goods are continually supplied through coordinated action, driven by trust and reciprocity that are predicated on stable and enduring institutional arrangements designed by villagers themselves. Such coordinated efforts to supply and maintain public goods can outperform state-driven initiatives. In a comparison of community-initiated and state-managed development initiatives, Shivakoti (2002) finds that communities assess their own efforts as far superior than those of the local government.

This is not to idealize communities but rather to underscore the point that communities and local governments are able to acquire the necessary capacity to overcome the many barriers to acting collectively to realize sustainable development. The specter of the free-rider problem in the provision of health, education and other public goods is always present. Uncertainty, distrust and conflict are a continuous challenge to a community's ability to collaborate and provide social services that affect the many (Yadama 2003). A good understanding of these dimensions is essential in capacity-building efforts where the emphasis should be on strengthening the ability of communities to realize their collective efficacy. It is in this way that fostering coordinated efforts within communities and between local governments and communities must be an important aspect of capacity building for local development.

CAPACITY BUILDING FOR LOCAL DEVELOPMENT

So far, we have discussed participation, empowerment, sustainability and collective action as important dimensions of capacity building. Intervening to raise the capacity of communities, local governments and NGOs toward sustainable local development should be the primary mission of all capacity building in development. Sustainability is achieved when capacity building of local actors in development is accomplished. When the three significant actors in local development—communities, governments and NGOs—are endowed with the capacity to enhance each other's respective roles in development, there is a greater propensity for sustainable development. What are these respective roles, and how can capacity-building efforts enhance the ability of these three entities to undertake their roles effectively?

Local governments—whether it is municipalities in urban areas of the world or *Panchayats* or *Baghs* in the case of rural India and Mongolia—have the responsibility to work with communities in delivering services and ensuring that a variety of public policies and their mandates are met. At the same time, communities must also mobilize to work with local governments to ensure effective realization of services and public policy goals. In this context, NGOs have assumed the key role of catalyzing communities and local governments to work effectively toward realizing sustainable development outcomes. Capacity building should focus on strengthening all three actors in realizing local development through effective delivery of social services, and social and economic development programs.

To enable effective local development, capacity building at the community level should focus on three interrelated aspects of sustainable development: collective action endogenous to communities, coproduction of public goods with local governments and governability. The capacity to act collectively is central to ensuring that a community realizes and maintains public goods such as health, education, roads and sanitation that raise their quality of living and well-being. Collective action, however, is predicated on overcoming the temptation to free ride on other people's efforts, and the provision of labor, time and resources by a wide range of members of a community. Many communities are unable to overcome their diverse preferences, heterogeneous interests and differential access to resources and act collectively, with some self-restraint, to gain a higher level of goods and services for the many. Capacity-building efforts should target underlying social, economic and political processes that are barriers to productive collective self-efficacy. In addition, capacity building should be tailored toward increasing coproduction of public goods and services on the part of communities and local governments. Capacity building efforts should equip a community to identify nonredundant resources and capabilities that complement local government resources and make it possible for the two parties to engage in the supply and maintenance of critical public goods.

Ostrom (1996) defines coproduction "as a process through which inputs used to produce a good or service are contributed by individuals who are not 'in' the same organization" (1073). Coproduction is rooted in the idea that citizens can be active participants in production of public goods that are consequential to them, and that state bureaucracy, wherever possible, should actively seek citizen involvement in the production of public goods. Such partnerships between state and community are sometimes necessary in the production of public goods because "not all of the inputs that could potentially be used to produce an output are under full control of a single, public-sector principal" (1079). When inputs of a state and community are redundant, then coproduction is not possible, as there is no potential for synergy. On the other hand, when the necessary resources to produce a public good are distributed between the public sector and a community, and these resources are not substitutable, then a public good is best produced using a combination of government and local community resources (1079–1080). According to Ostrom, "[C]oproduction of many goods and services normally considered to be public goods by government agencies and citizens organized into polycentric systems is crucial for achieving higher levels of welfare in developing countries, particularly for those who are poor" (1083). Therefore, capacity building of both communities and local governments to enable greater coproduction of public goods is fundamental to achieving sustainable local development.

Finally, yet importantly, capacity building should also be about increasing the capability of communities to engage in governance. It is empowering when citizens are able to hold both community-governing institutions and local governments accountable and transparent in their transactions with citizens. Capacity-building efforts to enable citizens to engage in seeking information and advocacy toward more transparent practices on the part of community institutions and local governments will significantly enable local development. One of the shortest routes of accountability is from the communities to local service providers, instead of communities asserting pressure on governments at a higher level to bring local service providers to deliver on public goods (World Bank 2004). Capacity-building efforts should strengthen the ability of communities to exercise accountability over service providers directly and as a routine matter.

Equally significant are capacity-building efforts to strengthen local government openness toward communities and the ability of NGOs to mediate between communities and local governments. Local governments that are informed about the needs and resources of a community are better suited to engage in coproduction of public goods. Capacity-building efforts should target the ability of local governments to seek and understand the resources and preferences of communities. Capacity building should also seek to soften traditional bureaucratic standoffishness toward communities' increasing the capacity of local governments to view service to communities as their primary mission. Capacity building for local development must ensure that local governments realize the merit in working closely with communities and the rewards of delivering development to communities. Strengthening the efforts of local governments with local communities are NGOs.

The value added by NGOs in development is in building alliances between communities and local governments toward sustainable development. In particular, the value of NGOs is in their capacity to elicit trust on the part of communities and to leverage that trust in bringing local governments to work with communities to deliver critical public goods and services. Such mediating efforts by NGOs increase the level of public goods provision, but also diminish elite capture of development efforts. Capacity-building efforts should target the ability of NGOs to forge such partnerships between communities and local governments and to enable a broader and deeper penetration of development programs in communities. Another critical dimension of NGOs is their ability to mobilize communities to advocate for their needs and to represent their interests using all the available provisions of extant public policy and legal institutions.

In order for NGOs to undertake such advocacy, they must train their professionals in envisioning ways in which current policy and legal provisions assist communities in securing new development goods and services. For example, very poor communities with ill-defined property rights cannot realistically undertake development investments until they are assured of tenurial rights to land, and so on. NGOs in such situations, instead of providing services, must first work to establish an equitable structure of property rights. The capacity of NGOs to undertake development efforts targeting fundamental social structural inequalities is underdeveloped. When an NGO is willing and able to tackle such structural inequalities in communities, the longer-term impact of their development efforts are more penetrating and sustainable. NGOs, such as Samata in Andhra Pradesh, India, have exclusively focused on addressing fundamental inequalities in property rights and political rights, and over the long haul have forged alliances with all forms of governmental agencies to empower tribal communities (Yadama and DeWeese-Boyd 2001).

To address fundamental structural inequalities, however, NGOs must focus on building the capacity of their staff to understand the social and economic processes that are underway in a community. The returns to addressing those fundamental processes in a community are many. In tandem, when NGOs are also capable of forging alliances with local governments, they multiply their development impact on communities. These capabilities are also critical when decentralization processes are underway in a country. The premise of decentralization is to allow local governments and communities to determine development priorities and realize more sustainable development outcomes. If the history of community and government relations is fraught with distrust, then NGOs are thrust into a position of mediating between communities and local governments. In a decentralizing context, if governments do not work closely with communities, and NGOs are incapable of forging alliances between communities and governments, then development outcomes will surely be skewed toward the elite. Decentralization under such conditions, instead of resulting in strong development outcomes, is likely to reinforce entrenched inequalities in communities. Capacity building of local governments enabling them to be aware of elite capture and of the preferences of the broad spectrum of a community, of NGOs to be effective mediators, and of communities to actively mobilize and advocate for themselves will help in realizing equitable and sustainable development outcomes.

DECENTRALIZATION WITHOUT CAPACITY BUILDING

When communities do not mobilize to assert their preferences on local governments, decentralization will only strengthen local governments and relatively weaken the position of communities vis-à-vis the state. Therefore, building the capacity of communities to mobilize and advocate for their rights as well as resources, and to work alongside local governments, will significantly increase the probability that decentralization will result in salutary development outcomes (Yadama and Menon 2003). Moreover, effective decentralization is predicated on good governance where communities are able to hold local governments accountable, and in turn local governments are engaged in transparent and accountable practices. Decentralization aims to "improve democratic governance by bringing government closer to the people and thereby increasing state responsiveness and accountability" (Selee and Tulchin 2004, 296). Discussions of decentralization often center on the necessity to strengthen the capacities of local governments to carry out their work in an effective and transparent manner (Hussein 2006). Building the capacities of local governments is essential; however, overlooking the importance of building the capacity of local communities privileges local governments over communities in decentralization.

As we previously described, when communities are able to act collectively, they become capable of asserting their preferences to local governments and collaborating with local governments to coproduce public goods. The primary goal of decentralization is to provide the right incentives to both communities and local governments to instigate local development.

In decentralization, NGOs also have a key role to play: they can ensure that decentralization unfolds in the best interest of communities. However, many times decentralization is pursued in the midst of incapable local governments, communities or NGOs. The outcomes of decentralization are both ambiguous and contradictory (Oxhorn 2004). Evidence indicates that transferring power from the state to the local level does not automatically lead to increased access to public services, transparency and accountability. Oxhorn (2004) indicates that, in the Philippines, decentralization benefits larger organizations that have sufficient capacities and know-how to influence policy. Most civil society organizations are too weak to take advantage of opportunities for participation in the local sphere.

Decentralization is sure to fail in the absence of capacity in local governments to focus on community preferences, or communities that are unable to mobilize to leverage newly gained resources by local governments, or NGOs that are oblivious to their role as trust builders and mediators between communities and local governments. In the absence of capacity-building efforts targeting all three actors—local governments, communities and NGOs—decentralization is sure to fail. Capacity building of communities, local governments and NGOs strengthens decentralization to realize sustainable local development. Responsive governments, assertive communities and facilitating NGOs make for successful local development. Capacity-building efforts should work toward strengthening all three entities of local development, especially when decentralization is underway, thus giving local governments and communities a greater role in undertaking development.

CONCLUSIONS

Our chapter provides an overarching view of capacity building and its role in development. In particular, we stress that capacity-building efforts should significantly strengthen communities to play a more active role in development. Along with strengthening communities, we also advocate for capacity building of local governments to give adequate attention to community needs, elite capture of development efforts and, where possible, enable them to collaborate with communities to provide public goods and services. While communities and local governments are central to undertaking sustainable local development, we also find a critical role for NGOs. NGOs should not merely deliver services, but also engage in mobilizing communities to advocate for their preferences. Moreover, we argue that NGOs are at their best when they mediate between communities and local governments. Advocacy and mediation to achieve sustainable local development require NGOs to be more than service delivery organizations. Their capacity building should adequately prepare them to understand the social, economic and political processes underway in communities, and to work with local governments instead of in opposition.

Understanding development as a political process, and bringing communities to advocate effectively for themselves within this process, is the most important task for NGOs. Performing such tasks strengthens capacities of people and their community-based organizations and facilitates local level development.

REFERENCES

Abraham, A., and Platteau, J.-P. 2004. Participatory development: Where culture creeps in. In *Culture and public action*, ed. V. Rao and M. Walton, 210–233. Stanford, CA: Stanford University Press.

Baldacci, E., Clements, B., Cui, Q., and Gupta, S. 2005. What does it take to help the poor? *Finance and Development* 42(2): 20–31.

Borren, S. 2003. Changing partners: Changing assumptions. In *Ownership and partnership: What role for civil society in poverty reduction strategies?* ed. I. Smillie and H-B. S. Lecomte, 19–27. Paris: Development Centre of the Organization for Economic Co-operation and Development.

Drydyk, J. 2005. When is development more democratic? *Journal of Human Development* 6(2): 247–267.

Eade, D. 1997. *Capacity-building: An approach to people-centred development.* Oxford: Oxfam.

———. 2007. Capacity building: Who builds whose capacity? *Development in Practice* 17(4): 630–639.

Girgis, M. 2007. The capacity-building paradox: Using friendship to build capacity in the South. *Development in Practice* 13(3): 353–363.

Gunnarsson, C. 2001. *Capacity building, institutional crisis and the issue of recurrent costs.* Stockholm: Almkvist & Wiksell International.

Hanushek, E. A. 2005. Why quality matters in education? *Finance and Development* 42(2): 15–19.

Hardin, G. 1968. The tragedy of the commons. *Science* 162:1243–1248.

Haq, M. 1995. *Reflections on human development.* New York: Oxford University Press.

Hohe, T. 2005. Developing local governance. In *Postconflict development: Meeting new challenges*, ed. G. Junne and W. Verkoren, 59–72. London: Lynne Rienner.

Hussein, M. K. 2006. Capacity building challenges in Malawi's local government reform programme. *Development Southern Africa* 23(3): 371–383.

Keng, K. 2006. China's unbalanced economic growth. *Journal of Contemporary China* 15(46): 183–214.

Laverack, G. 2005. Evaluating community capacity: Visual representation and interpretation. *Community Development Journal* 41(3): 266–276.

———. 2006. Using a "domains" approach to build community empowerment. *Community Development Journal* 41(1): 4–12.

Lecomte, B. J. 1986. *Project aid: Limitations and alternatives.* Paris: Development Centre of the Organization for Economic Co-Operation and Development.

Maconick, R., and Morgan, P., eds. 1999. *Capacity building supported by the United Nations: Some evaluations and some lessons.* New York: United Nations.

Mangones, K. 2001. Alternative food aid strategies and local capacity building in Haiti. In *Patronage or partnership: Local capacity building in humanitarian crises*, ed. I. Smillie, 51–76. Westport, CT: Kumarian Press.

Mason, K. O. 2006. Measuring women's empowerment: Learning from cross-national research. In *Measuring empowerment: Cross-disciplinary perspectives*, ed. D. Narayan, 88–102. New Delhi: Oxford University Press.

Narayan, D. 2006. Conceptual framework and methodological challenges. In *Measuring empowerment: Cross-disciplinary perspectives*, ed. D. Narayan, 3–39. New Delhi: Oxford University Press.

Ostrom, E. 1996. Crossing the great divide: Coproduction, synergy, and development. *World Development* 24(6): 1073–1087.

———. 2002. The challenge of underperformance. In *Improving irrigation governance and management in Nepal*, ed. G. P. Shivakoti and E. Ostrom, 3–33. Oakland, CA: Institute for Contemporary Studies.

Ostrom, E., Schroeder, L., and Wynne, S. 1993. *Institutional incentives and sustainable development: Infrastructure policies in perspective.* Boulder, CO: Westview Press.

Oxhorn, P. 2004. Unraveling the puzzle of decentralization. In *Decentralization, democratic governance, and civil society in comparative perspective: Africa, Asia, and Latin America*, ed. P. Oxhorn, J. S. Tulchin, and A. D. Selee, 3–27. Baltimore: Johns Hopkins University Press.

Parakrama, A. 2001. Means without end: Humanitarian assistance in Sri Lanka. In *Patronage or partnership: Local capacity building in humanitarian crises*, ed. I. Smillie, 107–130. Westport, CT: Kumarian Press.

Rahnema, M. 1992. Participation. In *The development dictionary: A guide to knowledge as power*, ed. W. Sachs, 116–131. London: Zed Books Ltd.

Rankin, K. N. 2002. Social capital, microfinance, and the politics of development. *Feminist Economics* 8(1): 1–24.

Selee, A. D., and Tulchin, J. S. 2004. Decentralization and democratic governance: Lessons and challenges. In *Decentralization, democratic governance, and civil society in comparative perspective: Africa, Asia, and Latin America*, ed. P. Oxhorn, J. S. Tulchin, and A. D. Selee, 295–318. Baltimore: Johns Hopkins University Press.

Shivakoti, G. P. 2002. Farmers' perceptions of performance in farmer-managed and agency-managed irrigation systems in Nepal. In *Improving irrigation governance and management in Nepal*, ed. G. P. Shivakoti and E. Ostrom, 126–149. Oakland, CA: Institute for Contemporary Studies.

Smillie, I. 2001. Capacity building and the humanitarian enterprise. In *Patronage or partnership: Local capacity building in humanitarian crises*, ed. I. Smillie, 7–23. Westport, CT: Kumarian Press.

Smillie, I., and Todorović, B. 2001. Reconstructing Bosnia, constructing civil society. In *Patronage or partnership: Local capacity building in humanitarian crises*, ed. I. Smillie, 25–50. Westport, CT: Kumarian Press.

Sumner, A. 2005. Is foreign direct investment good for the poor? A review and stocktake. *Development in Practice* 15(3–4): 269–285.

Taylor, M. 1995. *The possibility of cooperation.* New York: Cambridge University Press.

Taft, P. and Ladnier, J. 2005. *The capacity to protect: The role of civil society.* http://www.fundforpeace.org/programs/rriw/building_capacity/bc-civil-society.pdf (accessed May 16, 2007).

Turay, T. M. 2001. Peacebuilding in purgatory. In *Patronage or partnership: Local capacity building in humanitarian crises*, ed. I. Smillie, 157–174. Westport, CT: Kumarian Press.

United Nations Development Programme (UNDP). 1997. *Capacity development.* New York: UNDP, Management Development and Governance Division, Bureau for Policy Development.

————. 2005. *Human development report, 2005: International cooperation at a crossroads. Aid, trade and security in an unequal world.* http://hdr.undp.org/en/media/hdr05_complete.pdf, (accessed December 2, 2007).

Van der Plaat, M. and Barrett, G. 2006. Building community capacity in governance and decision making. *Community Development Journal* 41(1): 25–36.

Waddington, H. 2004. *Linking economic policy to childhood poverty: A review of the evidence on growth, trade reform and macroeconomic policy.* London: Childhood Poverty Research and Policy Centre.

World Bank. 2004. *World development report, 2004: Making services work for poor people.* New York: Oxford University Press.

————. 2006. *World development report, 2006: Equity and development.* http://go.worldbank.org/UWYLBR43C0, (accessed May 16, 2007).

Yadama, G. N. 2003. Co-production of forests in Andhra Pradesh, India: Theoretical and practical implications. In *Co-management of natural resources in Asia: A comparative perspective,* ed. G. A. Persoon, D. M. E. van Est, and P. E. Sajise, 215–238. Copenhagen, Denmark: NIAS Press.

Yadama, G. N., and DeWeese-Boyd, M. 2001. Co-management of forests in the Tribal regions of Andhra Pradesh, India: A study in the making and unmaking of social capital. In *Analytical issues in participatory natural resource management,* ed. B. Vira and R. Jeffery, 90–107. New York: Palgrave.

Yadama, G. N., and Menon, N. 2003. Fostering social development through civic and political engagement: How confidence in institutions and agency matter. *Social Development Issues* 25(1–2): 162–174.

7 Building Partnerships for Social Development

Ingrid Burkett and Alex Ruhunda

INTRODUCTION

"Partnership," like so many concepts in the field of social development, has become a platitude for good practice. It is a term that is overused and underdefined, profoundly important to the work of development but often lacking conceptual rigor, and basically meaning whatever the user wants it to mean. Added to this, the theoretical analysis and research that has been undertaken around partnerships in social development, while growing, is still focused on exploring what it is rather than examining how it works (or otherwise) in practice. The result is a degree of cynicism around the concept and a wariness around practices associated with it—for, as one commentator has said, "today's rule of thumb in international development is that everybody wants to be a partner with everyone else on everything, everywhere" (Fowler 2000, 26). Despite the debate and general distrust surrounding the concept, we propose that there is something worth reclaiming within the kernels of practice around partnerships in social development. Indeed, we suggest that an expanded and more complex understanding of partnership could help us to address some of the legacies of colonial power relations still lingering under the cover of social development.

In this chapter, we outline how partnership fits into the organizational and stakeholder relationships within the field of social development, and thereby frame what a "partnership approach" may look like. We illustrate the complexities of a partnership approach with case studies from our own practice experience and research (in various parts of the world, but principally in Australia and Uganda) and conclude with some of the core challenges of partnerships that could contribute to a more complex understanding of the role and nature of partnership in social development.

A SHORT HISTORY OF PARTNERSHIPS IN SOCIAL DEVELOPMENT

Partnership is not an entirely new concept in social development. In the 1970s, some of the more progressive international non-governmental organizations (NGOs) (mostly based in the global North) developed the idea of working in partnership with local NGOs and community-based organizations (CBOs) rather than setting up their own infrastructures in the countries they were targeting. This was seen as a way of authenticating and indigenizing development work, while also addressing issues of colonization in development practice. In the 1980s, there was interest in the development of partnerships between governments and NGOs, with this being seen as a way for governments to engage in more "bottom-up" processes, and for public funds to be spent more effectively through the work of NGOs (see, e.g., Holloway 1989). This period also saw the publication of a seminal work that was to influence many development practitioners— Riane Eisler's *The Chalice and the Blade* (1987), which proposed that there are two core systems at work in the world: the "dominator system," which is driven by a "command and control" imperative, and a "partnership system," which is built on mutuality, support and what she terms "actualising hierarchies." Though the original book focused particularly on these systems in gender relations, the thinking has permeated development thought, politics and economics.

In the 1980s and 1990s, there was a surge of interest in partnerships with an emphasis on developing public–private partnerships, particularly around infrastructure development. More recently, there has been a renewed interest in partnerships in the context of "cross-sector partnerships" between government, corporations and civil society organizations to address what are seen as complex, intractable issues in social development. This was strengthened in 2002 with the World Summit on Sustainable Development (in Johannesburg, South Africa) stressing the importance of cross-sector partnerships in social development (see, e.g., Jørgensen 2006). This summit also contributed to a growing link between a partnership model or approach to social development and the burgeoning area of corporate social responsibility (CSR), a link that is reflected in much recent literature on partnerships.

Throughout the history of partnerships in social development, there have been questions raised as to the motivations behind interest in partnerships. Critics have suggested that the concept, because it seems good and right and proper, has the potential to hide and mystify more negative motivations such as unequal power relations, donor domination of the local development process, government divestment of responsibility and corporate largesse in the face of environmental or social irresponsibility. It is unfortunate that the practice of partnership in social development (especially partnerships between the global North and South) is still plagued with many of the same issues and criticisms made throughout the history of partnerships. As one commentator, summarizing the views of a large number of social development practitioners, recently suggested, "Many of the issues (related to partnership) which were identified as issues for Northern and Southern NGOs for the 1990s, remain issues for the 21st Century" (Drew 2003). In this arena, it is very easy to be caught up either in strong cynicism about the "real" motivations behind partnerships or in an emerging "partnership industry" that presents a glowing view and uncritical enthusiasm that "the answers" to poverty, environmental degradation and all other global ills lie in partnership. The challenge, then, is to find ways to walk the rocky and more complicated path between these two extremes, and to examine what contributions partnerships can make in social development, while acknowledging and accepting what their limitations are.

THE NATURE OF PARTNERSHIPS IN SOCIAL DEVELOPMENT

In social development work, partnerships most often refer to *organizational relationships*—between Northern and Southern NGOs for example, or government bodies and NGOs, or corporations and government bodies. Although a great deal of development-oriented organizational relationships are now being named "partnerships," an honest assessment of the realities of such relationships shows a much more complex picture. NGOs, as key players in the on-the-ground practice of social development, often have a complex array of relationships with other organizations and key stakeholders. They work with other NGOs, foundations and philanthropic bodies, with more informal groupings and associations, with coordinating and peak bodies, and with various other structures including government structures (at local, regional, central and sometimes international levels). More recently, NGOs have also begun to engage with corporate bodies, such as corporate foundations, or directly with corporations and large businesses.[1] Indeed, the organizational relationships within the social development field as a whole are becoming more complex, now that civil society organizations (NGOs included), government bodies and corporations are all seen as stakeholders and actors in the development process. Interestingly, each of these sectors brings with it particularities of definition when it comes to partnership, and these are all impacting on how partnership is interpreted in the realm of social development.

Further, it is difficult to say that organizational relationships in the preceding contexts are singular and solid in nature. A relationship can have elements of partnership, but it can also have other characteristics that could include gifting, contracting, solidarity or other relational qualities. It is somewhat naive to think that relationships are all mutual or all good. Relationships between organizations are just as complex, dynamic and nuanced as relationships between individuals, and this complexity needs to be acknowledged in practice as well as in research into partnerships in social development. Furthermore, as the enthusiasm for cross-sector partnerships gains momentum, we must not forget that it is now also increasingly important for intra-sector partnerships to be negotiated and supported. This is especially necessary under neoliberal policy frameworks that can encourage competition amongst organizations such as NGOs, rather than promoting cooperation and collaboration.

It is therefore important to distinguish partnership relationships from other forms of relationships that operate in the realm of social development—and sometimes get subsumed under the more noble title of "partnership." Some of these relationships include:

- *Contractual relationships*, between contractor and service provider, where one organization contracts another to undertake a particular job or provide a specific service. This form of relationship is more and more common between NGOs and government departments, and unfortunately it is commonly referred to as a "partnership." Contractual relationships are not mutual, as one party is contracted to the other and paid to undertake a particular piece of work. There can, however, be mutual elements to the contract (e.g., we know of a social enterprise in Australia recently being contracted to undertake a large piece of work for a local council, and included in the contract was a great deal of monetary and in-kind assistance from the local council to build the infrastructure and capacity of the social enterprise).
- *Alliance and collaboration relationships*: these relationships often develop around a specific issue or situation where two or more organizations work together to achieve particular goals over a certain timeframe. In relation to NGOs, such alliances are common for advocacy and campaigning work. They are more akin to joint ventures than to partnerships as they involve less wholistic engagement and are more centered on specific goals. Further, they do not necessarily require an agreed alignment of methods or processes. Many so-called corporate–NGO partnerships are actually "project alliances," which focus on the development of a specific project rather than any broader or institutionally based partnership (see Shiller 2005). Another version of this relationship could be described as a "solidarity" relationship, whereby an organization supports particular work or campaigns of another organization from afar. For example, in West Papua, many of the NGOs and CBOs are restricted in their advocacy activities, while NGOs in Australia and elsewhere advocate publicly on their behalf to protect the NGO workers involved in West Papua. Another version still is more "assistance" oriented than "alliance" oriented, and is focused on capacity building or other forms of support (often with self-interest in mind in addition to supporting the interests of the other parties). For example, in Case Study 6, which follows, an NGO that had been advocating against the activities of a multinational resource company agreed to work with them to train key workers in how to engage more developmentally with communities. They did this to try to change the way in which communities are affected by this company's and this industry's actions, not merely to build the capacity of the corporation.

- *Donor–recipient relationships*: these relationships can be centered on project, program or operational levels of the organizations involved. Most often, it is Northern-based NGOs, government departments, corporations or philanthropists who constitute the donors, and their economic power can have a large impact on determination of planning, implementation and evaluation of the recipient's work. It is neither appropriate nor prudent to name such relationships "partnerships," particularly if donations are conditional on compliance with certain imposed terms or timeframes, outcomes or ideologies. Partnership cannot merely be a new and more sanitized term for a "donor–recipient" relationship. Some donor–recipient relationships include a broader range of support other than financial donations. Fowler (2000) calls such relationships "supporter" relationships and suggests that they can involve support at a programmatic level (i.e., support of a financial or technical nature, or access to networks to support a theme or program of the recipient organization—which also usually aligns with a key theme of interest to the donor) or support at an institutional level that focuses on supporting "an organisation's overall effectiveness and viability" (46).

Given the conflation of "partnership" with these other forms of relationships, it is important to highlight what makes "partnership" different. The overuse of the rhetoric of "partnerships" and the resultant cynicism and mistrust of the term have led some to look for ways to add on to the term for greater conceptual leverage and clarity. For example, Fowler (2000) calls for "authentic partnerships," and Smith (2007) argues for "inclusive partnerships."

The core general characteristics of what constitutes an "effective" or "authentic" or "inclusive" partnership are normative and somewhat idealistic; however, they seem to be quite consistent across literature and research (see, e.g., Brinkerhoff 2002b; Fowler 2000; Lister 2000; Drew 2003). They include

- Mutuality—in accountability, capacity-building, communication and decision making
- Recognition of the complexity of the relationship—and support for other engagements within the partnership (e.g., constructive advocacy)
- Trust, honesty, openness and transparency
- Equality of voice and recognition of any power differentials
- Agreed objectives and agendas on the goal and process of the partnership and a commitment across the organization to achieving these goals within the process
- Acknowledgement and support for each organization's identity and specific roles and responsibilities
- Voluntary and mutual decisions regarding the form and nature of the partnership—"partnerships" cannot be enforced or conditional.

According to Fowler (2000), partnerships are "holistic and comprehensive, with no limits—in principle—to what the relationship would embrace" (46). Partnerships go further than any of the preceding forms of relationship and can extend to much longer timeframes. They can be an extremely challenging form of organizational relationship. They can be conflictual, require self-reflection and ongoing dialogue, be time-consuming and, unless they are clearly focused on achieving certain objectives, can seem to become the ends rather than the means of the work. Partnerships are not the easiest of the possible forms of relationship, and they are not always suitable for the task at hand (Burkett 2007). Careful consideration should be given as to whether "partnership" is actually the most appropriate form of relationship for organizations to enter in to.

From our experience, a "partnership" could be considered an appropriate response in social development when

- the situation at hand is *complex*, the causes are multiple and perhaps multisectoral, and action requires the skills, resources and creativity of more than one actor or sector;
- there are clear advantages in *effectiveness and efficiency* for the development process;
- there are identifiable *alignments at the level of values and worldviews*, and yet enough differences in reach, location, relationships or influence to ensure that the purpose of the relationship is predominately mutual rather than adversarial, symbiotic rather than proprietorial, and dynamic rather than static or momentary;
- there is enough *respect for the core mission and identity of each of the organizations involved* and the differences in approach and culture that this will inevitably bring, and yet there is a commitment to engage in whatever crosscultural learning is required to ensure that the partnership is nurtured; and
- there is ongoing focus, passion and commitment to addressing the issues at hand—that is, a shared understanding of the purpose and expectations of the partnership, and *acknowledgement that the partnership is the means to the end* of addressing the issue at hand, rather than an end in and of itself.

Ultimately, a partnership is only as good as the impact it leverages for the constituents[2] or beneficiaries of the process.

A PARTNERSHIP APPROACH TO SOCIAL DEVELOPMENT

A "partnership approach" is not about the proliferation of partnerships as the quintessential organizational relationship in social development. Indeed, it is an approach that recognizes the value and importance of varied organizational relationships and seeks to maximize the potential learning and impact of each for the benefit of the poorest members of our society. A partnership approach certainly advocates that the core elements and values of partnership (particularly mutuality, trust and respect) be woven in to all organizational relationships to the degree that it is possible. However, at the same time, such an approach advocates transparent and honest communication about the nature of relationships within the realm of social development. If a relationship is essentially based on a donor–recipient frame of reference, then it should be named as such, even if the mutuality elements are maximized.

Morse and McNamara (2006) distinguish between concepts of "partnership," which relate to an NGO's relationship with other organizations and donors, and "participation," which relates to the intended beneficiaries or what we term the constituents of the NGOs. Conversely, we argue that the term "partnership" be extended to cover the range of relationships and stakeholders involved in a development relationship—that is, relationships between organizations and relationships between organizations and their constituents (see Figure 7.1). It is widely recognized that the features of partnership (i.e., mutuality, honesty, a sense of ownership of the process and outcomes) are equally vital elements of organization–constituent relationships if the development process is to be sustainable, relevant and equitable. Engaging in a "partnership" with our constituents (and not just external organizations) ensures that any mutual accountability includes them (not just the donors or external partners) and opens up the possibilities

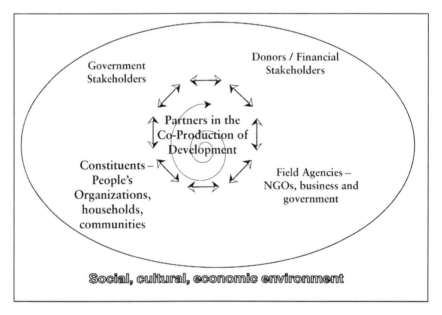

Figure 7.1 The stakeholders and context of partnerships in social development.

of a much more active engagement with constituents within the process of development. Development then becomes a "co-production,"[3] not something that is produced for or by one group for another. The importance of this "wholistic partnership" cannot be underestimated in the current context where we have seen constituents of NGOs being paid to participate in their own development or paid to advocate for their own rights. If we separate out "partnership" and "participation," we risk seeing one group of stakeholders in the development process as different to other groups, and this merely reinforces old colonial and patriarchal divisions. Including constituents as active partners in the development process is one way of ensuring that their "realities count" (Chambers 2004), that the voices of poor women, men, children and elders are part of the whole development process, not merely left in the realm of beneficiary participation.

Further, in applying a "partnership" approach, an organization cannot only focus their attention on *external* stakeholders of the development process. Partnership needs to be applied to the relationships and power structures *within* the organization engaged in social development work. Therefore, the governance structure, the management structure and the relationships and processes underpinning these structures all need to reflect the principles of partnership. If there are unnamed or unaddressed power issues, or corruption or mistrust internally within an organization, there can be no hope that external partnerships with other organizations, or with constituents will not reflect these internal struggles (see Case Study 1 and Case Study 3).

Case Study 1

An NGO involved in community development in Australia was reviewing its future after a major source of funds was lost. The review included its external relationships and partnerships, and its internal structure. Many external (actual and potential) partnerships were identified, and the excitement and hope in the NGO planning meeting was palpable. However, then the internal relationships were reviewed and it was realized that the types of relationships within the organization did not reflect the hopes and dreams for the organization's external relationships. While the external relationships were characterized as involving high degrees of trust, honesty, mutuality, reciprocity and equality, the internal relationships in the organization (especially between staff members and managers, and between board members and staff members) were characterized by distrust, a sense of dishonesty, unequal power and influence, a feeling of disrespect and a culture of competition. The governance structure was one that emphasized control and command. The extent of the mismatch between the organization's external focus and its internal relationships shocked the board and staff alike. The focus of the work was then changed to ensure that it was not just the external relationships that were considered to be "partnerships," but also the internal relationships. The board explored partnership models of governance, and the managers also introduced partnership qualities into manager–staff relations. The result was a much more consistent and effective approach to the work both within and outside the organization.

A partnership approach is based on addressing some of the core imbalances within relationships, whether they be organizational or individual, that continue to permeate social development. In what follows, we explore three elements of a framework for a partnership approach to social development. The framework builds on our experience as development practitioners and is informed by research undertaken into the practice of partnerships in development. The elements are by no means prescriptive or exhaustive. There are many resources available that point to tools and techniques for the development of effective partnerships. The elements presented next do not constitute tools. They are merely signposts for the organic journey of engaging with a partnership approach. It should be emphasized, however, that a partnership approach links all three of the elements—mindsets/language, behavior and systems—intimately, and each is dependent on the others. It is too common in the current environment to implement a highly developed policy and procedure system, without any changes in mindsets, language or behavior either at an organizational level or at the level of individual staff members.

MINDSETS AND LANGUAGE

> *The power of vocabulary to change how we think and what we do is easy to underestimate. It influences the course of development in many ways: through changing the agenda; through modifying mindsets; through legitimating new actions; and through stimulating and focussing research and learning. (Chambers 2004, 3)*

A partnership approach requires, first and foremost, an approach to social development that recognizes the importance of the worldviews, paradigms, mindsets and the language that we bring to our practice. Although the importance of this is often downplayed by those who argue that development is merely a technical or instrumental activity, many practice researchers and practitioners alike suggest that mindsets and language are critical to the development process (see, e.g., Chambers 2004; Kaplan 1989; Rahnema and Bawtree 1994). Without examining the mindsets and language underpinning a partnership approach, we could very well be implementing an empty, meaningless and rhetorical concept, rather than attempting to change the way we "do" development and the outcomes we are seeking to create.

One of the key critiques of the way in which partnership is being used in social development is that it is merely pretty window dressing used to cover up the same old power dynamics, dominations and inequitable economic relationships that have plagued particularly North–South interactions for decades. A mindset that is enquiring, recognizes and openly acknowledges power imbalances, seeks out honest communication and engaged learning will not settle for this rhetorical shell of partnership. A partnership approach cannot be built on a mindset that is centered on control, bureaucratic agreements, instrumentalism or coercion.

A partnership approach calls for the acknowledgement that all the stakeholders involved bring different strengths, knowledge and skills, while each also has gaps in their knowledge and limitations in their skills.[4] Further, partnerships in social development are emergent and organic relationships, rather than being static and linear outcomes. Therefore, a partnership approach requires action learning—a constant cycle of action, reflection, change and learning—rather than a toolkit or a "how-to" manual that can be read and applied. Such an approach requires a worldview that embraces learning, is reflective about how change happens and can engage reflection, self-consciousness and awareness, where practitioners are prepared to engage in transformation of themselves and not just the other.

Finally, a partnership approach requires a degree of confidence. This may seem like a strange statement. However, it is our experience that often there are both "pushers" and "pullers" in a partnership. Many studies have explored the role of the "pusher"—the dominant player, usually holding the economic power (and usually using this power through their role as donor), who can "push" their ideas and systems onto the other party in the partnership. Few, on the other hand, have focused on the role and experience of the "pullers"— the party who holds less economic power, who is often organizationally flattered by the attention given to them by the dominant player and who often more readily accepts conditions of the "partnership" lest they rock the boat and cause the donor party to look elsewhere. What is the effect on a partnership or the prospect of a partnership, of a mindset that is enveloped in a sense of powerlessness? What does such a mindset mean an organization is prepared to sacrifice in the name of a "partnership"? And what effect does this sacrifice have on the effectiveness of the partnership as a whole? In Burkett's (2007) work, which examined cross-sector partnerships in relation to microfinance and asset-building work in Australia, one of the issues raised was a perceived lack of confidence within NGOs in relation to the other two sectors (government and private). As one interviewee in this research suggested,

> [W]hen considering a partnership with business or government, it's important to be clear, get back to your values and your purpose. Then once you're clear about that you'll be able to go in and say well this is what we can do, this is what we can't do, and we're equal partners— we're not third rate citizens. And it's important for us to know that it's OK to walk away if it's not right. (in Burkett 2007, 29)

This is similar for NGOs in the global South, who, in our experience, will often accept the rhetoric of partnership (while being fully cognizant of the fact that it is rhetoric) so long as the status and the funds from the so-called partner organization continue to flow. Indeed, Drew (2003) highlights the asymmetric power evident between Northern and Southern NGOs and points to a number of reports in which Southern NGOs see these relation-ships as being "parent–child in nature" (7). Certainly, there is a need to address the push and pull of power within a partnership relationship. A partnership approach certainly involves addressing the power imbalances inherent in relationship where one organization holds resources over the other. However, it also advocates for the building of organizational confi-dence (particularly among NGOs, and then particularly among Southern or community-based NGOs) to name what objectives, values, principles and practice frameworks are central to their work, and to hold to these in the face of attractive partnership offers that may result in mission drift or other compromises. Case Study 2 illustrates this point.

Case Study 2: Resisting the Allure of "Partnership"

GTS* is a small NGO working in the field of microfinance and poverty alleviation in India. They had been approached by a number of larger NGOs and some corpo-rations with a view to forming a partnership. They attended a number of meetings with the potential partners, but when the ideas for the partnership were laid out on the table, it was clear that GTS was not an equal player in relation to the other organizations. GTS was asked to take the majority of the risks, and they were to undertake most of the more difficult work. The larger NGOs and the corporate players seemed to want to take the "glory" (by promoting the partnership's work through their media and public relations systems) and were prepared to put in the initial monies, but they did not want to take the risks or do the hard work of putting the initiatives into practice with constituents (mostly poor women living in slum areas of a large city). In addition, they only wanted to fund the costs of the actual project work, not the associated costs of infrastructure and organizational support. It was only project funding not core funding for GTS. Finally, to add insult to injury, the larger NGOs started to speak of all the changes to methodology that could be tried when the partnership was underway, as they had conducted research in other countries that was disputing some of the methodologies successfully used by GTS for many years. It all seemed very unequal, and GTS decided that if they entered the partnerships, although it all appeared very alluring and the promise of funding was difficult to resist, they would ultimately not benefit either themselves as an NGO or their constituents. They decided not to pursue the partnerships.

* *The name of the NGO in this case study has been changed at their request.*

BEHAVIORS

[W]e need to be continually observing our actions rather than simply acting. Put another way, we need to be continuously conscious of what we are doing, rather than simply doing. This, after all, is what "raising consciousness", "developing awareness" is all about. We tend to use these phrases almost exclusively with respect to "what is out there", but this is a dangerous misconception because it constitutes a denial of ourselves as responsible, integral players in the game. So we have to become conscious and we have to become observers, both of ourselves and of what surrounds us. (Kaplan, 1989, 3)

Developing a partner-oriented language and mindset can help us to espouse the necessary theory needed for effective or "authentic" partnerships. What is central, however, to the implementation of effective partnerships is how this espoused theory becomes a "theory-in-use" (Argyris and Schon 1974). Our mindsets and worldviews impact on how we behave in a partnership— how we speak with others, how we listen, how we observe, how we facilitate the process. A partnership approach demands behaviors that are conducive to putting the principles of partnership into practice, but most importantly, it demands an ability to be able to insightfully reflect on how our behavior is impacting on the process and to be able to learn from such reflections.

At its core, partnership is about power relations, and a partnership approach requires behaviors that acknowledge and address, in whatever ways possible, inequalities in such relations. A partnership approach moves relations of power from "power over" each other to "power with" one another. Adopting a position of "power with" means engaging in behaviors of collegiality, mutual trust, joint learning and collaboration (Eyben, in Chambers 2004). "Power with" requires processes that are facilitated and guided but not controlled or engineered. "Power with" does not mean that the relationship is always convivial and peaceful—indeed, central to a partnership approach are behaviors that acknowledge and engage with conflict (rather than hiding or ignoring it). "Power with" is, however, relational in the true and whole sense of this word. Thus, it is very difficult to enact a partnership approach if organizational structures are too fluid or when people only occupy organizational roles for short periods of time. Much of the research on partnerships in social development suggests that the behaviors and the relationships of individuals within organizations are crucial to the ongoing effectiveness of partnerships. It is very difficult to embed any kind of partnership in organizations if the people involved are constantly in flux. Thus, while we next suggest that processes and systems for partnership can be developed, we wish to emphasize the humanness of partnerships—they need to be peopled if they are to be effective; they cannot merely be systematized or contractual in nature.

Case Study 3: Some Personal Reflections on the Importance of "Peopled Partnerships" in KRC, an NGO in Uganda

Partnership has to begin with individuals and not structures. One has to acknowledge that behind any partnership there are people. The degree in which a given partnership succeeds will largely depend on in-depth knowledge the different individuals have of the partnership and how each views their stake in making the partnership work. We shall use our personal experience in the partnership approach we used in the establishment of Kabarole Research Center, now one of the most successful NGOs in Uganda. The partnership approach applies within our organization not just in relation to our external organizational relationships.

Continued

Continued

The notion of going beyond the frameworks that define partnerships into individual's inner feelings on the partnerships is very important. One has to take into consideration the passion each individual has within the partnership. The sharing of the passion goes with openness, which calls for a very transparent and accountable environment that makes every individual accountable to another irrespective of the position one holds. This practice has seen not only a huge increase in innovations from the staff, but also a high spirit of ownership of the organization by the staff. The recognition of what shapes behavior in the organization, and less attention to top-down managerial practices, has simplified and demystified the monitoring and management role of the top leadership. This shift of management behavior has led KRC not only to produce good managers but also thinkers and leaders in the development of the rural communities. It means that everyone shares a responsibility in the running and the success of the organization.

PROCESSES AND PRACTICES, SYSTEMS AND PROCEDURES

A number of researchers have found that effective or successful partnerships are often characterized by the development of strong personal relationships (see, e.g., Lister 2000). Burkett (2007), in a study of the practices associated with cross-sector partnerships, found that most of the partnerships had either begun out of, or been strengthened through, personal relationships, and that one of the key challenges within the partnerships was how these strong personal relationships could be institutionalized or broadened into the cultures of the organizations involved. Lister's (2000) research also indicated that "partnerships are strongest if there are multiple linkages that connect the organizations involved" (238). The question remains, then, how the processes, practice, systems and procedures can build on strong personal relationships that help to establish and grow the partnership. Further, how can they ensure that the qualities that the personal relationships bring to a partnership are not buried under bureaucratic systems, policies, tomes and organizational mandates? In other words, how can processes and systems maintain the quality of organic development rather than become static and instrumental in nature? Brinkerhoff and Brinkerhoff (2004) identify a gap that frequently exists between the "egalitarian relationship implied by the language *(in policy documents for example)* and the principal-agent reality embodied in the donor's operational system" (264; emphasis added). This is particularly pertinent (if much more complex) when we consider organizations that have many partnerships with all sorts of other organizations. Next, we outline five key ways in which this *can* happen, based on our practice research and on the findings of Burkett (2007).

1. *Developing an organizational questioning and learning framework.*
   This is a shared organizational framework that is used to determine whether the partnership is going to be mutually beneficial in

the first place, and that can enable organizations to continue to question and monitor who is benefiting from the partnership. Put simply, organizations need to ask questions about why they are seeking to engage in partnerships in the first place and continue this questioning for the life of the partnership. Basic questions, answered honestly, could help to focus on what organizations are hoping to achieve from a partnership—what is the partnership for? Who is it for? What will the partnership look like? Who will the partnership ultimately benefit? How will we know if the partnership is working? Or more specifically, how is the action I am about to undertake reflective of our partnership approach? How are mutuality and trust reflected in the accountability between the organizations? Such basic questions, though seemingly simple and innocuous, are often forgotten in the complexity of organizational life. They can, however, provide a quick and sharp reminder of the key elements of partnership and can be an essential part both of the pre-partnership processes and the ongoing evaluation of the effectiveness of the partnership. Their simplicity should not belie their power in terms of sharpening behaviors and processes.

2. *Moving from paper trails to cultural change.*

One of the key ways used by the organizations in Burkett's (2007) study to "institutionalize" partnerships or ensure their sustainability after the personalities who held the partnership together moved on was to leave a paper trail for others to follow. This paper trail was to document the history, the processes, the learnings, and so forth, of the partnership. Yet this represents a very limited form of institutionalization—as has been demonstrated in many partnerships around the world, once the key people leave an organization there is very often an impasse in the work of the partnership (at least until new relationships are established). For example, Morse and McNamara (2006), in their study of a "partnership" over a thirty-five-year period, concluded, "As for institutionalisation of mindset and skill set this simply did not occur. There was no institutional memory at the donor, and each desk officer came in with his/her agenda and personal attributes" (333). Paper trails can only go so far in creating a partnership footprint in organizations. What is needed is much broader than this and is more in the realm of cultural change than documentation and filing procedures. Such cultural change may involve the telling and retelling of the story of the partnership, various celebrations of the partnership and of a partnership approach within the organization, development of a partnership "ritual" that may be in the form of a creed or acknowledgement that appears in public spaces in the organization and/or is spoken at the beginning or end of public meetings. The forms of the processes used to build a culture of partnership within an organization are many and varied, and only limited by the imaginations of those within the organization. Again, such processes may seem banal or trivial, but if a partnership is to move off the paper files and into the life of an organization, then ways must be found to enliven the concept of partnership.

3. *Building systems and practices of transparency and mutual accountability.*

It is still the case that many so-called "partnerships" are based on applications by NGOs for funding from either other NGOs or large social-service foundations, governments or corporations. Often the guidelines for these funds are written by the donor organizations, and the recipient organizations "fit" their programs in to these guidelines in order to access the funds. A partnership approach demands a much more rigorous and honest system for the development of partnerships. In the first instance, it is crucial to the effectiveness of a partnership that there is recognition and respect given to each party's organizational mission, values, methodologies and strategies (see, e.g., Brinkerhoff 2004). This means that a process of openly sharing these markers of organizational identity must be found, rather than "fitting" one organization's identity into the others. Some form of alignment, complementarity or congruence between the different identities must be found for the partnership to be initiated. Further, it is important for an understanding to be developed about how decision making happens in the partnership and how (in what ways and using what frames of reference) the work and the partnership itself are to be evaluated. Effectively, what are needed are processes and practices that enact the laudable terms of "transparency" and "mutual accountability." Like many of the concepts that define partnership (and the concept of partnership itself), these terms need to move off the pages of policy and into action if the partnership is to be enacted.

4. *Challenging systems of control.*

At the same time as developing systems of transparency and mutual accountability, a partnership approach requires what could be termed "robust dialogue" about the systems of social development that seek to control and dominate. Among these is the particularly insidious system of time frames. This frequently comes to the fore in donor–recipient relationships where donors demand results and value for money and put pressure on the recipient organizations. The urgency for results, and the frequently unrealistic demands that are generated from this urgency, often create intense frustration among field workers and community development workers. Robust dialogue happens in a space where all parties can question assumptions and ideologies. So, in the instance of inappropriate time frames being determined, the recipient NGO could challenge the donor to reveal the nature of their urgency, or they could challenge their monochronic view of time, and in the context of the relationship, this challenge would be engaged in openly and without threat. Equally, the "donor" could challenge the NGO to reveal their process and speak openly about the challenges—in the spirit of dialogue rather than reporting. The curtailing of an NGO's voice within a partnership also needs to be challenged through robust dialogue. As Smith (2007) highlights, "Unfortunately, the experience of many civil society organisations in partnerships with government and business is that they are required to suspend critical voices, tone down public advocacy and tow the line of the more powerful partners" (4). Such systems and mechanisms of control need to be challenged before the partnership begins, during the partnership and through evaluation of the partnership after it ends.

5. Moving beyond "equality as sameness."

A partnership approach recognizes that equality in partnerships needs to appreciate a range of different and often complex contributions and benefits that flow through the partnership. Too often, the nonfinancial or noneconomic resources and assets of organizations involved in social development (e.g., their experience, expertise, cultural skills, relationships with local people and groups) are overlooked. And yet without these resources, the development process may merely involve a transfer of money. Hakim and Musendo (in Drew 2003, 6) highlight the different contributions to and benefits from partnerships between Southern NGOs and Northern NGOs. They suggest that the differences may not be as problematic if roles and responsibilities of different players were more clearly articulated and respected. Equality in partnerships is not about "sameness." It is about recognizing the variety of strengths, assets and resources that each stakeholder brings to the partnership. Further, it is about valuing and respecting what these differences bring to the process of meeting the objectives of the partnership. Finally, it is about acknowledging and respecting the different benefits that stakeholders derive from the partnership, ensuring that they all do benefit in some real and articulated ways. This is important for the endurance of the partnership—as Brinkerhoff (2002a) points out, "[W]hen partners generally benefit equally from their relationship, partnerships tend to be more enduring and high performing" (22). The processes, practices, systems and procedures that can be applied to support a partnership are many and varied. The danger is that these processes are translated into managerial control systems, which are the antithesis of a partnership approach. If mindsets, language, behavior, processes and systems are separated out and not treated as an integrated whole, then the whole basis of partnership can be undermined. For example, fear and lack of trust can take an upper hand and entrench the unrealistic demands, keeping both parties extremely busy in managing systems that shape an artificial culture under the guise of a partnership. Some of the complexities of this application and the importance of taking into account the context and environment of the stakeholders within the partnership when designing or planning these practices are explored further in Case Study 4.

Case Study 4: The Partnership between HIVOS and KRC

The partnership between KRC and HIVOS is one of the most fortunate happenings in the history of KRC. KRC was founded on very strong liberating principles that challenged the role of NGOs in the development of rural communities in Africa. The core principles and values are based on the realization that one of the major causes of poverty in Africa is largely a result of perpetual dependency that has stifled people's capacity to think through their own development challenges. The ideology of KRC strongly advocates for people-led development, and considers inputs from elsewhere as a mere catalyst and *not* the solution to people's development challenges. Much emphasis is put on processes that change the attitudes and perceptions of local communities to steer their own development with less external support. The relationship between KRC and HIVOS was founded on the recognition of the shared values and principles that shape the vision of the two organizations.

HIVOS as an external partner identifies and supports ideas and plans that are generated locally and owned by the local partners who take responsibility in fulfillment of the agreed obligations. The respect of the partner's context and diversity is taken seriously in the partnership, which makes HIVOS more knowledgeable and able to be relevant in supporting realistic and achievable programs. The practice by HIVOS of empowering the local partner to make critical decisions in the implementation of the supported programs without imposing their own perspectives, contributes greatly to the successes of the work of the local partners.

What many development partners (read donors) have failed to understand is that their top-down imposition on the local partners has created a negative perpetual cycle in which a group of people keep chasing and trying to read the donor's mindsets for the purpose of securing funding, even when they know it will not produce the desired results. This has more or less become a trade, and when a project fails, this is seen as a need to modify the support, and so the cycle continues. This distortion of development aid has been heavily criticized, with NGOs mainly left to do the expensively managed humanitarian emergency support. This has painted a negative picture of Africa in the eyes of people from the developed world.

HIVOS and KRC believe strongly in a long-term partnership that provides room for the experimentation and learning that is essential for the transformation of rural communities. The support by HIVOS of the entire institution, focused through program funding as opposed to project funding, has led to the increased growth in confidence of KRC in relations with the local development actors—including the government. The confidence created in this treasured partnership has created room for innovations that have been instrumental in the transformation process of the local communities in the Rwenzori region in Uganda.   *Continued*

Continued

There is nothing worse than having an unsure organization sending unsure staff into unsure communities. This is further worsened by having an organization focused on the short-term sending of short-term driven staff (always in a hurry to spend donor funds) to short-term stricken communities (who are in dire need of basic needs for survival). This scenario explains the dilemma facing development aid, which again impacts heavily on lopsided partnerships that always leave the rural people much worse than they found them. Usually, these short-term partnerships involve a lot of money that has to be spent in a short period of time, so that the communities get a lot of handouts through un-necessary allowances and grants. This bad practice has eroded the values of sacrifice and volunteerism and has affected ownership of the community development processes.

KRC and HIVOS have, for the last eight years, been committed to building processes that empower the rural communities to be in charge of their own development. The communities have to come up with their own ideas, which are brainstormed in a participatory manner, and each party agrees on their roles with very clear sustainability plans. The monitoring role of progress is a primary concern of the communities themselves and, later, KRC and HIVOS. This means that every member in the given community group takes pride in ensuring success, and not for the sake of pleasing a donor but for their own satisfaction. This process needs patience and long-term commitment that will enable the much desired confidence among the staff and the local communities.

The increasing pressure from the different funding partners for results is destabilizing the partnerships of organizations like HIVOS and KRC. This is slowly causing mixed feelings about the future, as a number of governments in Europe are putting stringent conditions in place that make it difficult for long-term- oriented funding agencies. As we continue to experience the effects of globalization with the rapid spread of information technology, the majority of rural communities stand out as more vulnerable, and they desperately need this long-term commitment that is now being threatened by the usual top-down drivers in the control of the global resources. HIVOS and KRC, through the lessons in our partnership and the strong recognition of broader processes of community development, are embarking on a new horizon of knowledge building that can inform more complex global processes about the real knowledge that works for the majority of the poor in the world.

THE CONTRIBUTION OF PARTNERSHIPS TO SOCIAL DEVELOPMENT

The contribution of partnerships to social development has been decidedly mixed. Among the rhetoric, grand claims and espoused benefits of partnerships, it is true that there have been some positive results, as Brinkerhoff (2006) highlights:

[I]n some pockets of international development practice, partnership has yielded significant improvements in efficiency, sustainability and, most importantly, effectiveness that in turn have improved quality of life. The less good news is that many areas are still plodding forward through trial and error: the lessons of what makes for an effective partnerships have not been systematised or mainstreamed. (1)

There is still a large gap between the rhetoric and the reality of partnerships, and between the theory and practice. Further, there remains a "dearth of literature that critically evaluates the performance of partnership" (Davies, in Morse and McNamara 2006, 324), with much research focused on specific case studies and contention about the variety and definition of partnership. There is also a danger that development practitioners become consumed by evaluating a partnership itself, rather than determining whether this partnership has actually resulted in "better development" (Morse and McNamara 2006, 327). The purpose of a partnership approach is to build more effective development processes, not to perfect the art of partnership in and of itself.

What can be discerned from the research to date is that the contribution of partnerships and of a partnership approach in social development centers on three areas, as illustrated in Figure 7.2.

Researchers and practitioners place different emphases on the importance of these areas, with some suggesting that "learning" is potentially at the heart of the contribution of partnership (see, e.g., Drew 2003; Hyatt

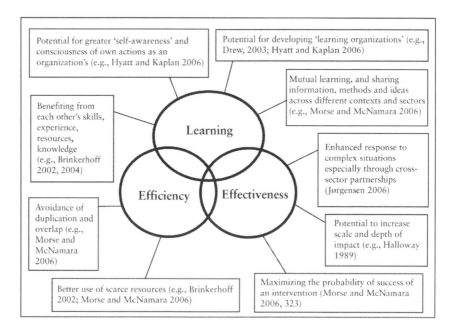

Figure 7.2 Potential and actual contributions of partnerships to social development.

and Kaplan 2006—interestingly both these articles also suggest that the "doing" of learning within partnerships has a long way to develop). Meanwhile, others suggest that effectiveness, or bettering the outcomes and outputs of development interventions, should be the focus of partnership (see, e.g., Morse and McNamara 2006). In many ways, the evaluation of the actual contributions of partnerships to social development suffer from the same limitations as articulations of the benefits of partnership, namely, that there is a difference between the espoused contributions of partnerships and the actual, evaluated and agreed upon contributions that individual partnerships and partnerships as a whole have made to social development.

While there are some frameworks for evaluating the performance of partnerships (see, e.g., Brinkerhoff 2002a), stakeholders would do well to take some of the normative principles of partnerships and apply these to the evaluation of the effectiveness of this approach. For example, an evaluation of a partnership could begin with the identification of mutually acceptable indicators as to how the work within the partnership is progressing. Or there could be a commitment to exploring the shifts and changes, challenges and tensions over time, rather than relying on snapshot evaluations or short-term results (see, e.g., Morse and McNamara 2006). Evaluation of the success of the partnership needs to be part of the overall process of the partnership itself, not an external or separate activity.

THE CURRENT CHALLENGES OF PARTNERSHIPS IN SOCIAL DEVELOPMENT

Though many of the challenges of partnership in social development have been outlined through our analysis of a partnership approach, it is worth highlighting some of the key issues facing the practice of partnership in the current global context. In what follows, we briefly summarize five key challenges facing partnerships in social development.

Beyond the Rhetoric: Naming and Accepting the Reality of Power in Partnership Relationships

This has been a challenge for partnerships in social development since their beginnings. Because the notion of "development" is ensconced in power, it is probably inevitable that any attempts to equalize power relationships in this field becomes both attractive and fraught. The oversimplification of power in partnerships, and the use of partnership terminology to dress the wolves of donor–recipient relationships in sheep's clothing, have meant that, in practice, power remains the unspoken about elephant in the room of partnerships. To mix metaphors even further, Hyatt and Kaplan (2006) confront the dangers of this: "[T]he rhetoric of partnership has buried power yet deeper in the psyche of (donor-grantee-beneficiary) communication. Yet, like the skeleton in the family cupboard, everyone is affected by the unspoken as much as by what is said" (28). A partnership approach acknowledges and names the whole range of possible organizational and stakeholder relationships in social development. The challenge now is for organizations of all kinds to *honestly* assess the quality of their relationships, maximize the potentials for mutuality, but refrain from calling all relationships partnerships, when they clearly are not!

The Ongoing Impact of Money and Funding on Partnerships

The first challenge is related to the second challenge, which really focuses on how significantly money and funding impacts on a partnership relationship. Most organizational relationships that are termed "partnerships" are based on some kind of funding or transfer of financial and other resources. Yet, according to Lister (2000), the control of money is "the most frequently cited constraint to the formation of authentic partnership" (230). There are two important points to be made in relation to this. First, it is necessary to understand the impact that transfer of money has had on social development as a whole. Often, action is tied to money (i.e., "We can't do anything until we have the funding"), and as the pools of money available shrink, it is inevitable that the "poorest" sectors (mostly the NGOs) will focus on maximizing their share of available resources. Therefore, what becomes attractive is not necessarily the partnership, but access to resources. Conversely, money often drives the cycles of donors, and once they establish a connection to an entity that can deliver what they are seeking in terms of social development goals, then the pump can flow too hard and too fast for monies to be used effectively. And if initiatives are donor-driven, then pumping in monies for a period of time can not only kill local initiatives and social movements, but it can worsen the situation of local people once the pump is turned off and the monies for action dry up. Money and the flow of resources is a very complex and probably underacknowledged issue in social development. So when we add partnership to this volatile mix, we can appreciate the additional layers of complexity that are added. The way to engage with this complexity is to acknowledge the whole flow of resources, to name the power of money (and the associated accountabilities) in the relationship and to make sure that any "partnerships" go far beyond the money. Case Study 5 illustrates this last point. Second, also illustrated in Case Study 5 is the current focus on funding discrete "projects" and still calling the relationship around the project a "partnership." As is seen in this case study, however, the partnership extended a long way beyond particular "projects." While "projects" could be part of a broader partnership, it is rarely the case that funding relationships centered around specific "projects" will demonstrate many of the qualities of partnership, and they are more likely to fall into the "donor–recipient" or "contractual" relationship (see Hakim, in Drew 2003, 4). Relationships between organizations that are built squarely around funding are probably rarely going to develop into partnerships. Partnerships are much more institutional and longer term in nature than focused on specific projects or funding cycles.

Case Study 5: Reflections on the Extent of Partnership

We visited a large and well-established NGO in northern India while working for an international NGO and donor organization. We were aware of the long history of association between the Indian NGO and the international NGO. We asked about the nature of this relationship. The reply was, "We are partners—we have been partners for around twenty-five years and we continue to be partners in the process of development." We were surprised by the strength of conviction shown by the workers as to their relationship with the international NGO. We enquired further about the relationship. We learned that the international organization had funded the Indian NGO at a time when few other donors were interested—and that they were funded largely on the strength of the relationship between the local field office of the international NGO and their observations of the work that was being undertaken with local communities. The funding was relatively small, but crucial in the growth of the Indian NGO. The funding was recurrent for around ten years, and then over a period of time, it was deemed no longer necessary. We enquired about whether this changed the nature of the partnership relationship: "Not at all . . . we are not partners because we received money or funding. We are partners because we share a belief in a common goal, and we share information, skills, knowledge, friendship and advocacy, we participate in each other's campaigns, we have exchanges and we build our capacities together. Money has never made the partnership . . . that's why we are still partners today and no money has changed hands for fifteen years or so." This is now a large NGO that is "chased" and "courted" by many international donors of all varieties because of the success of their work. They are very careful about who they "partner" with, when the offer to "partner" is centered only on money.

The Limitations of Idealizing Partnerships and Overrating Expectations of Partnerships

Much of the literature on partnerships in social development is normative in nature and presents an "ideal type" of relationship that constitutes a partnership. The practice of social development needs to recognize the limitations of such ideal types, for they are only very rarely achieved in full, and the reality of partnerships is much more contested, fragile, imperfect and complex than any ideal type representation. Brinkerhoff (2002b) argues that this recognition can help practitioners to avoid cynicism regarding the concept of partnership, while at the same time it can open up opportunities for asking questions that can help to shape the reality and practicality of a partnership or potential partnership. So, for example, "using the partnership model, actors can assess their relative tolerance for mutuality and their willingness to invest in protecting the organisational identity of their potential partners. This may lead actors to rule out the partnership option in favour of more acceptable alternatives" (27). Case Study 6 examines how an NGO's relationship with a large multinational corporation developed into something other than a partnership because there was only a limited focus for mutuality, and the core objectives of each organization made it difficult to conceive of either "protecting" the other's identity.

Related to the idealization of what constitutes a partnership are the often heightened expectations of what can happen through and in a partnership. When high expectations are not met, and the idealism is brought down by the difficulties of reality, then the potential impact is a reduction of trust and cynicism about the value of partnerships as a whole. For this reason, realistic timeframes and pragmatism are important in a partnership approach. Vangen and Huxham suggest the use of a "cyclical trust-building loop" in partnerships—that is, "having enough trust to start, pursuing modest goals that can be met and which will thus reinforce trust; then developing more ambitious initiatives" (in Johnson and Wilson 2006, 15).

The Attractions and Dangers of New Partnerships between NGOs and Corporations

This challenge requires a whole chapter in its own right, and we cannot do it justice in the space that is left. The question concerns what is now a very real challenge in the field of social development, that is, the proliferation of new partnerships, specifically involving NGOs and corporations. While there are many popular reports and public relations documents surrounding such partnerships, there are relatively few objective analyses and little research on the effectiveness and challenges of such partnerships. Of all the forms of partnership in social development, cross-sector partnerships—and more particularly partnerships between NGOs and corporations—are subject to the most prolific rhetoric. As one commentator recently suggested, "[T]hough still very early days in the formation of multi-sector partnerships, expectations (and rhetoric) run high while the reality lags well behind" (Caplan 2003, 31).

Historically, most of the literature focused on partnerships in social development has focused on relationships between donor NGOs (often referred to as Northern NGOs) and recipient NGOs (Southern NGOs) or on relations between NGOs and government organizations. One would think that the power issues highlighted in this literature, along with the tensions of aligning values, goals and strategies, must be manifested tenfold in relationships between NGOs and corporations. In Burkett's (2007) study of cross-sector partnerships, however, many of the NGO staff members reported that "partnership" between their NGOs and corporations were actually "easier," or at least less contested, than they were between NGOs and government bodies, which, it was argued, were much more burdened with the historical baggage of donor-recipient mindsets whilst dressing these relationships up as "partnerships." In truth, however, many of the so-called "partnerships" studied by Burkett (2007) were, in reality, more like "project alliances" (Shiller 2005), relationships that were focused on specific, discrete projects rather than wholesale "partnerships." Corporate–NGO relationships are potentially fraught with complexities and tensions, only some of which are beginning to be documented (see, e.g., Jørgensen 2006; Shiller 2005; Burkett 2007; Caplan 2003). The challenge will be to see if the concept of "partnership," and a partnership approach to social development, will become clearer or even more muddied as corporations (with their legal and company partnership histories) enter the fray.

Case Study 6

A large international NGO had engaged in a number of public campaigns against the actions and impacts on communities of a multinational resource corporation. Some of the campaigns resulted in legal actions undertaken by communities against the company. Simultaneously, however, the company responded by initiating a dialogue group (including a number of NGO representatives) to discuss how they could improve their corporate–community relations, and they also sent some of their community relations staff on an exposure trip with the NGO to see first hand the impact of resource development on poor communities. This resulted in a specific exposure program that focused on giving the company staff and managers an opportunity to see how resource development impacted on communities, and to demonstrate how the company could do things differently so that the negative impacts on communities could be reduced. This in turn led to a training program where the resource company paid the NGO to train their community-engagement staff in many of the most sensitive regions of their activities. The training involved introducing staff to the principles and practices of effective participatory development work—in contrast to the public- relations and community- relations paradigm in which they had previously been working.

This has been a long-term engagement or relationship between an NGO and a resource corporation (five years to date). However, it was decided very early in the relationship that this could not be termed a "partnership," as the values and approaches of the two entities were too divergent. What was common was a belief that the private sector has an increasingly large influence on the welfare and well-being of people—especially in the global South, and especially in poorer regions. It was decided that advocacy and campaigning by NGOs could only go so far in ensuring that this impact by the private sector was not devastating for local people and their environment. Their response also needed to include dialogue and mutual exchanges between NGOs and corporations.

The challenges of this relationship lie in three areas:
–   There have been impacts of the training in the company; however, it is still unclear what these are in objective, practical and global terms

Continued

Continued

– It is clear that sustainability of the resource development sector in environmental and social terms requires the involvement of government bodies—both within country and internationally. NGO–corporation relationships can only go so far, and it is imperative that government involvement occurs in the long term; however, governments have thus far not been involved in this process;

– There have been great challenges in terms of honesty and trust (from both sides), and it has been important in this to recognize the needs, approaches and values of each entity, and to reinforce the nature of the relationship (given that it was decided that this was not to be a partnership) and how this shapes their interactions.

In many ways, it was an enlightened decision not to refer to nor consider this relationship to have the qualities of a "partnership"—particularly in a political context that revered and gave great status to corporate–community partnerships. It demonstrates that there are a variety of possibilities for cross-organizational and cross-sectoral relationships being other than partnerships, and it highlights the particular and specific place of partnerships in this context. The concept of partnerships was not and should not be used lightly.

CONCLUSION

Authentic partnerships are comparatively rare in social development. There are many relationships that are called "partnerships" but that neither have the normative aspirations nor the relational qualities of actual partnership. These are often very specifically project focused, or they are donor–recipient or contractual relationships under the mask of partnership. Along with other concepts considered to represent "good" development (such as participation, empowerment, capacity building, and so on), partnership has come to represent the sort of relationships that people and organizations aspire to, but few can enact on a practical level. This does not render the concept or the aspiration redundant. On the contrary, it becomes an important signpost for practitioners and organizations alike. It is a signpost, however, that makes demands—a demand for honesty of engagement (naming when a partnership is not a partnership), confidence (to do the naming in the face of power relations and funding agreements) and learning (to understand and enact the bedrocks that can help people to build authentic partnerships in their own organizations and contexts). Partnerships do not offer a panacea for social development, and, as a recent commentator has suggested, "partnerships—multi-sector or multi-stakeholder—are not in themselves an answer to the ills of a globalised, vastly unequal world. . . . Partnerships are not a substitute for politics, leadership, citizen action and long-term development processes" (Smith 2007, 1). They can, however, be part of the picture, and with a little more rigor, a little more truthfulness and a lot more action learning, a partnership approach can make a real contribution to the development of communities and societies, both in the global South and in the global North.

NOTES

1. It should be noted that many local NGOs have worked with local businesses for a long time; their relationships with the larger or multinational corporate sector, in other than advocacy terms, as outlined here is, however, a more recent phenomenon.
2. We prefer the term "constituents" to describe people involved in the development process (rather than "beneficiaries" or other terms). A constituent is an active citizen of the process—a contributor, a resource, bringing knowledge, strengths and skills to the process. A constituent is a coproducer of development, not a passive recipient or beneficiary of the outcomes.
3. For a wider exploration of the notions of coproduction (which, incidentally, is now a trademarked term), see Cahn (2004) and Ostrom (1996).
4. See Johari Window for a detailed explanation of this aspect of mindset (Chambers 2000; Srinivsan 1993).

REFERENCES

Argyris, M., and Schön, D. 1974. Theory in practice: Increasing professional effectiveness. San Francisco: Jossey-Bass.

Brinkerhoff, J. 2002b. Assessing and improving partnership relationships and outcomes: A proposed framework. *Evaluation and Program Planning* 25:215–231.

———. 2002a. Government–nonprofit partnerships: A defining framework. *Public Administration and Development* 22(1): 9–33.

———. 2004. *Partnership for international development: Rhetoric or results?* Boulder, CO: Lynne Rienner Publishers.

———. 2006. The partnership imperative. In *Monday Developments* (Interaction report). http://www.interaction.org/newswire/detail.php?id=5237 (accessed November 30, 2007).

Burkett, I. 2007. *Asset building: Partnerships out of poverty.* Research report written for the Agora Think Tank, Melbourne, Australia. http://www.agorathink-tank.org/lib/PDFs/Agora_Asset_Building_Report.pdf (accessed December 2, 2007).

Cahn, E. 2004. *No more throw away people: The co-production imperative.* 2nd ed. New York: Essential Books.

Caplan, K. 2003. The purist's partnership: Debunking the terminology of partnerships. *Partnership Matters* 1:31–37.

Chambers, R. 2004. Ideas for development: Reflecting forwards (IDS Working Paper no. 238). Brighton: Institute for Development Studies.

Drew, R. 2003. Learning in partnership: What constitutes learning in the context of South–North partnerships. Discussion Paper for BOND/Exchange Program, April. www.bond.org.uk/pubs/lte/nsworkshopdiss2.pdf (accessed December 1, 2007).

Eisler, R. 1987. *The chalice and the blade: Our history, our future.* New York: Harper and Row.

Fowler, A. 2000. *Civil society, NGDOs and social development: Changing the rules of the game* (UNRISD Occasional Paper, no. 1, January). http://www.unrisd.org/ (accessed November 30, 2007).

Holloway, R. 1989. Partners in development? The government and NGOs in Indonesia. In *Doing Development—government, NGOs and the rural poor in Asia*, ed. R. Holloway, 136–160. London: Earthscan.

Hyatt, J., and Kaplan, A. 2006. Space for learning? *Alliance Magazine*, June, pp. 26–29.

Johnson, H., and Wilson, G. 2006. North–South/South–North partnerships: Closing the "mutuality gap." *Public Administation and Development* 26(1): 71–80.

Jørgensen, M. 2006. *Evaluating cross-sector partnerships*. Working paper presented at the conference, "Public-Private Partnerships in the Post WSSD Context," Copenhagen Business School, August 14.

Kaplan, A. 1989. *Evaluation for development*. Paper written for the Community Development Resource Association, South Africa.

Kaul, I. 2006. Exploring the policy space between markets and states: Global public–private partnerships. In *The new public finance*, ed. I. Kaul and P. Conceição, 219–268. Oxford: Oxford University Press.

Lister, S. 2000. Power in partnership? An analysis of an NGO's relationship with its partners. *Journal of International Development* 12(2): 227–239.

Morse, S., and McNamara, N. 2006. Analysing institutional partnerships in development: A contract between equals or a loaded process? *Progress in Development Studies* 6(4): 321–336.

Ostrom, E. 1996. Crossing the great divide: Coproduction, synergy and development. *World Development* 24(6): 1073–1087.

Rahnema, M., and Bawtree, V., eds. 1994. *The post-development reader*. London: Earthscan.

Shiller, B. 2005. *Business–NGO partnerships*. Ethical Corporation report. http://www.ethicalcorp.com/londonpartnership/FINAL_REPORT_Jan_10.pdf (accessed December 2, 2007).

Smith, B. 2007. *Building inclusive development partnerships: Some reflections and questions for practitioners*. Guest writing published on the Community Development Resources Association's Web site. www.cdra.org.za, (accessed December 3, 2007).

Srinivasan, L. 1993. *Tools for community participation: A manual for training trainers in participatory techniques* (PROWWESS/UNDP Technical Series). New York: PROWWESS/UNDP.

8 Personnel for Local Level Social Development

David R. Cox and Manohar S. Pawar

INTRODUCTION

In areas of professional practice, we usually find that an area of practice has been identified and arrangements put in place for preparing and accrediting personnel for that area of practice. However, this is clearly not the case with the development field. Development is not a clearly defined area of practice, nor has it given rise to a profession to work in the field. There certainly exist a plethora of courses that are promoted as covering aspects of international development. Many of these are at the postgraduate level, and they are advertised, to take some recent examples, under titles such as human resources management; management and implementation of development projects; organizational change and development; industry, trade and development; development economics and policy; sustainable environmental management; and social policy and development. Who, then, are social development personnel?

When one places the emphasis on social development as that concept is presented in Chapter 2, the comprehensive and integrated nature of the process presupposes the involvement of many, if not all, of the professions as they apply their professional expertise to the development field. Social development personnel will therefore include doctors, nurses, lawyers, agricultural scientists, forestry personnel, engineers, social workers, community development workers and a wide range of others. What seems to happen essentially is that personnel from a wide range of professional and vocational backgrounds either become involved, or seek to become involved, in social development work. Some of these will develop specific development skills in the field, over and above their basic vocational skills; some will have access to in-service training and short courses; and some will do postgraduate studies with a focus appropriate to their work or interests. There would appear to be no significant concerns regarding this prevailing situation, and therefore no widespread attempts to change it. However, we would argue that social development will often require, in addition to the range of professions referred to previously, personnel with a firm grasp of the social development field as it presents, and able to provide, in addition to any direct intervention roles, planning, management and integrating roles within a nation's overall social development strategy.

Where the personnel issue becomes clearly problematic and a matter of stated concern is in the area of local level social development, as that practice is outlined in Chapter 3. Several situations seem to exist in relation to personnel for this level of development in the field, and these are often discussed in the literature. One situation is that government and non-government agencies wishing to engage in local level social development simply seek out locally available personnel. The personnel sought will vary in their backgrounds and levels of competence. They may be from among the more well-to-do section of the local population—usually in our experience women, such as the wives of local officials—and engaged without further training on a largely voluntary or unpaid basis. Alternatively, they may be locally recruited persons who are deployed within their own communities and paid to provide leadership in local development. Hopefully these personnel are provided with some training. However, neither of these strategies, in some well-documented examples, has been evaluated as effective personnel strategies for local social development, although one can see their attraction to government. This seems to be especially the case when the programs employing such personnel are initiated by national governments, such as nationwide community development programs.

A third alternative personnel strategy, which uses local personnel and is discussed in the literature, focuses on personnel already employed locally. For example, in 1979, a UN report suggested that "local social service personnel" could be employed to perform important social development roles such as "change agents," liaison personnel and "helping to establish and strengthen local institutions" (1979, 24–7). As a second example, the UN Economic and Social Commission for Asia and the Pacific (ESCAP) Jakarta Plan published in 1988 and 1994 argues the need for "appropriate enablers" who "can catalyze the human resources development process." The only stated qualification to be possessed by these enablers is that they be persons "who come into direct contact with the disadvantaged." The report then goes on to suggest that any local government officials, or local social service personnel such as teachers, or local non-governmental organization (NGO) staff, or even local mass media personnel, could be engaged in such work—presumably over and above their existing important, and often very demanding, local roles, and presumably without training or supervision. We regard this approach as highly problematic from every point of view.

Moving on from the use of local personnel, a second situation is where the personnel for local level social development are recruited from the ranks of university graduates who are not immediately able to secure work in their chosen field because of high levels of graduate unemployment. This has been at times the case in Bangladesh, the Philippines and Sri Lanka. The graduates recruited are given some specialized training and then employed at the local level for a year or two, or until they secure the employment they are seeking. There are advantages in this approach, where it is feasible, in that personnel with various qualifications are available, are likely to benefit from the experience and, from our observations, will often make a valuable contribution. However, it is clearly not an ideal solution for meeting this personnel need and, in some national contexts, it will simply not be possible on any large scale. On the other hand, if university graduates from across the spectrum of courses can be motivated to devote a few years to local social development, with appropriate supervision or mentoring, this can be highly beneficial to both those graduates and the local situations in which they work. A recent well-known developed-country example of this involved the current president of the U.S., Barack Obama. He has recorded in some detail the nature and significance of his work as a community organizer in Chicago (Obama 2007, Chs. 7–10). Many graduates have thus engaged in local social development across a wide range of countries, including one of the authors, D. Cox, in both Australia and Europe when he went as a young graduate to work in the refugee field.

A third situation, frequently depicted in the literature and observed in the field, highlights simply a lack of personnel for local social development. As a result, across a wide range of situations, very little such development takes place, especially on a deliberate and systematic basis, largely because no personnel stream exists for carrying out such work. Chambers (1983, 1993) is one writer who has stressed strongly the need for a new type of professional social development worker for the local level. Also, in 1991, a UN report stated simply, "Sufficiently trained local workers are usually lacking" (14). A 1997 UN/ESCAP report stated that, although social development programs required professional personnel with appropriate capabilities, very few countries in the Asia-Pacific region had developed "a comprehensive training plan for social development personnel at various levels," including particularly the local level (4). While such publications emphasize a strong need for such work and for a personnel stream to carry it out, it is not usually clear whether a demand for such workers currently exists but is not met, or whether work is required on both the demand and supply aspects of the situation. We suspect that the second situation is in fact often the case and that this represents a vicious circle in that agencies are reluctant to establish programs for which there exist no appropriate personnel, while training programs are then not established because there is not a clear demand for such. Hence the common conclusion that the local level of social development is frequently a neglected level of development—and this was confirmed again by a review of the literature undertaken by M. Pawar in 2009 that found that either the personnel issue was ignored or a passing reference made to a shortage of personnel. While clearly many government organizations and NGOs provide short training courses around specific programs, it is clear that both developed and developing countries face significant personnel shortages in many areas of social welfare and social development, yet seemingly have no strategies for overcoming this situation. This suggests that certain areas of need, or of rights, especially involving the more disadvantaged population groupings, are considered in effect a low priority.

A fourth situation clearly observable in the field is the existence of a probably very large number of local level social development programs, usually targeting specific situations through focusing on one dimension of social development rather than implementing comprehensive or multidimensional social development programs This situation is more commonly found in some countries than in others. Many of these single dimension programs have provided, and continue to provide, excellent models of what can be achieved in social development in a one-dimensional sense at the local level. What they do not provide, however, are clear models of how to handle either the ideal comprehensive approach (see Chapters 2–3) or the personnel issue. Indeed, no one clear model for either seems to exist, but an emphasis here is on the personnel issue. Some of these programs employ local graduates in interim employment, as discussed previously; some employ expatriate personnel from a wide range of professional and vocational backgrounds, usually supported by local personnel engaged in a range of roles and hopefully receiving some appropriate on-the-job training; and some employ local recruits, with again a wide range of backgrounds and capabilities, on a more long-term basis and usually with some training provided. The impression sometimes received is that those administering such programs cope with recruiting, preparing and retaining personnel as best they can, with many frustrations. On the other hand, these initiatives do demonstrate beyond doubt the viability and success of many such local social development, or one-dimensional development programs, including the possibility of the short-term recruitment and deployment of local personnel, usually working in close partnership with personnel from outside the location.

If this review of the personnel situation in local level social development is at all accurate, there remains a major personnel need to overcome—assuming, of course, that one accepts the arguments put forward in Chapter 3 regarding the importance of such work. In this chapter, we assume that it is essential to engage, methodically and consistently, in much more local level social development than we have seen to date, and that such initiatives will require a personnel stream of appropriate nature and size. We therefore endeavor to outline what a personnel strategy for local level social development might entail, in general terms, accepting always that countries will vary greatly in the precise nature and levels of personnel required and available for such work.

LEVELS OF PERSONNEL REQUIRED IN
LOCAL LEVEL SOCIAL DEVELOPMENT

When local level social development is placed in its broader social development context, it becomes clear that personnel will be required at three levels. Some personnel will be involved in what might be termed hands-on work—direct service delivery, working with local communities or operating as local level catalysts in local level development. These are often referred to in the literature as front-line or grassroots workers. Behind this level, it is logical to assume the need for a level of supervisors and administrators, and the literature often confirms this. A common way of differentiating these two levels is by using the terms professional and paraprofessional, although the situation is really more complex than this terminology suggests, while the latter term is often used very vaguely in the development literature. Finally, a third logical and commonly referred-to level is that of planners, program designers, policy personnel and so on, usually located at a central level. Let us consider each of these three levels of personnel.

Local Level Catalysts

In countries or regions possessing low levels of development and high levels of poverty, the local level constitutes a major concern. Such situations are particularly likely to occur in rural areas, overcrowded and depressed urban areas, and in the communities of indigenous minorities and other marginalized peoples. In many such situations, catalysts seem essential for initiating a development process aimed at eradicating, or at least alleviating, poverty and bringing the quality of life level to the point where all people possess the capabilities, and have access to at least the basic opportunities, for realizing their potential and contributing to local development. These catalysts need to be trusted by the people, so that they can slowly begin the process of bringing people together to discuss their needs, consider their options, become cognizant of available local and external resources, and so to develop the abilities needed to arrange for action on selected fronts. To achieve these goals, catalysts need to be perceived locally as possessing relevant knowledge and skills, as having access to external resources and as working closely with the communities and with the best interests of the community as the major goal. Ideally, they need to possess also at least a basic multidisciplinary understanding of development, and so an ability to range across the breadth of development, including productivity enhancement, education and health services provision, income-earning opportunities such as microcredit schemes, political issues including local governance, and a plethora of other issues. In other words, local level catalysts should not be what the UN (1979) once referred to as "single-purpose personnel," such as health or literacy or microcredit workers, but rather multipurpose personnel able to understand and respond to the multidimensional nature of social development.

Intermediate Level Facilitators

The intermediate level is where facilitators are deployed through a network of regional government and nongovernment agencies to facilitate development at the local level. These facilitators represent an essential support to local level catalysts. They provide a back-up service to catalysts in situations that go beyond their skills, provide them with in-service training, facilitate their linkages with national and international level agencies and generally support them in the field. These personnel also facilitate the delivery of a range of services at the local level in a manner commensurate with local culture and need, and play a role in coordinating services in ways most conducive to enhancing well-being and promoting social development. These facilitators should be part of a vertically integrated team responsible for local level social development, professionally trained and experienced in providing local level catalysts with supportive supervision and in coordinating the work across their region. This latter role will require that these workers appreciate the work of, and be able to liaise with, a wide range of professional personnel employed at an intermediate level with responsibility for local level social development in its various dimensions. In some situations, however, there will be no agricultural, medical, educational and other personnel at either the intermediate or local levels, rendering the task of both intermediate facilitators and local level catalysts in local social development all the more complex, difficult and important.

Central Level Promoters

The importance of having social development personnel deployed at the central—usually national, but sometimes regional—level stems primarily from the importance generally of that central level. While the local level is the critical one in tackling local poverty and meeting other specific development needs, ultimately the level of prosperity a country achieves will depend on its central level planning and development, based on a set of national economic and social policies and programs. The type and location of manufacturing, the control of urbanization processes, the balance between rural and urban development, the basic health and education policies and programs, the provision of income security measures, the national development of infrastructure, the opening up of markets and the promotion of trade, taxation and other fiscal policies, and so on, all work together to create the parameters within which social development at all levels takes place—the so-called national, or at least regional, enabling environment (UN 1995). Hence, effective social development at all levels will require social development promoters at the central level, with crucial planning, implementation and coordination roles. In relation to local level social development, their roles are to promote, at the central level, the following: an understanding of, and effective responses to, local level realities, including the need to recruit and deploy local level workers; participation of local level representatives in central planning and decision-making processes; and the integration and coordination of all central initiatives in the interests of local people's well-being.

We might note that this basic notion of three levels of workers being required to bring about successful local level development is not uncommon in field discussions and reports. As one example of the latter, a report on community-based rehabilitation in South Asia that focused on personnel and training issues suggested a three-level personnel model. This consisted of professionals, managers and grassroots workers, with the respective roles not unlike those outlined previously (Wirz and Chalker n.d.). While seeing the need for such a model, the study found that there were widespread significant shortages of appropriate personnel. One reason why the three-level idea is not uncommon is because it presents not only to us but also to others in the field as an eminently logical and practical approach to the personnel question, and one that also provides the framework for a discussion of recruitment and training issues. Before we turn to those, however, some reflection on the important question of personnel numbers is called for.

PERSONNEL NUMBERS AND LOCAL LEVEL SOCIAL DEVELOPMENT

Following on from the aforementioned personnel model, a crucial question—especially for recruitment, training and deployment purposes—is how many local level catalysts are likely to be required in any national or local regional context. At the national level, the overall need for local level social development can be determined by identifying remote areas that are mainly missing out on the benefits of national level development; rural areas that remain underdeveloped and beset by poverty; urban areas that are overcrowded and economically impoverished; disadvantaged populations that tend to be significantly marginalized from mainstream development; and areas significantly affected by recent or frequently occurring natural disasters or internal conflict. It can be assumed that all such areas will either desperately require, or at least significantly benefit from, a series of local level social development initiatives, and that the introduction of such will require the services of local level catalysts.

The first step, then, in determining the necessary or ideal number of local level catalysts would be to list the areas in need of local level social development, calculate the populations of such and, on the basis of an agreed formula, determine the numbers of local level workers required. No formula can have universal application, but a very general one could be used as a starting point, such as one worker for every three or five thousand persons in the designated areas, or one worker for every three villages of not less than one thousand persons each. It should be pointed out, however, that there have been local level social development programs in the Philippines that have deployed, in one case, one worker per village, whatever its size, and, in another case, one worker for a period of one year for just ten to twelve families scattered over a remote highland area with no village structure (see Cox

1998). The final determination of numbers of workers required in any specific local context will depend, in the final analysis, on the extent and severity of the need, local geographical factors such as ease of access, and resources available to the agencies undertaking the program. Even a very general idea of numbers, however, can become the basis of a national social development personnel plan, with responsibility for the education and training of the approximately determined number of personnel allocated to appropriately structured and located education and training institutions.

Then, once the number of local level catalysts has been determined, the question of the required number of intermediate and central personnel is a relatively easy one. Most of the areas in need of local level social development will possess provincial centers where intermediate level facilitators should be located, with the numbers in any center being determined by several factors, including the size and population of the region, the levels of local need, the extent of the existing development of essential social service delivery networks and hence the numbers of local level catalysts who should ideally be deployed across the region. Adding up the required numbers across all the relevant regional centers will then determine the number of intermediate personnel who should be being prepared for this role. Similarly, work related to local level social development required at the central level can be determined, and the necessary number of central level promoters will then be clear.

Longer-term planning of numbers of graduates of various courses required will need also to take into account worker retention rates. If local level catalysts are offered the opportunity of upward mobility within the development field, or indeed within a profession such as social work, a number will take advantage of this and so be lost to the local level. Furthermore, given that this work at the local level is highly demanding in many ways, retention rates at the local level should probably be seen as likely to be relatively low. However, many other factors, such as the backgrounds, gender and marital status of those recruited into this work, will also affect these retention rates.

What is most important to note in this context is that currently, and in virtually all countries, there exist neither a national personnel plan for social development that identifies the numbers required at any level nor an effective and adequate stream of qualified local level social development personnel to meet development needs at the local level. Let us therefore turn our attention to the recruitment and education or training of personnel for such work.

THE RECRUITMENT OF PERSONNEL FOR
LOCAL LEVEL SOCIAL DEVELOPMENT

To the best of our knowledge, the question of possible sources for the recruitment of local level social development personnel has not been addressed in the literature in any meaningful way, and no model for it exists in any country beyond at an agency or educational institution level. Yet it is a question that must be addressed if local level social development is to become an integral aspect of the development field. If we take the analogy of social work, it is quite commonly stated that the main recruitment ground for social workers in developing countries is, or at least has been until comparatively recent times, the urban middle class. Although there are probably several reasons for this, two critical ones are, first, that social work education is located mainly in universities, to which only the middle class has access, and, second, that the basic notion of social work is scarcely known, or at least understood, beyond middle-class ranks (and often not even there). As a result of this prevailing recruitment process into social work, it is commonly said that the great majority of these graduates have no inclination to work in rural areas or even with disadvantaged populations in urban areas.

Similarly, if the ranks of the urban educated middle class are unlikely to produce recruits for social work willing to work in rural, remote or impoverished regions, this appears also to be true of those recruited from a similar background into the government civil service, as a UN report back in 1979 argued and which has been since confirmed quite frequently. As this report stated,

> The civil service ethos in many countries does not foster empathy with the poor in general and the rural poor in particular. Since the traditional national elites predominate in the upper administrative echelons, the result is a widening of the social distance between the development personnel and the rural residents. (3)

The recruitment process in effect largely determines the professional profile that emerges. Hence, if we wish to recruit and train either social workers or local level social development workers for deployment in remote, rural or disadvantaged areas, we must start by ensuring an appropriate recruitment process.

The significant question appears, therefore, to be, from what population sectors does one recruit for local level social development? Or, more specifically, from what sectors of the population does one recruit into what aspects of the work?

In terms of the sources from which local level social development personnel can be recruited, we would suggest that the following general conclusions flow from all the available evidence. It is clear that the range of sources must contain or reflect, to a significant degree, the localities and peoples most in need of local level social development. This may mean recruits from rural backgrounds, from the more remote and impoverished areas of the nation, from the membership of indigenous and other types of minority populations, and, to at least some extent, from among females where the gender issue is significant (as is frequently the case), and so on.

Inevitably, this will often mean the recruitment of personnel who, at the time of recruitment, have not reached a high educational level, but rather have reached at best, perhaps, only the middle years of secondary schooling.

It may be appropriate in some contexts to recruit young people who are currently undertaking their secondary education, offering them a specific education and career pathway. This approach has been used occasionally in Indonesia. Alternatively, or in addition, it may be appropriate to offer particular professional and paraprofessional training within the geographical areas in need of local level social development, perhaps under the auspices of centralized training institutions with the use of staff from the central campus and other arrangements. Very frequently, recruitment into such courses would then need to have a set of recruitment prerequisites that were consistent with regional characteristics, potential applicants' backgrounds, and local level development staffing needs. These would inevitably differ from those prevailing in urban areas. What is clear from the evidence is that there need to be close links between the type and location of training offered, the sources from which participants in such training are drawn, and the nature of the populations among whom recruits are being trained to work.

In terms of our second question relating to the types or levels of work for which recruits are being trained, we suggest that the preceding conclusions apply particularly to the recruitment of local level catalysts. However, in some situations, even formal training in secondary schools or in local training institutions will be unlikely to provide the numbers of local level catalysts required, at least initially. It may therefore be that such personnel will need to be recruited directly into such work with little prior preparation, while ensuring that they possess the capacity to benefit in the long run from in-service training, workshops, short courses, and so on, and with the possibility of receiving credits for such which will assist in making them eligible for more formal training at a later date. On the other hand, recruits for intermediate level positions may well come from providing a special stream within pregraduate and undergraduate courses for recruits with some form of links with disadvantaged and underdeveloped populations, or at least possessing empathy with such people and their development needs. Finally, central level personnel should be able to be recruited from among the ranks of those entering appropriate existing courses and offered some additional training in social development at perhaps a postgraduate level. Central level personnel need to be highly qualified in social development and with the skills required to promote local level social development across all sectors, and their recruitment should ideally reflect these requirements.

EDUCATION AND TRAINING ISSUES

Many issues surround the education and training of local level social development personnel. Following their recruitment, the following questions arise: what are the levels at which they are to be educated or trained? Within which institutions and courses, existing or newly and specially established, are they to be trained? How does one ensure a ready supply of appropriate trainers? What training models could be used? And who should carry overall responsibility for the provision of training? Before we consider each of these questions, let us briefly review the relevant literature.

Once again, we encounter a relative absence of detail in the literature relating to education and training issues. The following examples seem typical of what one finds.

A UN/ESCAP 1994 Plan of Action for Social Development comments simply that "the personnel staffing these enabler organizations themselves require appropriate education, training, awareness-raising, provision of incentives and other means to ensure that they fulfill their special role" (21–22). Similarly, UN/ESCAP's 1995 Manila Declaration emphasizes the need for governments to engage in "training, re-training and advanced training" for social development (35), but provides no detail. Then in 1997, reporting on the implementation of the UN/ESCAP Social Development Agenda, training is covered in a recommendation with only limited detail:

> Training of personnel should aim at increasing their knowledge of social issues and providing the analytical and technical skills necessary to diagnose social development problems, and evolve policy and program measures through increased understanding of the linkages between the economic and social sectors, and the three major interacting goals of the Agenda For Action ... They should also receive training in facilitating participatory development, including the participation of the poor and vulnerable groups. (17)

As a final example from the literature, in his outline of "The Social Development Paradigm," Falk (1984) states that social development workers "will incorporate a variety of skills" (10), but how these skills are acquired is not explored. The tendency in the literature simply to state or imply a need for training seems all too common, and there is little guidance pertaining to the questions we have raised.

The Levels of Education and Training

The question as to the level of education or training for local level social development includes the decision as to whether it is professionals or paraprofessionals who are being trained. For example, Chambers (1983, 1993) regards the personnel required for local level social development as professionals, and many others share this view, including those who regard social workers as adequately and appropriately equipped to fulfill this role (see, e.g., UN 1972, 1991; Gore 1988; Sanders 1988). Others, however, argue that this role is best filled by paraprofessional personnel. For example,

Brawley and Schindler (1988) write extensively about "the front-line para-professional in social development." They do so largely because, in their view, "the great majority of persons involved in front-line human service or social development activities are persons who have received limited or no specific training for the jobs they perform" (1). This prevailing situation is seen as partly due to the inadequate numbers of professional personnel but also as reflecting the reality that paraprofessionals are better suited to front-line work (2). These authors go on to emphasize the particular importance of "indigenous paraprofessionals" (4–5; see also Schindler and Brawley 1987).

In addition to this question of professional or paraprofessional, there is also the question of education levels reflected in the common division between pregraduate, undergraduate and postgraduate. Elsewhere, we have argued that, in many developing country contexts, social workers should be educated at each of these three levels, reflecting the need for three levels of workers with each possessing education and training levels commensurate with the nature of their future work in the field (Cox and Pawar 2006, 362). The same arguments can be applied to the three levels of local level social development personnel set out previously, provided always that the model is applied flexibly and in a manner consistent with prevailing realities. We are strongly of the opinion that a three-level personnel model such as we have proposed is preferable to distinguishing between professional and paraprofessional workers, which seems always to imply a clear barrier between the two that often reduces greatly the possibilities of cooperation in the field and mobility within a profession or field. Clearly, the multilevel nature of social development calls for a multilevel approach to the recruitment, training and deployment of social development personnel, especially when the local level is included as a very important focus of attention.

Settings for Education and Training

The discussion so far has already suggested that the nature and location of the courses where training in local level social development is organized is an extremely important question. If, for example, training is offered in urban settings, either recruits will tend to come largely from urban areas or, if recruited from rural areas, they may well opt, after graduation, to remain in the urban areas where many actual or perceived advantages exist. An alternative is to establish new social development courses within those regions where local level social development is vitally important, so that recruitment and deployment of trainees is from and to the region. The nature of such rural-based courses is likely to vary greatly. They may be established as rural-based universities, or the rural campuses of central and urban universities. They may be short courses, full- or part-time, run within existing premises and not requiring a new establishment. Countries such as China and India are currently using a variety of such approaches. Alternatively, they may be something more like the mobile training schemes for social development that operated for a time in Nepal, Afghanistan and Bangladesh (UN 1979, 24), but which we have not come across in more recent times. In most developing countries, a flexible approach that offers a range of training opportunities is likely to be called for in catering for the inevitable diversity across the nation, and we can see this situation developing in, for example, India.

A further related question is whether training in local level social development should be attached to an existing profession or established as a new field of practice. We can see real advantages, in at least some national contexts, in expanding social work into rural and remote areas and with a focus on local level social development. These advantages include the fact that social work is an established profession internationally and so able to offer support to such an extension within a specific state. Already, we can see in several countries efforts to expand social work into rural and remote areas, into work with indigenous minorities, and even specifically into the field of social development. We believe that we can learn from these developments to date and build upon them. However, it may well be that in some national contexts, it is preferable to start with an exclusive focus on local level social development, allowing the future links of such courses and such work to evolve as circumstances dictate. This may be especially necessary where social work scarcely exists, where social development needs are clearly dominant, and where a social development focus would receive more official support than a social work focus. In any case, there is no inherent reason why local level social development personnel should not be drawn from a range of sources, as is currently the case, as long as at least some sources are available and promoted.

Whatever the conclusion reached in any context, the nature and location of the education and training offered in social development requires careful consideration.

The Availability of Trainers

Wherever courses in local level social development are located, and however they are structured, the question of trainers will probably emerge as a key one. It is highly likely that within a particular state, there will be few people who are not only experienced in social development, but who possess the ability to work as trainers, and willing to work in the regions where training courses are being established. As Guerrero (1989) concludes, "Without adequately-trained trainers in sufficient numbers, a situation which is common in most Asian and Pacific countries, training in local social development will not advance in improving the quality of life of underprivileged people" (267–268). How, then, can one proceed?

In some situations, it may be necessary to bring in trainers from those countries in the region where local level social development is further advanced and use them to train an initial team of trainers. This would need to be done with care, especially if those brought in were unfamiliar with conditions prevailing in the country. As Diaz (1989) emphasizes, trainers need to understand "the conditions and pressures that trainees are exposed to in the work world" if they are to train effectively (246). However, even local trainers may not meet this requirement, especially if they come from urban areas or academic ranks. Guerrero (1989) implies this when she comments that "most university staff members do not have much experience in practical work, and they are not familiar with how people in remote areas and urban slums live" (267–268). She goes on to point out that, in the Asia-Pacific region, "very few university staff members have been trained in the social development discipline as it should apply to developing countries." In the 1980s, however, she sees alternative trainers as being in very short supply.

An alternative to bringing in outsiders, either from other countries or from urban areas, is to appoint local trainers able "to learn together with trainees," as Diaz (1989) puts it. This may well be possible with trainers with particular types of backgrounds and personalities able to live and work initially without answers to many questions. However, it should represent only a temporary solution with appropriate field research and in-service training ensuring that a high level of understanding is obtained as quickly as possible. Diaz also emphasizes the need for trainers to learn from each other and from all others involved in social development, at whatever level and from whatever discipline. As he puts it,

> The nature of social development itself is multisectoral and interdisciplinary. Hence trainers have to learn how to understand each other across sectors and disciplines, by first getting out of an isolated frame of mind and becoming more open to the intersectoral and interdisciplinary panorama of social development through a multitude of dialogue sessions and readings. (247)

It is, of course, also possible to send personnel to another country for training, and we note that in 2005, a program was introduced in which community development personnel were sent from South Africa to India for training in rural development. After a successful trial course with eight trainees, the decision was to send groups of thirty community development workers at a time to learn from India's long experience in the community and rural development fields (NIRD 2005).

A more long-term solution to the shortage of trainers is to introduce appropriate courses within existing schools within the state, such as schools of social work or schools of development studies. Some graduates may be able to accommodate and benefit from intensive courses that are perhaps also broken into short segments to accommodate access while working. This step will be necessary anyway to guarantee a supply of intermediate and central level social development personnel, while also serving to prepare the trainers of local level catalysts.

However the need for trainers is responded to in any context, it needs to be a priority in the early stages of establishing training in local level social development.

Training Models for Local Level Social Development

What constitutes an appropriate training model for trainees destined for work in local level social development? It is clear that there exists no one answer to this question. However, addressing it enables us to consider some of the possible alternatives suggested. For example, Guerrero's 1989 field-work in seven Asian countries and one Pacific country resulted in the following summary overview of methods of training:

> Training programs in the eight countries surveyed employ a variety of methods, ranging from conventional lectures, seminars and panel discussions, to more experimental, evocative, and participatory techniques where trainers serve primarily as facilitators helping to analyze trainees' experiences and put them into appropriate perspective. The most used techniques of this kind are field trips, case studies, simulations, structured learning experiences, audiovisuals, films and creative dramatics. Other techniques are employed to raise consciousness. Among high-level planners and policymakers, for example, community immersion requires them to live, work and interact with the village poor during training. This is intended to deepen their sense of commitment and service to the poor. (264)

Much will clearly depend on the characteristics of trainees. Some of these may have significant work experience in the field that can and should be used within the learning process. Some, however, will never have set foot in the type of local situation within which they will be employed as local level catalysts, and will require a very different approach. Similarly, the ability to work with concepts will vary, and presentations will often need to be grounded in existing realities. For this reason, commentators such as Diaz (1989) and Guerrero (1989) emphasize the use of, for example, reports of programs and projects, videotapes of program processes, the involvement of community people in the classroom, case studies and field visits that preferably span some days or weeks. What is clearly important is that the possible training models are carefully canvassed and the selection made on the basis of trainee characteristics, trainer's level of expertise, proximity to future possible work settings and their characteristics, time available for training, and so on.

Overall Responsibility for the Provision of Training

It will be clear that education and training for local level social development requires a careful estimate of the numbers of graduates required, consideration of the best locations for training courses, the recruitment of educators and trainers, decisions regarding the nature and structure of courses and the learning methods to be used, arrangements for the production of suitable learning materials and ideas regarding coordination across a complex field of activity. The development and provision of such a program suggests a role for the national government, but carried out with high levels of participation by all interested parties and often involving a significant degree of decentralization in the process. If, however, a government views and treats this aspect of development as a low priority, a different approach might be called for. This might be the giving of responsibility to a profession such as social work, ideally organized in country but at the international level where this becomes necessary. Alternatively, responsibility for a particular country might be assumed, with agreement, by a UN agency or a regional intergovernmental association, which could carry many advantages.

In addition to the question as to which body assumes responsibility for the provision of training in local level social development within a specific context, there is little doubt that the process across the board would be facilitated by an international body or network that would assume responsibility in several areas, including the development of lists of trainers available internationally; the development and dissemination of a range of teaching and learning materials; the provision of information regarding existing initiatives in this field of work; the promotion of appropriate research in this field and the dissemination of its outcomes; the promotion of education-training needs in this field at government and other levels; and an advisory service available to any country or agency. This may well be a role for the International Consortium on Social Development.

DEPLOYMENT ISSUES

If little local level social development is being undertaken in a country, beyond perhaps the odd program or project, the recruitment and training of ideally adequate numbers of appropriate personnel will result only in widespread unemployment among those trained. It is important, therefore, that work on supply-and-demand aspects of the promotion of local level development occurs in tandem. How, then, can the demand aspects be addressed?

One possible approach is for a government to initiate a large-scale program designed to extend local social service delivery in neglected areas, establish local microcredit and microenterprise schemes, and promote community development, with the ultimate aims of alleviating poverty and engaging in local level social development. For example, at one point the South African post-apartheid government considered the deployment of some thousands of local social development workers, before recognizing that such workers would not be readily available, at least not personnel with training. In such circumstances, the government would need to embark on a complementary training and deployment strategy. Moreover, such a scheme would be unlikely to be as successful as it might otherwise have been unless intermediate level facilitators were also deployed to support and supervise the local level catalysts and provide them with appropriate ongoing support and training. While such a scheme would often require a significant external grant, its benefits could be highly significant.

Another approach would be either to encourage existing NGOs, or new ones established for the purpose, to undertake such work. They would receive a grant to implement an appropriate program in designated areas, with the overall program designed, supported and monitored by an appropriate central agency or committee. This central structure would be also responsible for ensuring that personnel were appropriately trained and available for recruitment.

In some circumstances, local communities might be sufficiently well advanced in their development to benefit from the appointment for a given period of a local level catalyst to work largely under their direction but with external support. This situation could occur where an aspect of local level social development had been significantly advanced but now required an expansion into a more comprehensive approach to local development. For example, a community may have run a successful microcredit scheme, or been the recipient of a literacy or community health care program, which had in turn stimulated local interest in further local development and identified potential leadership resources. Such a community could be encouraged and enabled to undertake a more comprehensive social development program.

In each of these three approaches, some central leadership to motivate and facilitate the initial development would seem critical. Local level social development will often require stimulation at the local level; grants will usually be required to fund the deployment of workers; training arrangements will need to be put in place and monitored; and all such developments should be carefully evaluated and the approach being adopted modified accordingly. This leadership may come from central government, from an established NGO, or even from an external agency invited by government to come in and initiate an extensive local level social development program. This external agency could be part of the UN, an international NGO or an appropriate donor government. It would be critical, however, that local nationals always play a major role, given the importance of sound local knowledge on many levels.

The selection of localities for a local development program will be important. Clearly, the initial or potential participation of the local community will be vital, and situations where communities ask to be included in such a program would be ideal. In some situations, however, local participation will need to be sought as a first step. Second, it may be important, at least in the early stages of the program, to select localities that offer a reasonable chance of some success. Some localities may have such deeply entrenched and serious problems that any local level social development initiative will require greatly enhanced efforts and resources over a significant period. They will also require very carefully selected workers, who will often be difficult to find. On the other hand, however, local level social development is essentially a response to need, so that the choice of localities that do present a significant level of need should also be a major consideration.

Finally, the deployment of personnel for local level social development must also consider the needs of those being deployed. We have seen situations where local level catalysts have been placed in isolated villages experiencing high poverty levels and been forced to operate almost exclusively on their own resources for long periods of time. Yet steps can be taken to avoid this happening. For example, in one such situation, the NGO running the scheme deployed workers to separate villages experiencing great need but did so effectively in teams of two (UN/ESCAP, 1996). That is to say, two workers would be placed in different villages but in reasonably close proximity to each other so as to have some interaction fortnightly, and such interaction was strongly encouraged. In addition to the team-of-two approach, all workers deployed in this program were withdrawn from the field once a month for a three day break together. These periods were times of sharing experiences, successes and difficulties, and so learning from and supporting each other. There was also some debriefing by a skilled person and the provision of in-service training where such seemed to be important. Finally, such deployment was for periods of a year at a time, with a decision made annually in each case regarding whether to extend the deployment or move the worker to another village or position. All the workers involved were from the country in question, and all had received significant preparation prior to their first deployment.

If a scheme such as that outlined is not feasible, there should be at least an intermediate level facilitator available to each local level catalyst, with ease of regular communication ensured by devices such as two-way radios and, preferable, periodic visits by the facilitator to the location of each local level catalyst. We have seen both strategies operating successfully. The precise arrangements in any particular situation will be determined by prevailing circumstances, and it is accepted that, in some circumstances, significant ingenuity will be required to provide local level workers with adequate support and supervision.

The key point in relation to the deployment of local level catalysts in particular is that the inherent difficulties in such work are appreciated, along with the possible impact on the worker of isolation, frustration if the program is not seen to be making progress and very real dilemmas as to how to handle particular situations. It is essential that the deployment of such personnel is always accompanied by the provision of appropriate support and supervision arrangements.

A NATIONAL PERSONNEL PLAN FOR LOCAL LEVEL SOCIAL DEVELOPMENT

Given the range of interacting issues pertaining to the recruitment, training and deployment of personnel for local level social development, it is difficult not to conclude that a national personnel plan is crucial. The foundation of any such plan should be the careful delineation, based on an analysis of prevailing development needs, of the types of workers called for and the numbers in which they are required. It appears widely accepted that workers at the local or grassroots level are of primary importance, and that, whatever name these workers are given, their basic role is to stimulate development at the local level by operating as catalysts. It is further acknowledged that, at a level above these grassroots workers, the deployment of facilitators is necessary. These personnel have the task of supporting local level development and the workers engaged in it in various ways. Finally, an effective social development strategy requires considerable action at the central or national level, in the areas of leadership, planning, coordinating and integrating activities at the various levels, and developing and implementing appropriate policies and programs.

Having identified the workers required, in terms of levels and approximate numbers, a personnel plan will need to address the related education and training issues. It will be necessary to specify the levels and types of education institution required, the question of recruitment into these courses, a range of curriculum issues, and the possible need for additional training arrangements at the field level.

Finally, a number of broader issues need to be addressed. These will include the place of local level social development within a nation's existing development programs, an understanding of the necessary links with existing professions, career paths generally for those entering the social development field, articulation between the various levels and types of training, salary levels and work conditions, further education and training generally, arrangements for ongoing research in this field and arrangements for personnel across this field to share with each other and benefit from each other's experience. One crucial basic question will be whether social development is to be established as an independent profession or as part of an existing profession such as social work or community development. We can see real benefits from the latter approach, assuming that there are existing social work or community development structures that can be used in the implementation of a personnel plan for local level social development, or that the establishment of such professional structures will benefit a range of areas to which social workers and others contribute as well as the area of local level social development (see Healy 2001; Lyons and Lawrence 2006).

REFERENCES

Brawley E. A., and Schindler, R. 1988. The front-line professional in social development: An international perspective. *Social Development Issues* 11(3): 1–12.

Chambers, R. 1983. *Rural development: Putting the last first.* Harlow, UK: Longman.

———. 1993. *Challenging the professions: Frontiers for rural development.* London: Intermediate Technology.

Cox, D. R. 1998. Community rebuilding in the Philippines. In *Sustainable community development: Studies in economic, environmental and cultural revitalization*, ed. M. D. Hoff, 45–62. Boca Raton, FL: Lewis.

Cox, D. R., and Pawar, M. 2006. *International social work: Issues, strategies, and programs*. Thousand Oaks, CA: Sage.

Diaz, R. 1989. Research and training on local social development. *Regional Development Dialogue* 10(2): 243–258.

Falk, D. 1984. The social development paradigm. *Social Development Issues* 8(3): 4–14.

Gore, M. 1988. Levels of social work provision in relation to need in a developing society. *Indian Journal of Social Work* 49(1): 1–9.

Guerrero, S. H. 1989. Training on local social development in Asia and the Pacific. *Regional Development Dialogue* 10(2): 259–271.

Healy, L. 2001. *International social work: Professional action in an interdependent world*. New York: Oxford University Press.

Lyons, K., and Lawrence, S., eds. 2006. *Social work in Europe: Educating for change*. Birmingham: IASSW/Basic Venture Press.

National Institute of Rural Development. 2005. Report of the community development workers delegation on the training in India on rural development, with emphasis on micro planning, 28 February to 30 March 2005. http://www.pmg.org.za/docs/2005/051109report.doc (accessed December 4, 2009).

Obama, B. 2007. *Dreams from my father*. Edinburgh: Canongate Books.

Sanders, D. S. 1988. Social work concerns related to peace and people oriented development in the international context. *Journal of Sociology & Social Welfare* 15(2): 57–72.

Schindler, R., and Brawley, E. A. 1987. *Social care at the front line*. New York: Tavistock Publications

United Nations. 1972. *Problems and prospects in schools of social work contributing to development in the ECAFE region*. Bangkok: Author.

———. 1979. *Social services in rural development*. New York: Author.

———. 1991. *Social development: Questions relating to the world social situation and to youth, ageing, disabled persons and the family*. New York: Author.

———. 1994. *Implementation of the guiding principles for developmental social welfare policies and programmes in the near future*. New York: Author.

United Nations Economic and Social Commission for Asia and the Pacific (UN/ESCAP). 1988. *Jakarta plan of action on human resources development in the ESCAP region*. Bangkok: Author.

———. 1994. *Jakarta Plan as revised in 1994*. Bangkok: Author.

———. 1995. *Manila declaration on the agenda for action on social development in the ESCAP region*. Bangkok: Author.

———. 1996. *Making an impact: Innovative HRD approaches to poverty alleviation*. Bangkok: Author.

———. 1997. *Proposals for accelerating the implementation of the agenda for action on social development in the ESCVAP region: National action on policy and programme development, and administration*. Bangkok: Author.

Wirz, S., and Chalker, P. n.d. Training issues in community based rehabilitation in South Asia. www.aifo.it/english/resources/online/apdrj/selread102/wirz.doc (accessed December 3, 2009).

9 Importance to Poverty Alleviation of Bottom-Up Approaches to Social Development

Rufus Akindola

INTRODUCTION

This chapter is concerned with rural poverty alleviation, as an important aspect of social development, and with which strategies are best suited to this task. Its central argument is that poor people's perceptions of their own poverty often differ significantly from the perceptions of outsiders. Hence, the designs of poverty alleviation strategies developed by outsiders are frequently found to be conceptually inappropriate and in practice unsuccessful in achieving their key objective of significant poverty reduction. Outsiders usually design a top-down approach to poverty alleviation based on their own perceptions of the nature of the poverty in question. This chapter argues that when the alternative of a bottom-up approach is used, one which reflects the people's understanding of the nature of their poverty reality, the outcome can be much better and more sustainable.

The chapter moves from a discussion of the nature of poverty to a comparison of top-down and bottom-up approaches to poverty alleviation, drawing significantly on the literature and on the author's experience of the Sub-Saharan African situation where bottom-up approaches have been relatively uncommon. While the focus is on the deficiencies of top-down approaches when compared with bottom-up approaches, it is accepted that, in reality, both are important and are ideally complementary. If the bottom-up approaches are emphasized here, it is because in many places, and especially in parts of Africa, they are effectively ignored with their potential importance significantly underestimated.

THE NATURE OF POVERTY

The concept of poverty is both vague and complex. Poverty can be defined either in absolute or relative terms. According to Devas (2004), absolute poverty relates to those who lack sufficient income to afford a minimum level of nutrition and basic needs, while relative poverty is concerned with the position of the poor in relation to the rest of society and so is an indicator of the degree of inequality. Nevertheless, the most common definitions for the purposes of government programs have been based on data concerning the estimated cost of subsistence (Stein 2004). In such definitions, poverty is regarded as low income, making it much easier to measure and seemingly more straightforward to address. Moreover, the nature of poverty varies between urban and rural areas. Most urban dwellers, for example, are able to find at least occasional income sources, whereas many in rural areas rarely can. In terms of quality-of-life indicators, rural people, on average, have a lower quality of life compared to their urban counterparts, and rural public services, as measured by per capita public expenditure, are approximately one half those of urban areas (World Bank 2003). This can be an important distinction when poverty alleviation strategies are devised by urban-based personnel having little familiarity with rural conditions.

Basically, the choice of definition of poverty tends to determine how poverty is measured. Intervention strategies to reduce poverty also differ greatly, partly reflecting the definition of poverty being employed, and partly reflecting which agencies in society are responsible for poverty-re-duction programs, and the perceptions of those agencies as to how they should operate. The approach of many economists, for example, tends to view poverty in terms of economic growth and suggests that central government is responsible for poverty reduction. In this case, it is experts at both the planning and implementation levels who guide the process of poverty reduction. This usually means that there is a lack of any specific role for poor people themselves as poverty reduction is made dependent on what Olaniyan (1997) describes as the macroeconomic development model, with trickle-down effects.

By contrast, there is the people-centered approach that sees poverty as requiring poor people's participation at all stages. This approach recognizes the importance of sociocultural aspects and therefore recommends that non-governmental organizations (NGOs) and local organizations facilitate the process of poverty reduction (Cooke and Kothari 2001). The focus is, therefore, on people's active involvement and participation. On the other hand, the social development approach, pioneered by the UN, tends to combine these two extremes. This approach recognizes the roles for government, private enterprise, NGOs and communities. It also views the economic, social, political and cultural dimensions as all important, while regarding values as crucial—for example, the values of participation, self-reliance and equity (Keare 2001).

At the national poverty-reduction level, however, the range of understandings of addressing poverty can, in the majority of contexts, be divided basically into the top-down and bottom-up approaches, rather than the greatly preferred combination of these two approaches, and this chapter explores the significance of differences between the two while arguing for a much greater emphasis than we have seen to date on bottom-up approaches within the overall context of local level social development.

TOP-DOWN APPROACHES

Top-down approaches to development have tended to rest on the assumption that economic growth will be central and that any economic growth will automatically trickle down to improve the conditions of the population. It is therefore generally income that becomes the principal criterion for defining who is poor (Robb 2001). With top-down approaches, there is little use of participatory techniques, despite these being better able to determine the full range of those in poverty and the range of their needs. The main issue with this top-down approach to definition, which also remains a major impediment to implementing successful poverty-reduction strategies, is who actually defines poverty and how they do so. The actual process of defining poverty is critical to recognizing and analyzing the economically and socially disadvantaged by location, and to devising locally effective reduction strategies. Centrally controlled public policies almost invariably spring from different definitions to locally sponsored policies and result in different outcomes (Desai and Shah 1998).

The top-down approaches, for example, tend to define poverty as deprivation of economic resources that are required to meet food, shelter and clothing needs necessary for physical well-being (Sarlo 1996; Ross, Shillington and Lochhead 1994). In other words, there is a perceived lack of income for people to meet their basic survival needs, as emphases are mainly on economic deprivation rather than personal and physical, social, cultural and political deprivation. This represents an official definition compiled by experts who are not themselves poor, and it is often based on decisions about the best proxy (income or consumption) for material deprivation (Short and Thesia 2002). Despite criticisms of this approach, income definitions are still frequently adopted by governments and have mostly retained their dominance in the description and analysis of poverty, both nationally and internationally (Ligon and Schechter 2003). This poses serious implications for poverty-reduction strategies because, in reality, poor people are not confronted by income poverty alone. For example, Chambers (1995) argues that the realities of poor people are local, complex and dynamic, and that income poverty, though important, is only one aspect of deprivation. A striking feature of income-based definitions is a tendency to pragmatically set social priorities and implement policies based on these. However, such policies, as Dixon and Macarov (1998) explain, are not necessarily targeted at absolute deprivation; instead, they merely establish poverty lines, which serve as guideposts for various social welfare benefits. In this case, the extent of access to clean water, education, health care and other basic services is frequently not considered important enough to target directly.

The limitations of top-down approaches in capturing the extent and dynamics of poverty, and the political connotations of income-based definitions, are the basis of Chambers' (1995) concerns. He argues that "our views of the realities of the poor, and of what should be done, are constructed mainly from a distance, and can be seen to be constructed mainly for our convenience" (175). Chambers is not alone in making this salient point. Webster and Engberg-Pedersen (2002) also suggest that the world should take as a point of departure the actions and strategies of poor people themselves. They refer to the point of departure as recognition of the fact that what may be labeled poverty covers a very wide and diverse range of experiences and processes of marginalization, which are excluded if one considers only economic factors such as low income. Similarly, Fusco (2003) argues that since the general well-being of people in a given society is fundamental to their survival, the monetary definition of poverty severely limits their opportunities and choices. Fusco further explains that the individual freedom to choose is a fundamental constituent of well-being and that, when an individual is deprived of that right, it constitutes a clear reduction in well-being.

The definition of poverty as employed by top-down approaches demonstrates that the major concern rests with economic deprivation. In these contexts, little tends to be known or taken into account about other dimensions of poverty that poor people may also experience. This is due to a lack of opportunity for the poor to participate in the process of defining the nature of their poverty. The implication of top-down income definitions of poverty is that income is also used as a parameter to measure poverty, in order to determine the proportion of the population who are experiencing income poverty. How poverty is measured by these approaches is the focus of the next section.

Top-down Approaches and Measurement of Poverty

The definition of poverty thus leads to the selection of the poverty-measurement approach, with the most common types of measures being those based on income. When poverty is defined as low income, an income-based measurement approach is then employed. In this case, the extent of poverty is generalized into a single representative statistic—the poverty line (Barrington 1997), which separates the poor from the non-poor. Accordingly, people are counted poor when their measured standard of living in terms of income or consumption is below that poverty line (Osinubi and Amaghion-veodiwe 2004).

Depending on their economic status and policy objectives, different countries construct different poverty lines. Yet there is an international poverty line designed to compare economic welfare levels. For example, in measuring income or consumption expenditure poverty in developing countries, the World Bank has widely adopted the US$1 a day standard as a lower boundary (Pritchet 2006). As a result, the World Bank publishes an annual set of estimates about levels and trends of poverty in the world, and also sets of data about intracountry income inequality, which permits an assessment of the differences and trends (Gwatkin 2000). The main reason why the World Bank followed the income-based concept of poverty until lately is clear. In the 1950s and 1960s, reducing poverty was not seen as a goal in itself, but as a by-product of economic growth (Gerster 2000), which was considered as the key to development. However, Townsend (1993) and Easton (1997) believe that the World Bank's US$1 a day definition is an acceptable improvisation, being a convenient and understandable temporary standard on which to base research and policy. They further argue that the importance of income poverty measures is to enable the identification and proper targeting of problem areas, with the aim of generating appropriate remedial policies. This justifies the popularity of income measures, not only because they enhance comparisons across places, but also because they are, as Destremau (2001) puts it, simple to set up since they rest on variables that are relatively easy to quantify.

In spite of the simplicity of income measures, there are implications of using them. For example, they substantially hide the extent of poverty while also understating the challenges that the reduction of poverty poses for developing countries. Income measures also make no distinction between the desperately poor, with hardly any income, and those just below the poverty threshold (Tsui 2002). What this implies is that there is insufficient information for policy; hence, income measures are not revealing the true condition of the poor. In this case, the extent of access of the poor to safe water, health care and education is not revealed. Yet these services are important for better quality-of-life expectancy. This is why Burkey (2000) proposes the adoption of a Physical Quality of Life Index based on the selection and measurement of quality of life expectancy—the state of people's health and welfare. Burkey's main point is that Physical Quality of Life Indices give a better indication of the standard of living for an average person than do national economic statistics.

Although this does not constitute an attempt to trivialize the significance of income, it serves to underscore that other important aspects of deprivation are not being measured with top-down approaches. Mayfield (1997) and Bourguignon and Chakravarty (2003) have rightly pointed out that increased income is important, as this may at least enable individuals to improve the position of their monetary and nonmonetary attributes. In other words, money gives individuals the purchasing power to meet certain needs that are important for improving their well-being. On the other hand, the authors note that it may be that some nonmonetary attributes, like public goods, do not exist in a location, and that it may also be the case that the unemployed petty traders and peasant farmers in the rural areas are deprived of the benefits of economic growth. In their conclusion, they argue that monetary income often represents a small fraction of the resources available to a given family, especially in rural areas of developing countries. This suggests that income measures are not adequate for determining the extent of poverty among the rural poor. In this case, the understanding of poverty should go beyond mere statistics. It should examine the processes and events that, according to Saunders (2004), expose people to poverty and to the conditions that prevent their escape from it.

Top-down Approaches and Poverty Reduction

Top-down approaches to poverty reduction commonly mirror top-down approaches to the definition and measurement of poverty. The definition of poverty as inadequate income automatically leads to the adoption of monetary measurements that identify the population whose income or consumption falls below a certain level. This also leads to the adoption of an economic growth strategy to address the shortfall in income. The central objective of the economic growth strategy is to achieve sustainable levels of growth in national production (Obadan 1997). In spite of the projected benefits of growth, the conventional development-oriented approaches have proved narrow and limited in their capacity to impact on the well-being of poor people (Smith 1997). A major reason is that economic growth has not been accompanied by social development policies, particularly at the local level. Even in cases where growth was recorded, empirical evidence suggests that it did not benefit the poorest citizens (Mafeje 2001). For example,

> Argentina grew 2 per cent per capita a year in the 1950s, yet saw income poverty rise. Honduras grew 2 per cent a year in 1986–1989 and saw income poverty double. New Zealand, the United Kingdom and the United States all experienced good average growth during 1975–1995, yet the proportion of population in poverty increased. (UNDP 1997, 7)

This would appear to demonstrate that poverty cannot be reduced by economic growth alone. It needs to also address other areas of deprivation.

Poor people's inability to benefit from growth has been attributed to a lack of capabilities, which in turn has been largely neglected by growth-oriented policies. Olavarria-Gambi (2003) argues that it is true that greater economic activity increases the demand for labor, increases wages and ultimately leads to an improvement in the situation of the poor. However, Olavarria-Gambi also identifies two basic conditions that people must satisfy to get into the job market: they must be educated and healthy. The basis of this argument is that these factors are critical to poverty reduction, yet they are trivialized by narrow economic policies that seem invariably to lead to ineffective poverty reduction efforts. Evidence from countries that have strong economic growth but still experience poverty shows that these economic policies have not been pro-poor. Adams (2004) and Hoeven and Shorrocks (2003) argue that the relationship between growth and poverty lies at the heart of development economics. In this case, the extent of poverty reduction depends on how economic growth is defined. Even development orthodoxy, based on macroeconomic theory, stresses the importance of physical and human capital accumulation as necessary elements for economic growth (Owens, 2004). With even low economic growth, but alongside a certain level of social development, there are opportunities for poor people to improve their quality of life. As people become healthier, better nourished and educated, they will find themselves in a better position to both gain from and contribute more to economic growth (Ranis et al. 2000).

Existing data point to inadequate access to basic needs in rural areas as depriving poor people of opportunities to contribute to economic development. Delamonica, Vandemoortele and Minujin (2002), for example, give an account of how each year about 11 million children under the age of five die as a result of preventable or easily treatable diseases. Most of these children belong to poor households in rural areas. The authors conclude that universal access to basic health services and quality education is not only a fundamental right; it is also one of the paths toward poverty reduction and economic and social development.

The results of econometric analysis carried out by Balisacan, Pernia and Asra (2003) in Indonesia show that growth was not the only factor that helped to reduce poverty. Other critical factors, including education, health care and agricultural price incentives, also directly influenced the welfare of the poor, as well as having an indirect effect through their impact on growth. Given the important role of these factors, these authors argue that while economic growth is crucial, a more complete poverty reduction strategy needs to take these relevant factors into account. Importantly, such factors revolve around what Sen (1999) refers to as substantive freedoms. They include elementary capabilities, like being able to avoid such deprivation as starvation, undernourishment, escapable morbidity, and premature mortality, as well as being literate, numerate and enjoying political participation. Therefore, poverty-reduction strategies must, along with growth, possess a strong element of human development.

Similarly, Christiaensen, Demery and Paternostro (2003) review trends in poverty, economic policies and growth in a sample of African countries during the 1990s. They found that, while in some countries overall economic growth has been pro-poor, in others this has not been the case. Their evidence suggests that market connectedness is crucial to enabling participation in the gains from economic growth. In addition, some regions and households, by virtue of their remoteness, were left behind when growth picked up. What this implies is that countries that promote social development alongside economic growth, including improvements in roads that facilitate access to markets, are more likely to benefit from growth than countries that only concentrate on economic development. Finally, and importantly, the evidence shows that education and access to land emerged as key private endowments that helped households benefit from new economic opportunities.

These examples demonstrate that poverty is not just the consequence of economic deprivation, but also the result of many other reinforcing factors that include lack of productive resources, illiteracy and ill-health. As Destremau (2001) explains, access to income cannot constitute a sufficient means for poverty to be reduced, given the extent of vulnerability of poor families and individuals. In this case, poverty reduction will entail public investment to improve infrastructure and efficient delivery of functional health and educational systems. This also gives people the basis to participate in the economic growth process.

In the context of the limited success of the top-down, growth-oriented approaches of the past, there is the need to seek alternative strategies that promote participation and see poverty as going beyond the lack of adequate income. This is the concern of the following section, which examines bottom-up approaches to poverty definition, measurement and reduction strategies within the context of local level social development.

BOTTOM-UP APPROACHES TO POVERTY ALLEVIATION

The limited success of the top-down, growth-oriented approach has shifted the debate from income-based analysis to the recognition of the multidimensional nature of poverty. Poverty in developing countries is a direct and indirect manifestation of several causal factors that are beyond just low income (Dike 1997). Designing an effective poverty-reduction strategy, therefore, requires an understanding of the dimensions and causes of poverty from the point of view of the poor. This will depend on the use of bottom-up approaches that emphasize the active participation of poor people in the process. In this case, the views of poor people are recognized and incorporated into poverty-reduction strategies. An important characteristic of these approaches is their qualitative nature that allows poor people to use their own criteria to define their poverty.

Blanco (2003) defines poverty as "the total absence of opportunities, accompanied by high levels of under-nourishment, hunger, illiteracy, lack of education, physical and mental ailments, emotional and social instability, unhappiness, sorrow and hopelessness for the future" (28). This definition suggests that poverty is not just the result of low income but of many factors often omitted by top-down definitions. In order not to restrict its definition to just a lack of monetary income, the UNDP (1997) also defines poverty from the perspectives of human development. It states that "human poverty is more than income; it is the denial of choices and opportunities for living a tolerable life" (2). The World Bank, too, in its *World Development Report* (2000b), presents poverty as "multidimensional, encompassing not only material deprivation, but also low achievements in education and health" (15). Its main objective is not only to portray development as a process of improvement in human well-being and quality of life, but also to show how the population of a given country has been affected by the development process and how this has strengthened the people as subjects of the process, not just as objects and recipients (Jolly, Emmeriji and Lapeyre 2004). In this case, people have a role to play in the development process, and this is in sharp contrast to those nonparticipatory approaches where outsiders tend to monopolize the entire process.

Despite the World Bank's commitment to poverty reduction and its dramatic shift from an income-focused to multidimensional approaches, many people are still skeptical about the Bank's sincerity. Two of those who have cast doubt on this are Verheul and Rowson (2001). They argue that a greater emphasis on poverty issues has barely challenged the old agenda of monetarist macroeconomic policies. They claim that the World Bank's policy has one section on poverty and another on economics. What this implies is that the Bank still subtly treats poverty as economic deprivation rather than a combination of income and non-income deprivation.

Townsend's (1979) description of poverty strongly reflects the human development dimension: "Individual families are in poverty when they lack the resources to obtain the type of diet or participate in the activities and have the living conditions and amenities which are widely approved in the societies to which they belong" (31). The key argument in Townsend's description is that families in poverty are in effect excluded from ordinary living patterns, customs and activities of the society. In other words, poverty is a combination of various factors that touch on different aspects of human life. This point has been further expanded by Desai and Shah (1988). They see poverty as a multidimensional phenomenon, with income being just one of these dimensions.

Given these definitions, three basic concepts—namely, sufficiency, access and vulnerability, as suggested by May and Norton (2005)—are of utmost importance to the whole poverty-reduction process. They relate to the extent of access of poor people to essential services as well as to safety, opportunities and other conditions for an acceptable life. When poverty is defined as low income or low consumption, these important dimensions are ignored or trivialized. Burkey (2000) and Mayfield (1997) argue that basic needs must, of necessity, include material comforts that are capable of giving people an element of choice, as well as having adequate resources to create options in the way they would live. Burkey (2000) divides these needs into two broad categories. First, he sees adequate food, safe drinking water, suitable shelter, clothing and simple household equipment as basic requirements for a family. Second, he identifies essential services such as public transport, health and educational facilities as also being important.

The International Labour Organisation (1977) also states that education itself is a basic need, and equality of access to educational services, particularly in the rural areas, is an important ingredient of a basic needs strategy. In this case, education is not only an instrument for the reduction of poverty, but also a measure of empowerment, as well as a right and an entitlement

(Tilak 2002). Burkey's emphasis on health is reflected in Bloom and Canning (2003). They note that, across the world, ill-health disproportionately afflicts poor people. This is why poverty remains a major factor in access to health care, and rural areas are often adversely affected. Yet, it is one of those important areas that are often ignored by monetary measures of poverty.

The relationship between economic growth and social development is complementary. While economic growth has the potential to generate opportunities, the people that take advantage of those opportunities are the ones exhibiting what Olavarria-Gambi (2003) describes as relatively high levels of schooling and good health. In other words, beyond needs as an end in themselves, they also serve as means to fulfill other necessities of life (Destremau 2001). For example, access to education and health care enables poor people to build their productive assets, which in turn facilitates their access to other important needs such as income and employment.

The Capability Theory and Bottom-up Rural Poverty Alleviation

The focus on means and ends within the development process to attain personal fulfillment underpins Sen's (1999) groundbreaking work on capability. Sen begins with freedom, which, as he argues, involves both the processes that allow individuals to take actions and decisions, and the actual opportunities that people have, irrespective of their personal and social circumstances. In this case, lack of freedom can result in inadequate opportunities for individuals to achieve those things that they desire. Against this background, Sen argues that, apart from the capability of better basic education and health care to improve the quality of life directly, they are also capable of increasing a person's ability to earn an income, thereby escaping income poverty as well. Therefore, capability serves as the means to earn an income, which is referred to as an end in this case. People with education and good health can have better access to well-paid job opportunities compared to those without education.

Despite Sen's innovative work, not everyone agrees with his capability theory. Alakire (2002) and Zuolo (2004), for example, are skeptical about the operational logic of Sen's capabilities framework. Paramount among their concerns is doubt over how to measure capabilities, such that one can evaluate changes brought about by economic initiatives. These concerns are grounded in disagreement about what, as a matter of fact, should be regarded as the important capabilities, and what might be the parameters for judging one set of capabilities against another, assuming one set was not strictly dominant. Alakire is in particular concerned about evaluating the possibilities of choice and functioning achieved by people. Zuolo, on the other hand, argues that not all that is obtained is good for a person. Accordingly, both authors see Sen's attempt to distinguish between simple and refined functioning as defective, and not an appropriate criterion as to whether these lead to real development.

Nonetheless, Sen's innovative ideas have significantly enhanced the debate on the multidimensionality of poverty and encouraged bottom-up participatory approaches. These approaches recognize a set of factors, such as access to basic needs, infrastructure and opportunities, that are essential for the poor to escape poverty. The rural poor are not able to contribute to, or benefit from, economic growth unless their potential is well developed through access to basic needs, both material and nonmaterial. As argued by Desai and Potter (2002), economic growth is not the same as human development, which can only occur through qualitative improvement in standards of living. This is why the validity of income as a measure of poverty has been challenged on many fronts: it basically fails to take many other variables of poverty, such as quality of life, into account. In this context, measurements that are based on the multidimensionality of poverty will now be discussed.

Bottom-up Approaches and Measurement of Poverty

The definition of poverty as a multidimensional concept suggests that measurement should take dimensions of poverty other than income into account. The proponents of multidimensional approaches emphasize not only income but also the fulfillment of basic needs, capabilities and participation. This is because poverty manifests itself in a variety of ways, including monetary and nonmonetary, which the traditional monetary measures fail to capture. Chambers (1995), for example, argues that the multiple and diverse realities of poverty and well-being defy capture by standard measures. Townsend (1993) also believes that the more the concept of poverty is restricted to an insufficiency of income, the easier it is to argue that economic growth is all that is required to overcome poverty. Townsend's argument is that the more the concept is widened from an insufficiency of income to cover basic needs like health, welfare and community participation, the more it becomes necessary to admit that a complex combination of growth, redistribution and reorganization of trading has to evolve. This is why poverty should be measured with several indicators that give complementary information on its different aspects (Moisio 2004). The UNDP, for example, has focused on the various dimensions of human development through its *Human Development Reports*. Its 1997 report stresses that, although income focuses on an important dimension of poverty, it gives only a partial picture of the many ways in which human lives can be blighted. Human poverty includes many aspects that cannot be measured, or are not being measured. The rural poor are a good example of a population that lacks most of the basic needs and that often fares poorly when top-down policies are devised to reduce poverty, especially when such policies are based mainly on monetary measures.

The UNDP (1997) points out that, in 1994, the population in Mexico with access to health services was 93% and to safe water 83%. By contrast, the population of Nigerians with access to health services for that same year was 51%, while 51% also represented the population with access to safe water. What this suggests is that the basic needs of people in Nigeria are not being met, and it is clear that the government there tends to focus more on growth than social development. Moreover, poor people in Nigeria are not being encouraged, or permitted, to give their accounts of their priority needs. Along similar lines, Sen's (1999) capability approach is seen by Laderchi, Saith and Stewart (2003) as rejecting monetary income as the measure of well-being, and instead focusing on indicators of the freedom to live a valued life. What Sen's approach epitomizes is individuals becoming active agents of change rather than being passive recipients of charity. Through this approach, poor people are able to have the freedom to do what they value by using available resources to engage in productive activities with significant impact on poverty reduction. With economic measures, poor people's opportunities and choices are severely constrained because the resources they need to enhance such opportunities are taken for granted.

Bottom-up Approaches and Poverty Reduction

The limited success recorded by most developing countries in reducing poverty to acceptable levels and the widespread reliance on top-down approaches strongly suggest that top-down approaches are not effective. This is why alternative approaches that recognize poverty as representing such conditions as inadequate capabilities are critical. Hence, improving poor people's access to education, health care and credit means increased productivity and income. Moreover, Barrett and Carter (2006) argue that the stock of productive assets that households and individuals control largely determines their structural position in a society, and their ability to avoid poverty or escape from it if they find themselves falling backward in the face of adverse shocks. The International Fund for Agricultural Development states in its 2000/2001 report that lack of access is both an effect and a cause of poverty—this is in terms of income opportunities, consumption and capability building of people and their own institutions. For instance, the lack of adequate access to health care can undermine the productive capacity of poor people, and, in the same manner, the lack of sufficient access to basic education can deprive poor people of the capability needed to survive, develop and thrive. People with education are more likely to access better remunerative employment than those who are deprived of access to education. The bottom line is that poor people's possession of assets can significantly offer them a pathway out of poverty.

The significance of access to services has been emphasized by the African Economic Outlook (2003). It predicts that while most Asian, Latin American and Caribbean countries are on course to meet many of the Millennium Development Goals (MDGs), most of the African countries are unlikely to achieve these. Yet even among African countries, according to the report, significant differences exist in terms of economic and social progress towards the MDGs. For example, northern Africa has the lowest poverty rate among all developing regions in the world, with only 2% of its population below the poverty line of US$1 a day. At the other extreme, Sub-Saharan Africa has the highest poverty ratio in the world, with 46% of its population living below the poverty line of US$1 a day. The report concludes that the large disparity between the two subregions reflects variations not only in past performance but also in the quality of growth and in human and social capital development. In other words, growth needs to be complemented with a set of social and related policies, which not only target the most impoverished but also empower the poor through productivity increases, access to productive employment, resources and delivery of basic social services (Obadan 1997). The case of northern Africa illustrates this point. Similarly, evidence across countries demonstrates that robust and sustained pro-poor economic growth is the single most important factor in attaining rapid poverty reduction. Linden (2004) explains that India, People's Republic of China, Thailand and Vietnam are among the countries where rapid growth has resulted in a significant drop in poverty in the last decade, mainly because of the availability of infrastructure and services in both urban and rural areas.

In this case, the inclusion of poor people through bottom-up participatory approaches creates an important avenue for capturing their perspective in a way that can be communicated to decision makers in government and development agencies. This is because, as Robb (1999) argues, an understanding of the nature and causes of poverty lies at the heart of designing economic and social strategies for development.

A bottom-up development strategy encompasses various approaches that reflect the multidimensionality of poverty, and the most frequently mentioned strategy, according to the World Bank (1994), is the inclusion of the poor in the design of interventions. Robert Chambers emphasizes this point in much of his work. He argues that it is inappropriate for those who are not poor to pronounce on what matters to those who are poor, as avoiding this will reduce distortions. Ayoola and others (2001) also assert that, because poor people are the true poverty experts, any policy document on poverty reduction has to be based essentially on the experiences, priorities, reflections and recommendations of poor people. Poor people's perceptions of their deprivation have many dimensions that include not only lack of income and wealth, but also social inferiority, physical weakness, disability and sickness (Chambers 1997). This is an important reason why this chapter deviates from the many studies by focusing on opportunities for the poor to present their personal experiences of poverty and solutions for its reduction.

An example of the benefits of participation is reflected in the work of Okali, Sumberg and Farrington (1994) titled *Farmer Participatory*

Research. This work extensively involved farmers in order to determine the effectiveness of their participation in fostering closer integration of farmers' own research and the formal agricultural research system. The research provides clear evidence of farmers' involvement in activities to identify problems, opportunities and possible solutions. The authors conclude that participatory methods provide efficient means of reaching the poor and disadvantaged. Similarly, Gujja and Pimbert (1998) present the case of villagers challenging the wetland management policies during a community meeting that also involved key government staff. The meeting focused on two sites of international importance: the Ucchali Wetland Complex in the province of Punjab, Pakistan, and Keoladeo National Park in the State of Rajastan, India. Local people believe that the grazing by buffalos inside the wetlands is part of ecosystem management. They also believe that grazing contributes to the health of the ecosystem and thus helps attract migratory birds, a major purpose of the park. On the other hand, the locals in Ucchali describe Lake Khabbaki as a disaster flood zone rather than a lake. The management, which is constantly driven by profit, agreed with the community to effect some changes to existing policies. At the meeting, it was emphasized that participation was not simply the application of a method but part of a process of dialogue, action, analysis, conflict resolution and change. Quite revealing was the degree to which shifts from normal top-down practices were encouraged and how participation was used to advocate bigger policy changes. More important was the empowerment of local communities through their participation in the entire process.

These case studies show that empowerment of the poor is a critical element of bottom-up approaches because it helps poor people to significantly remove major political, economic and social constraints in the pursuit of their aspirations. The *World Development Report* (World Bank 2000b) recognizes empowerment as an important and necessary aspect of bottom-up approaches for poverty reduction. It describes empowerment as enhancing the capacity of poor people to influence the state institutions that affect their lives, by strengthening their participation in political processes and local decision making.

Factors discussed in this chapter appear to have the potential to promote bottom-up approaches. However, good governance that can influence the form, extent and quality of participation is also critical. Many countries in Africa, such as Nigeria, have experienced military dictatorships that have used coercive power extensively to silence their citizens. In other countries, where governments have been democratically elected, their citizens still lack freedom and security, and corruption seems to have been institutionalized: "Voicelessness and powerlessness are key dimensions of poverty, and an important aspect of voice relates to political rights and civil liberties" (World Bank 2000b, 112). An enabling environment ensures that people have security, freedom to participate in decisions that affect their lives, and access to education, health-care services and safe drinking water. In this case, the constitutive role of freedom, as Sen (1999) explains, relates to the importance of substantive freedom in enriching human life. That is, freedom for individuals to access the means to achieve their goals and improve their well-being is critical.

CONCLUSIONS

This chapter has argued that poverty is a complex concept, and that inadequate attention has generally been paid to a detailed analysis of poverty as perceived by poor people themselves. Closely related to this is the lack of attention paid to the economic, social and political constraints that tend to hinder poor people's development. It is shown that the definition of poverty used tends to determine both the parameters for its measurement and the type of reduction strategies to be adopted. For example, when poverty is defined as a lack of income, income levels are seen as appropriate for measurement, which then leads to the adoption of a critical poverty line. Then economic growth is perceived to be the best strategy to take care of those falling below the poverty threshold. In this case, other forms of deprivation are not taken into account.

Furthermore, it is found that top-down approaches have had limited success in reducing poverty, essentially because poor people have no opportunity to provide their own understandings of the nature and dimensions of their poverty. In other words, there is no participation of poor people, either in the process of analyzing the nature and extent of poverty, or in the process of identifying the causes and solutions to poverty. Top-down approaches represent an attempt to help the disadvantaged and rural poor by offering them predetermined, outside-funded plans and programs that reflect what the outsider considers to be appropriate, rather than what the poor regard as appropriate for themselves (Mayfield 1997). Clearly, these poverty reduction strategies have been found to be largely ineffective because they are based on a growth strategy orchestrated by a group of experts, whereas poor peoples' needs are more than just a lack of income.

A critical review of literature on top-down and bottom-up approaches suggests that successful poverty reduction will depend to a great extent on bottom-up approaches. This is because emphases are then on grassroots strategies whereby poor people are not only protected from the counter-productive interventions of the outside world, but are also provided with limited resources to tackle their most pressing problems (Mayfield 1997). This is to enable them to use their initiative to tackle their own problems, which usually leads to greater self-reliance and self-sufficiency. It has to be recognized, therefore, that the opportunities for the poor to be heard and contribute to their own development are critical for effective poverty reduction. Although past studies have suggested radical changes to policies to benefit the poor in rural areas, rural neglect is still prevalent in developing countries. Even basic needs, regarded as the right of all human beings, are often not being met. Yet these people are voiceless and powerless. The requirement for meeting the challenges of development, which is the concern of this chapter, are the bottom-up approaches that are participatory and action-oriented, but ideally implemented in collaboration with sensitive top-down approaches.

REFERENCES

Adams, R. 2004. Economic growth, inequality and poverty: Estimating the growth elasticity of poverty. *World Development* 32(12): 1989–2014.

African Economic Outlook 2003/2004. African Economic Outlook, OECD Development Centre, Molineaux, France.

Aku, P. M., Ibrahim, M. J., and Bulus, Y. D. 1997. Perspectives on Poverty and Poverty Alleviation Strategies for Nigeria. In Selected Papers for the 1997 Annual Conference on Poverty Alleviation in Nigeria. Published by the Nigerian Economic Society. Ibadan, Nigeria, 41–53.

Alakire, S. 2002. *Valuing freedom: Sen's capability approach and poverty reduction*. Oxford: Oxford University Press.

Anyanwu, J. C. 1997. Analytical framework for poverty reduction: Issue of economic growth versus other strategies. In *Selected Papers for the 1997 Annual Conference on Poverty Alleviation in Nigeria*. Published by the Nigerian Economic Society. Ibadan, Nigeria, 65–74.

Ayoola, G. B., Okumadewa, F., Mamman, B., Nweze, N., Odebiyi, T., Zasha, J., Williams, O., Shehu, D., and Aina, A. 2001. Nigeria: Voice of the poor: Country synthesis report. In *World development report, 2000/2001: Consultation with the poor*. Washington, D.C.: World Bank.

Balisacan, A. M., Pernia, E. M., and Asra, A. 2003. Revisiting growth and poverty reduction in Indonesia: What do subnational data show? *Bulletin of Indonesian Economic Studies* 39(3): 329–351.

Barrett, C. B., and Carter, M. R. 2006. The economics of poverty traps and persistent poverty: An asset-based approach. *Journal of Development Studies* 42(2): 178–186.

Barrington, L. 1997. Estimating earnings poverty in 1939: A comparison of Orshasky- method and price-indexed definitions of poverty. *Review of Economics and Statistics* 79(3): 406–414.

Blanco, R. O. 2003. How we define poverty. *UN Chronicle* 39(4): 28.

Bloom, D. E., and Canning, D. 2003. The health and poverty of nations: From theory to practice. *Journal of Human Development* 4(1): 47–71.

Bourguignon, F., and Chakravarty, S. R. 2003. The measurement of multidimensional poverty. *Journal of Economic Inequality* 1:25–49.

Burkey, S. 2000. *People first: A guide to self-reliant participatory rural development*. London: Zed Books.

Chambers, R. 1995. Poverty and livelihoods: Whose reality counts? *Environment and Urbanisation* 7(1): 173–184.

———. 1997. *Whose reality counts? Putting the first last*. London: ITDG.

Christiaensen, L., Demery, L., and Paternostro, S. 2003, Macro and micro perspectives of growth and poverty in Africa. *The World Bank Economic Review* 17(3): 317–347.

Cooke, B., and Kothari, U. 2001. *Participation: The new tyranny*. London: Zed Books.

Delamonica, E., Vandemoortele, J., and Minujin, A. 2002. Economic growth, poverty and children. *Environment and Urbanisation* 14(2): 23–43.

Desai, M., and Shah, A. 1998. Relative deprivation and measurement of poverty. *Oxford Economic Papers* 40(3): 505–522.

Desai, V., and Potter, R. B. 2002. *The companion to development studies.* London: Arnold.

Destremau, B. 2001. *Poverty, discourse and state power: A case study of Morocco.* London: Zed Books.

Devas, N. 2004. *Urban governance, voice and poverty in the developing world.* London: Earthscan.

Dike, N. 1997. Understanding the multidimensional nature of poverty: *Poverty alleviation in Nigeria: Selected papers for the 1997 annual conference on poverty alleviation in Nigeria.* Ibadan: Nigerian Economic Society, 91–112.

Dixon, J., and Macarov, D. 1998. *Poverty: A persistent global reality.* London: Routledge.

Easton, B. 1997. Measuring poverty: Some problems. *Social Policy Journal of New Zealand* 9 (November): 171–179.

Fusco, A. 2003. *On the definition and measurement of poverty: The contribution of multidimensional analysis.* 3rd Conference on the Capability Approach: From Sustainable Development to Sustainable Freedom, September 7–9, University of Pavia.

Gerster, R. 2000. Alternative Approaches to Poverty Reduction Strategies. A Review of the World Bank Compared to Other Donors. Bern: SDC (Swiss Agency for Development and Cooperation) Working Paper 1/2000.

Gujja, B., and Pimbert, M. P. 1998. Village voices challenging wetland management policies: PRA experiences from India and Pakistan. *Nature and Resources* 33(1): 34–39.

Gwatkin, D. 2000. The health of the poor: What do we know? What can we do? *Bulletin of the World Health Organisation* 78(1): 1–16.

Hoeven, R., and Shorrocks, A. 2003. Perspectives on growth and poverty. Tokyo: United Nations University Press.

International Fund for Agricultural Development. 2001. *The challenge of ending rural poverty: Rural poverty report.* New York: Oxford University Press.

International Labour Organisation. 1977. *Meeting basic needs: Strategies for eradicating mass poverty and unemployment.* Geneva: Author.

Jolly, R. D., Emmeriji, G., and Lapeyre, F. 2004. *UN contributions to development thinking and practice.* Bloomington: Indiana University Press.

Keare, D. H. 2001. Learning to clap: Reflections on top-down versus bottom-up development. *Human Organization* 60(2): 159–165.

Laderchi, R., Saith, R., and Stewart, F. 2003. *Does it matter that we don't agree on the definition of poverty? A comparison of four approaches* (Queen Elizabeth House Working Paper Series QEHWPS107). Oxford: Queen Elizabeth House, University of Oxford.

Linden, G. V. 2004. The challenge is to halve extreme poverty and hunger by 2015. *Business World,* Manila, April 23, p. 1.

Mafeje, A. 2001. Conceptual and philosophical predispositions. In *Poverty reduction: What role for the state in today's globalised economy?* ed. F. Wilson, N. Kanji, and E. Braathen, 2–33. London: Zed Books.

Moisio, P. 2004. A latent class application to the multidimensional measurement of poverty. *Quality and Quantity* 38:703–717.

Okali, C., Sumberg, J., and Farrington, J. 1994. *Farmer participatory research: Rhetoric and reality.* London: Intermediate Technology Publications/Overseas Development Institute.

Olaniyan, I. F. 1997. Macroeconomic policy framework for poverty alleviation in Nigeria. In *Poverty alleviation in Nigeria: Selected papers for the 1997 annual conference on poverty alleviation in Nigeria.* Ibadan: Nigerian Economic Society.

Olavarria-Gambi, M. 2003. Poverty reduction in Chile: Has economic growth been enough? *Journal of Human Development* 4(1): 103–117.

Ranis, G., Stewart, F., and Ramirez, A. 2000. Economic Growth and Human Development. *World Development*, 28(2): 197–219.

Robb, C. 2001. *Can the poor influence policy?* Washington, D.C.: World Bank.

Ross D. P., Shillington, E. R., and Lochhead, C. 1994. *The Canadian fact book on poverty*. Ottawa, ON: Canadian Council on Social Development.

Sarlo, C. 1996. *Poverty in Canada*. Vancouver, BC: Fraser Institute.

Saunders, P. 2004. From income poverty to deprivation (Social Policy Research Centre Discussion Paper No. 31). Sydney: University of New South Wales, Australia.

Short, K., and Thesia, I. G. 2002. Experimental poverty measures. *Monthly Labour Review* 25(8): 3–11.

Stein, S. 2004. *The culture of education policy*. New York: Teachers College Press

Tilak, J. A. B. 2002. Education and poverty. *Journal of Human Development* 3(2): 191–207.

Townsend, P. 1979. *Poverty in the United Kingdom: A survey of household resources and standards of living*. Hammondsworth: Penguin Books,

———. 1993. *The international analysis of poverty*. New York: Harvester Wheatsheaf.

Tsui, K. 2002. Multidimensional poverty lines. *Social Choice and Welfare* 19(1): 69–93.

United Nations Development Programme (UNDP). 1997. *Human development report 1997*. New York: Oxford University Press.

Verheul, E., and Rowson, M., 2001. Poverty reduction strategy paper: It's too soon to say whether this new approach to aid will improve health. *British Medical Journal* 323(7305): 120–121.

Webster, N., and Engberg-Pedersen, L. 2002. *In the name of the poor: Contesting political space for poverty reduction*. London: Zed books.

World Bank. 1994. *Good practice in non-lending: Gender in poverty assessments, Benin: Towards a poverty alleviation strategy*. Washington: Population and Human Resources Division, Occidental and Central Africa Department.

———. 2000a. *Comprehensive development framework*. Washington D.C.: Author. http://www.worldbank.org/cdf/

———. 2000b. *World development report, 2000/2001: Attacking poverty*. New York: Oxford University Press.

———. 2003. *Reaching the rural poor: A renewed strategy for rural development*. Washington, D.C.: Author.

Zuolo, F. 2004. *Sen's capability theory: Spinoza beyond Aristotle*. Pavia, Italy: University of Pavia.

Part III

Ethical Issues in Social Development

10 The Ethics of Social Development[1]

Hartley Dean

INTRODUCTION

The title of this chapter, possibly, is somewhat pretentious. I should make clear from the outset that its purpose is quite modest and straightforward. My initial premises are that social development is an ethical project in its own right and not merely an adjunct to economic development, and that the goal of social development is to promote collectively guaranteed human well-being for all peoples across the whole of the life course. The principal complexities that arise from these simple premises relate, first, to a distinction between ethical principles and moral standards, and second, to a distinction between competing ideas about what constitutes human well-being. The chapter initially considers the conceptual distinction between morals and ethics, and the way this in turn relates to the distinction between social standards, on the one hand, and social rights, on the other. I then discuss the competing hedonic and eudaimonic ethical traditions before relating this to different conceptions of social policy and citizenship. This analysis is then applied to construct a heuristic taxonomy of currently prevailing strategies of social development. Finally, the chapter outlines a variety of contrasting ideas about the future of social development, before concluding with a quali-fied case for a rights-based eudaimonic ethic of social development.

MORAL STANDARDS AND ETHICAL PRINCIPLES

In ordinary English usage, "morality" and "ethics" are virtually syn-onymous terms, yet for some philosophers, it is important to distinguish between the two—generally in terms of abstract and contested distinctions between that which is "good" and that which is "right." The distinction I wish to draw is, perhaps, more sociological than philosophical. It is related in one sense to that which Habermas (1987) makes between "life world" and "system." Morals are concerned with cultural *mores*, ethics with cog-nitive *ethos*. Morality and ethics are, of course, closely related and exist in dialectical relation to each other. Morals may entail the (re)interpreta-tion of ethics. Ethics are a reflection upon morals. Morals are grounded;

their preoccupation is with norms and customary practices. Ethics are systemic; their preoccupation is with values and abstract principles. Morals are expressed in terms of codes, ethics in terms of doctrines. The process of social development may be informed by the setting of social or human welfare *standards* that may be imposed upon or adopted by countries or regions as they develop: such standards—though they may be specified with an expressly technical component—imply *moral* assumptions about what ought in practice to be achieved. Alternatively, the process of social development may be informed by a concept of social *rights*: the creation of rights—to such things as education, health care, housing and social security—requires some kind of *ethical* framework or systemic understanding of what may potentially be achieved.

The development of capitalist welfare states in the global North may be understood in terms of a transition from a postmedieval poor-law morality to a modern social citizenship ethic. The classic formulation was espoused by T. H. Marshall (1950/1992), who identified three kinds of citizenship rights: civil or legal rights, political or democratic rights, and social or welfare rights. It was the capitalist welfare state that gave expression to the last. Marshall's contention was that in liberal democracies, the struggles of past centuries had delivered first the rule of law and then the universal franchise. However, the crowning achievement of the twentieth century—brought finally to fruition following the end of World War II—had been the consolidation of more or less systematic forms of social policy across the capitalist world, providing certain rights to education, health care, housing, social protection and even such things as legal aid for the poor. Democratic welfare capitalism, Marshall supposed, would secure equality of status for the individual citizens of nation-states.

And it is citizenship rights that have in practice provided the ethical foundations upon which modern global conceptions of *human* rights have been constructed (e.g., P. Clarke 1996). The human rights instruments of the modern era—including and particularly the Universal Declaration of Human Rights (UDHR) of 1948—incorporated the same distinction that Marshall drew between a "first generation" of civil and political rights that had been defined through past struggles and a "second generation" of rights identified in the twentieth century. The UDHR characterizes this second generation of rights as economic, social and cultural. Such rights have to do with the means by which human beings obtain their livelihood and the ways in which they are allowed or enabled to participate in human society.

The form and substance of second generation or social rights[2] have always been contestable. Different welfare-state regimes (Esping-Andersen 1990) function with rather different notions of rights. T. H. Marshall, it should be noted, was a liberal, and it is within the liberal English-speaking tradition that there has been a certain tendency to look upon social rights in terms of safety nets for the relief of poverty or national minima for the prevention of poverty. In contrast, corporatist continental-European welfare states have tended to see welfare rights as compensatory rights for their nations' workers, whereas Nordic social-democratic welfare states have been inclined to regard welfare rather more in terms of universal rights for all their citizens. Fundamentally, however, social rights are rights that have in various ways been bestowed or demanded under capitalism in the global North.

Second generation human rights have been conceptually more abstract and practically more elusive than first generation rights. The form in which they were encapsulated in the UDHR of 1948 owed much to the Cold War tensions of that era (e.g., Hunt 1996). They represented an uncomfortable compromise between, on the one hand, a liberal legacy summed up in Franklin Roosevelt's celebrated aphorism that "a necessitous man is not a free man" (see Eide 2001) and, on the other, attempts by the Soviet communist bloc to move the agenda away from civil and political freedoms in favor of its own interpretation of human rights, based on state organized economic and social guarantees (e.g., Wronka 1992). Despite rhetorical assertions as to the indivisibility and interdependence of all human rights, these tensions as to their substance—and, more particularly, as to the manner of their implementation and enforcement—led to the development of separate international covenants: one for civil and political rights, the other for economic, social and cultural rights. The latter have been consistently marginalized in favor of the former (Dean 2002). Later, with the collapse of Soviet communism, human rights discourse became—for a time at least—less of a rhetorical propaganda medium (UN Development Programme [UNDP] 2003, 3). As a result, it has been argued, it has become increasingly feasible at the international level to entertain the possibility of global approaches to social policy issues (Deacon, Hulse and Stubbs 1997).

In the meantime, in response to the demands of the global South, the UN, through the Declaration of the Right to Development of 1986, had purported to institute a "third generation" of human rights. The Declaration, which is not binding, was intended in the words of the Senegalese delegate to express for the poorest people of the world "the right to live better." It sought to establish the principle that all human beings should be enabled to participate in a process of social, economic and political development (Rosas 2001). This new generation of rights incorporated demands for peace, for a healthy environment and for self-determination. It implied not only individual rights, but also collective, group and solidarity rights. In the process, however, it did not so much add to the canon of rights that had already been set out in the 1966 International Covenant on Economic, Social and Cultural Rights as bring an element of ambiguity to the question of whether "the right to live better" was a right to be demanded by citizens against individual nation-states or a right of poor nations to international cooperation and assistance. Paradoxically, perhaps, this has served further to marginalize the idea that social rights may be regarded as a global species of human rights that could or should in themselves be inalienable and unconditional. Certainly, aspirations based, for example, on group rights to self-determination or cultural freedom (Kymlicka 1995; Perez-Bustillo 2001) seek to enlarge our understanding of civil and political rights, not social rights. In the struggle for the right to development, social rights have tended to take a back seat.

It is now more widely acknowledged that notions of welfare state regimes and social rights do not readily translate to the poorest nations of the world (Gough et al. 2004). What is more, concerns have been expressed as to whether a rights-based approach to human welfare can be sustained in the face of economic globalization (Mishra 1999). Mishra had contended that in the postmodern era, the language of social rights is being progressively displaced by a language of social standards. A similar, if differently expressed, argument about the nature and consequences of globalization is offered by Gilbert (2004), who suggests that the resulting transformation of welfare states in the global North portend "the silent surrender of public responsibility"—a retreat, in effect, from ethical premises.

Some commentators are more optimistic. Globalization has brought a range of international governmental organizations and actors into play, and Deacon (2007) claims that the globalization of social policy is opening up a space for processes of "redistribution, regulation and rights." It is not that rights are off the agenda, but that they are ambiguously construed. Amartya Sen (in UNDP 2000, Ch. 1) draws upon Kant's distinction between perfect and imperfect duties to make the point that just because the rights demanded by or on behalf of the poor are neglected or repudiated by those with the power to honor them, this does not mean that such rights do not exist or cannot be inalienable. The Office of the High Commissioner for Human Rights has issued *Draft Guidelines for a Human Rights Approach to Poverty Reduction Strategies* (2002). However, these are intended, it would appear, to complement the UN's Millennium Development Goals (MDGs) (see UNDP 2003), and they seek to establish a set of indicators and benchmarks to ensure that economic development is matched in time by social development. The emphasis is on safety nets, good governance and performance monitoring; upon the interdependence of rights and responsibilities, such that, for example, the right to food should be linked to the right to work; and upon the accountability of state parties as well as global actors. The document defines a process for the setting of targets in relation to "rights" to food, health, education, work, housing, and so on (but, significantly, there is no mention of a right to social security). The *Guidelines*, at the time of writing, remain in draft and remain subordinate in policy terms to the MDGs, which they supplement and which do not create rights, but set standards to be achieved in the global South.

Insofar as processes of social development have accompanied economic development in the global North and are now promoted in the global South, they have been and are now informed by an element of ambiguity and a certain tension between morally pragmatic standards-based approaches and ethically principled rights-based approaches. Intersecting with that tension, however, is another source of ambiguity that has to do with an important distinction to be made between different kinds of well-being.

HEDONIC AND EUDAIMONIC TRADITIONS

The ancient Greek philosophers distinguished between hedonic and eudaimonic notions of well-being. The former is concerned with pleasure, the latter with ontological (or, some might claim, spiritual) well-being. While the Socratic tradition recognized both, other traditions have diverged. The Epicurean tradition supposed that a good life entailed the pursuit of pleasure (both mental and physical) and the avoidance of pain. This hedonic approach evolved in the nineteenth century into Utilitarianism and the idea that it is the role of policy makers to promote the greatest happiness for the greatest number of people: a philosophy that by implication justified inflicting pain upon any who threatened the happiness of the majority. The Aristotelian tradition, on the other hand, contended that the good life required more than pleasure; it also entailed shared duties and personal fulfillment. This eudaimonic approach translated during the eighteenth century onward into Kantian deontological ethics, notions of universal moral duty and the contention that not only does everybody have a right to well-being, but also nobody should be treated as a means of achieving happiness for another. Such thinking opened the door to modern concepts of social justice, such as that espoused by Rawls (1972).

I have previously argued that the hedonic–eudaimonic distinction is reflected in the competing ways in which post-Enlightenment concepts of citizenship have been constructed (Dean 2003). Conceptions of citizenship articulate distinctive assumptions about the basis of human relations. Liberal conceptions regard human relations in more or less Hobbesian terms, as a war or competition of all against all; dealings between people entail various forms of bargaining; citizenship is therefore construed in contractarian terms as a trade-off between the unrestrained pleasures of individual sovereignty or freedom in return for protection against the pain that may be occasioned through the predations of others. Republican conceptions regard human relations in terms of a collaboration between vulnerable but cooperative beings; dealings between people entail various forms of interpersonal attachment or belonging; and citizenship is therefore construed in solidaristic terms as a pooling of individual sovereignty and the promotion of social order, existential security and collective well-being.

The eudaimonic aspect of human well-being has received recognition from diverse quarters, including social psychologists (e.g., Maslow 1943) and Marxists (e.g., Fromm 1976). But a preference for a eudaimonic approach has also emerged from within the neo-Aristotelian tradition associated with Amartya Sen (1985, 1999). Sen has sought to promote the concept of human "capabilities." Capabilities are not the same as abilities.

The term refers not to what people are able to do, but to their freedom to choose and to lead the kind of lives they value. The concept cuts through the debate about whether human needs are absolute or culturally relative, but also the hierarchical distinction between base pleasures and "higher" forms of self-fulfillment. Sen's argument is that our need for and enjoyment of income and commodities will always be relative to the social and economic context. By contrast, our need for capabilities—for the freedom properly to function as members of human society—is absolute. Human capability is not necessarily the same as human capital since it is concerned with the integrity of the self, not with productive potential. For Sen, the test of well-being and the object of social development is not satisfaction; it is freedom.

Sen's approach is reflected in Doyal and Gough's influential theory of human need (1991), which specifies personal autonomy as a basic need. Doyal and Gough are concerned to define the "societal preconditions" that can ensure the optimal satisfaction of human need. From several quarters, then, there is explicit or implicit support for the idea that social development could or should contribute not to mere hedonic satisfaction, but to eudaimonic well-being. Put another way, "What we need in order to survive and what we need in order to flourish are two different things" (Ignatieff 1984, 10). The point from a eudaimonic perspective is not that survival and flourishing are different levels of human well-being, but that the fundamental nature of our humanity requires a particular *kind* of flourishing.

Arguably, however, despite his prominence, Sen's substantive influence upon the approach of the UNDP, for example, has been quite superficial. The prevailing establishment discourse assumes that human development and the reduction of poverty self-evidently require economic growth and that rights require liberal democracy. Each of these things requires a pluralistic context and a largely depoliticized public realm in which nongovernmental organizations (NGOs) and civil society groups can play a role as much as the state. It is claimed that—in the pursuit of human development—economic, social and cultural rights are as important as civil and political rights (UNDP 2000, 9). And yet, it would seem, the rights that matter most are rights to free trade. Fostering human development, therefore, is a matter of creating incentive structures, furnishing appropriate regulation and facilitating participation. Poor countries, it is supposed, should avail themselves of the opportunities that capitalist globalization can provide. And so, although it was Sen who set the initial tone of the *Human Development Report 2000* in its first chapter, subsequent chapters and reports take on the flavor of the new public managerialist discourse (J. Clarke 2004; Porter and Craig 2004): social development is to be achieved through standard setting and through technocratic processes, requiring such managerial techniques as self-assessment, benchmarking and culture change. The term "human capital" is insinuated as if it were a synonym for Sen's notion of "human capabilities." Sen himself has remarked upon the limitations of the term human capital on the grounds that "human beings are not merely means of production, but also the end of the exercise" (1999). The concept of human capital has become common currency within the dominant discourse. Though it may have had an application within critical sociological analysis (e.g., Bordieu 1997), as a metaphor in policy discourse, it takes on a distinctly reductive hedonic or utilitarian meaning. It is symptomatic of the economic and political orthodoxy once dubbed the "Washington Consensus" (Williamson 1990). Though the original proponents of the Washington Consensus may have learned from the worst excesses of the structural adjustment programs so disastrously visited on developing countries in the 1980s and 1990s (Townsend and Gordon 2002), the most favored recipe for social development still favors the liberalization of trade and financial markets, the privatization and deregulation of economic production, flexible labor markets, low public spending and taxation, and selective social "safety nets". The legacy of the consensus is an approach premised on a hedonic moral calculus of incentives and disincentives.

It is possible to bring together the intersecting distinctions between standards-based and rights-based approaches to social development, on the one hand, and hedonic and eudaimonic conceptions of well-being, on the other, to generate the taxonomy of social development strategies illustrated in Figure 10.1. The figure resembles but differs from that outlined in an earlier work (Dean 2001, 68) in which I used the distinctions developed by Mamdani (1996) between modernist/Eurocentrist and communitarian/Africanist approaches to development, on the one hand, and between authoritarian and emancipatory modes of politics, on the other. The former distinction resonates in part with the idea that rights-based approaches are "modernist", while the latter distinction equates to some extent with the idea that the eudaimonic tradition is emancipatory. However, the connections are, I concede, quite tenuous.

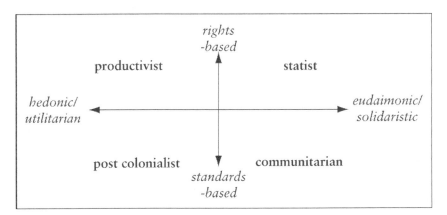

Figure 10.1 Competing strategies of social development.

The taxonomy may be compared in some aspects to that advanced by Midgley (1997), who has offered a threefold classification of externally imposed social development strategies: the enterprise or market-led strategy, which is linked to the "trickle-down" theory of economic development; the communitarian or community development strategy, which is linked to a trickle-up theory of economic development; and the statist or planned development strategy, which is linked to social democratic welfare economics. It may also be compared with a taxonomy proposed by Gough and Wood et al. (2004), which relates not to externally imposed social development strategies but to the substantive welfare regimes to be found in the global South: the "productivist," "insecurity," "informal security" and "welfare state" regimes (see also Dean 2003, 16).

What is here defined in Figure 10.1 as the **productivist** strategy, while it is rights-based, emphasizes civil and political rights, not social rights, and is concerned to promote social development and human well-being through wealth creation and the regulation of economic incentives. It is a version of Midgley's enterprise strategy, and it directly corresponds to the strategy attributed by Gough and Wood et al. to certain East Asian welfare regimes. A criticism of such strategy is that it may lead to uneven social development and social division. The **postcolonialist** strategy is standards-based, albeit that the standards are (more or less) beneficent prescriptions intended where possible to ensure the survival of the most disadvantaged. It is, in one sense, another less interventionist version of Midgley's enterprise strategy and, in another, it also corresponds to the substantive situation in the insecurity regimes to be found, according to Gough and Wood et al., amid the dysfunctional aftermath of colonial rule in—for example, much of Sub-Saharan Africa. A criticism of such strategy is that it will provide at best minimal well-being and at worst adverse forms of social inclusion. The **communitarian** strategy is based on standards that are commonly defined and is intended to allow every member of a community to flourish. It equates directly with the communitarian strategy defined by Midgley, and it corresponds to a certain extent to the substantive situation described by Gough and Wood et al. as informal security regimes in which—sometimes with assistance from the participatory antipoverty initiatives of external donors—human well-being is promoted through familial, kinship and community networks. A criticism of such strategy is that it may result in little more than the indirect manipulation of customary power and the reinforcement of patrimonial or clientalistic social relations. The **statist** strategy is rights based, emphasizing social rights, and is concerned to promote social development and human well-being through welfare provision guaranteed by the state. It equates directly with the statist strategy defined by Midgley and it corresponds to the welfare state strategy attributed by Gough and Wood et al. to certain Latin American welfare regimes, which can—up to a point—be considered with reference to the same kinds of criteria as those applied within welfare-state regime theories of Esping-Andersen and others. A criticism of such strategy is that it may lead to *dirigiste* and inflexible forms of provision that are inimical to well-being or to forms of relief that perpetuate rather than ameliorate structural inequalities.

The social development strategies defined by the taxonomy are, of course, ideal types. The taxonomy is no more than a model or heuristic device. It does not and is not intended to provide an adequate account of any actually existing welfare regime, since real welfare regimes are invariably hybrid in nature. Nonetheless, the taxonomy does provide a way of thinking about the ethical dimensions of social development.

FUTURE SCENARIOS

There is not the space in this chapter to develop and apply this model in any detail, nor is that my purpose. Our purpose here is briefly to discuss what ethical principles we might choose in the pursuit of social development. Though it is an oversimplification, the dominant consensus in social development, it would seem, is represented by the World Bank, on the one hand, and the World Trade Organisation (WTO), on the other (Deacon 2007; Deacon et al. 1997; Jordan 2006). Between them, these agencies envisage means-tested safety nets for the poorest, and self-provision through market-based insurance or investment products for those who can afford it. This strong productivist emphasis is tempered to an extent by the aspirations of the MDGs (see previous section) and by the development of various participatory antipoverty initiatives. But insofar as rights-based approaches are pursued, they are predominantly hedonic/utilitarian in their application, favoring civil and political rights above social rights. And insofar as eudaimonic/solidaristic approaches are accommodated, they are predominantly standards-based and broadly hostile to state-level intervention necessary to guarantee substantive social rights. It is possible, nonetheless, to point to a number of recent proposals that counter this consensus.

The Incremental Approach: The ILO

Within the UN's "family" of organizations, the International Labour Organisation (ILO) stands out, not least because it predates the UN, having been formed in 1919, and because since its Philadelphia Conference of 1944 it has remained committed to the cause of adequate social protection. As its name might imply, the ILO asserts that the best way that workers may achieve security is through "decent work"—that is, employment that is safe, dignified and adequately remunerated. In addition, nonetheless, the ILO has mounted what is billed as a *Global Campaign on Social Security and Coverage for All* (2001, 2006). It calls for nationally governed systems that provide income security during old age and in the event of sickness, disability or unemployment. Therefore, the ILO commits itself to the promotion of "standards" of social security provision through "social dialogue". The standards promulgated by the ILO are not legally enforceable, and their influence is entirely dependent upon the willingness of social actors to engage as social partners. Over the best part of a century, the ILO's progress in the face of opposing global interests has been at best modest.

The tradition to which the ILO has generally subscribed supports social insurance and universal forms of social security provision in preference to social assistance and means-tested safety nets. More recently, however, it has sought to engage not only with the gaps in social provision in the "developed" world but also with the absence of coverage throughout much of the "developing" world. Fundamentally, for any organization whose existence is premised upon the need for social protection in the context of a capitalist labor market, the problem from the ILO's perspective is that in parts of the global South, there is no labor market. Throughout much of Sub-Saharan Africa, for example, livelihoods remain dependent on subsistence agriculture. In regions such as Latin America, where extensive economic development has in fact occurred, a substantial proportion of the available employment is to be found in the informal economy and is beyond the reach of conventional contributory social insurance mechanisms (see also Beattie 2000). The issue, therefore, is not just about the affordability of social development in poor countries.

In exploring ways to promote social development, the ILO advocates the expansion of those existing compulsory social insurance schemes that have not yet achieved full coverage, but also the development of voluntary microinsurance schemes that might reach people not currently engaged in formal labor markets. There is nothing new about voluntary forms of social insurance (for health, pensions, etc.), but such schemes characteristically do not benefit the poorest sections of society and, if they do, they tend to deliver benefits that are both limited and short term in nature. There remains the possibility, however, that microinsurance schemes fostered at a local level with financial and technical assistance from the international community could represent an interim measure, establishing the basis for more extensive schemes in the future. To an extent, this might represent a more significant strategy than microfinance schemes (e.g., Yunus 1991) intended to promote individual enterprise, since it might in time provide a basis for reconciling the divide between formal and informal employment sectors.

The Pessimistic Approach: WeD

The Economic and Social Research Council's Well-being in Developing Countries (WeD) Research Group based at the University of Bath has been responsible for some innovative thinking about the application of welfare-regime theory to social policy in developing countries (Gough and Wood et al. 2004). This chapter has already drawn upon that body of work.

Geoff Wood and Julie Newton (2005) have attempted to move this agenda along in order practically to address the issues that apply in what they call "unsettled societies"—societies that lack not only a fully formalized labor market, but also a fully legitimized state apparatus. Their argument is that we should be thinking in terms of well-being rather than welfare regimes. The primary issue is capacity building, not social protection. Attention, they say, should shift from notions of human capability or autonomy to consider the substantive processes of alienation that deny well-being. In many parts of the world (Wood and Newton illustrate their arguments on the basis of their work in Bangladesh) and for much of the population, existential security can at present only be achieved by way of a "Faustian bargain" that perpetuates their material poverty. The process by which social development as a public good or a policy concession could come about is dependent upon the reform of the political order. Broader forms of social cohesion and integration are the conditions precedent for securing the enforceable security of livelihood.

The disturbing implication is that in parts of the world, more effective means of social development may for the time being remain an unachievable prospect. The essential insight that this offers, however, is that alternative mechanisms for promoting social solidarity are critical, and it is difficult to see how microlevel social development initiatives would provide a sufficient basis for this.

The Optimistic Approach: Townsend

In stark contrast, veteran social policy academic Peter Townsend (2002) advances the prospect and declaims the necessity of an international welfare state. Elements of what Townsend has in mind (see also Townsend 2007) may be summarized as follows:

- The international community must agree a more rigorous approach to the measurement of poverty and the monitoring of its alleviation.
- Means must be found effectively to enforce the observance of the rights to social security and to an adequate standard of living contained in UN human rights instruments—and the standards set by the ILO.
- A new international legal framework should be put in place so as to regulate the conduct of transnational corporations (as employers of labor and providers of services).
- Financial resources should be harnessed, partly by increasing the contributions made by the richest countries to overseas development aid, and partly through the introduction of a Tobin tax (a tax on international financial transactions).
- To give priority to the introduction and extension in developing countries of "universal" contributory social insurance and tax-financed

contingent benefit schemes—including and particularly child bene-fit—in preference to selective social safety nets.

The explicit emphasis is upon boldly translating the successful experiences of the developed welfare states—drawing especially upon those elements that promote eudaimonic well-being—to the developing world. And yet, when one considers what little headway the ILO have made in the face of the intransigence of other global interests and the telling insights offered by the WeD approach, one cannot help but feel that, despite the clarity of his analysis, Townsend is, perhaps, unduly optimistic.

The Radical Approach: The Global Left

Insofar as the historic Cold War between socialism and capitalism has ended with a global victory for capitalism (Fukuyama 1992), it is some-times supposed that socialism and "the Left" are now effectively dead. However, so long as anywhere in the world there is active resistance to capitalism, socialism is more than an atavistic curiosity. The clearest example of this is the emergence of the "antiglobalization" movement and the spectacular opposition it has mounted against the WTO and the G8 summits of rich nations. In practice, the antiglobalization movement represents an eclectic mixture of political groups, social movements and nongovernmental bodies. Nonetheless, the emergence of the Jubilee 2000 campaign for the reduction of "third world" debt and the burgeoning of movements like the World Social Forum (WSF) would seem to signal the basis of what amounts to an *anti-capitalist* alliance, with an alternative vision of a more "inclusive" form of globalization. The WSF has become in many ways a vehicle for a resurgent global Left. The WSF does not advance policy proposals, and there are those who would reject social development models originating in the global North (see discussion in Deacon 2007; Hardt and Negri 2000).

Nonetheless, some who have been active within the WSF, such as Alex Callinicos (2003), have envisioned a global campaign for an anticapitalist manifesto. This entails a transitional program that pragmatically incor-porates relatively familiar left-wing demands, including the introduction of universal basic income schemes, progressive and radically redistribu-tive forms of taxation, widespread reductions of working hours and the defense of public services, none of which by themselves would be sufficient to achieve socialism, but which together would amount to a fundamental challenge to capitalism.

Other academic activists within the WSF have argued that what should inform the global Left is an alternative epistemology. Boaventura de Sousa Santos (2006) has argued that the monocultural epistemology of the global North obscures and constrains alternative social ecologies, premised on different perceptions of knowledge, time, human identity, global scale and economic productivity. He refers to these alternatives as the "epistemology of the South": de Sousa Santos' analysis resonates with that of other critical postdevelopment theorists (e.g., Escobar 1995). The epistemology of the South, as the nascent alternative epistemology of the Global Left, implies a fundamentally eudaimonic conception of human well-being. De Sousa Santos contrasts what he calls the "axiology of progress and development that have justified untold destruction" with an "axiology of care". He alludes to this as an "ethical dimension" (2006, 31). He insists that "clues" to the future lie in the present, and this might imply support for the pragmatic strategy advocated by Callinicos, which, in turn, is not substantively speaking wholly dissimilar to Townsend's. Nor is such thinking necessarily out of step, for example, with some of the more radical ideas explored (but not adopted) by factions within the ILO, such as the notion of a Global Social Trust Network through which to redistribute funds from rich countries to fund social protection in poor countries (see Chicon et al. 2003).

SOCIAL DEVELOPMENT AND ETHICAL LIFE

My starting premise for this chapter was that social development is an ethical project. This claim is not an attempt to monopolize the moral high ground or to close down debate about the normative assumptions that inform competing conceptions of social development. The aim has been to focus on the extent to which social development can be conceived of in terms of ethical principles. Sen (1999), famously, contends that the object of development is freedom. Sen's capability approach—particularly in some theorists' hands (e.g., Nussbaum 2000, 2006)—entails an attempt to capture an essentially Aristotelian/eudaimonic vision of what constitutes a good life. For Sen, a good life must be freely chosen. But we might also speak of "ethical life," and one theorist who explicitly does so is Axel Honneth (1995).

Honneth has sought—drawing, inter alia, upon the work of Hegel and the social psychologist Mead—to reinterpret the development of human societies in terms of the struggle for recognition. For Honneth, "the reproduction of social life is governed by the imperative of mutual recognition" (1995, 92). His particular quest is for a normative theory premised on a distinctly eudaimonic interpretation of what is required for the good or ethical life. This normative theory rests on an empirical analysis of historical struggles that have progressed beyond conflicts between status groups to conflicts that bear upon individualized identity. There are three modes of intersubjective recognition that together play a part in the formation of identity and the realization of what Honneth would hold to be an ethical life: love, solidarity and rights.

Love provides the emotional substance of our more intimate relations of dependency. It is through caring for each other that we come to recognize, accommodate and respect each other as needy creatures. Honneth contends that love entails discovering and being oneself in and through another; love is therefore necessary for self-identity. Solidarity provides the basis on which to apprehend our shared responsibilities for strangers. It is through the sharing of ethical goals and cultural understandings with other members of a social group that we come to recognize, accommodate and respect each other as creatures defined though difference. Honneth contends that solidarity entails establishing one's traits and abilities though collective identity; solidarity is necessary for self-esteem. Finally, rights entail cognitive respect, a recognition of the subject's ethical capacity to make claims. Honneth contends that it is through rights that we come to recognize each other—not merely as proprietors, but as bearers of that universal capacity that characterizes human beings. There is an implicit affinity between this idea of a universal constitutive capacity and Sen's notion of capabilities. There is also an explicit affinity with Kant's categorical imperative, insofar as it is through rights, Honneth supposes, that we come to recognize each other as we would ourselves wish to be recognized; rights are necessary for self-respect. Honneth's argument is that all three modes of recognition are the subject of conflict and struggle.

Therefore, they must also, we might argue, be central to the process of social development. It is a very particular and somewhat abstractly drawn conception of what constitutes human well-being. Honneth is not a social development theorist, but the object of social development may be conceived in terms of promoting not only freedom but also "ethical life" for all peoples throughout the life course. It is an idea that captures a eudaimonic (and thick) rather than a hedonic (and thin) conception of well-being and that emphasizes the importance of substantive rights, not recommended standards. But what in this context is the basis of our rights—in particular, our rights to social provision? The question challenges us to reflect on the role of the state as the guarantor of social rights and on the nature of citizenship.

Turning to the question of the state, we might recall Gramsci's somewhat elusive notion of the "ethical state". An ethical state might reasonably be supposed to be, if not the precondition, then the medium for achieving ethical life. Gramsci (1988) equates the ethical state with a "regulated society" in which coercion is superseded and law subsumed. The state is not some "phantasmagorical entity", but a collective organism with a collective consciousness (244). The state, to use a different metaphor, distils the dominant ethos and, at any particular stage of social development, gives effect to social objectives. To this extent, existing states may be fatally flawed and forms of "statist" social development strategy (see Figure 10.1) may be ethically ill-conceived.

There is dispute as to the extent to which the nation-state is weakened by processes of globalization. Since the days of the nation-state *may* be numbered, commentators have variously argued that some form of transnational, postnational, global or cosmopolitan citizenship is likely in time to evolve (Dwyer 2004). Falk (1994), for example, has argued that quite apart from the consequences of economic globalization, there are a variety of grounds on which global as opposed to national citizenship might now be advocated: to satisfy aspirations for global peace and justice, to accommodate emerging forms of transnational political mobilization and to address the global ecological crisis. In particular, Held (1995) argues for a shift toward cosmopolitan governance, suggesting, among other things, the introduction over the longer term of an adequate and guaranteed basic income for all citizens and a new but unspecified form of international financial architecture to support this (see also Jordan 2006). It is relevant in this context that April 2007 saw the launch of a Campaign for the Establishment of a UN Parliamentary Assembly (see http://en.unpacampaign.org/index.php).

Nonetheless, in light of the obstacles outlined in the previous parts of this chapter, the idea of a form of cosmopolitan citizenship capable of delivering effective rights to social protection and human services is at best a distant prospect. For so long as the nation-state remains an actual or potential locus of policy-making for social development, it is necessary to address the capacity of the state to recognize, promote and protect the social as well as the civil and political rights of its citizens.

CONCLUSION

There can be no single "ethical path" to social development. Some of the arguments outlined in this chapter portend the possibility of approaches that transcend those characterized (or caricatured) in Figure 10.1. By and large, however, we must contend with approaches that are accommodated within the model that I have presented. If, in particular, there were a set of day-to-day principles that might be applied on the basis of a eudaimonic/ rights-based ideal, they would be as follows. They are ethical principles applicable to policy makers and practitioners, whether at an international, national or local level; whether working through governmental or nongovernmental agencies.

Social development initiatives would need to be, first, *universal in their approach*. That is to say, they should aim to reach "people as people". The phrase is redolent of aphorisms from Ubuntu philosophy (Ramose 2003), an ancient pan-African humanistic tradition and an example of an "epistemology of the South". Personhood is primarily defined not though productive or trading relations, but through the way that human beings care for and about each other. Social development should rest on deontological, not utilitarian assumptions: its purpose should be to underwrite the mutual obligations and attachments that people have for one another.

Second, they should be *nonconditional*. Interventions should put life needs first and should not be conditional upon compliance with particular norms of behavior. The primary aim should not be, for example, to promote the formation of human capital required for national productivity and competitiveness, but to guarantee the capabilities required for human development and "ethical life".

Finally, they should be *globally contextualized but locally grounded*. This applies in two senses. On the one hand, to achieve social development, it may be necessary in some instances to overcome the alienating or disabling effects of local relations of power; on the other hand, local demands and epistemologies may provide alternative understandings of human well-being that supersede hegemonic assumptions. This is not to suggest a relativistic compromise between top-down and bottom-up approaches, so much as to embrace the axiom that workable ethical principles have to be meaningful at both a global and a local level.

NOTES

1. This chapter draws extensively from other recently published work by the author, most particularly, Dean 2007a, 2007b, and 2008.
2. Like Marshall, I propose pragmatically to encompass within the term "social rights" the *economic* rights associated, for example, with employment, and the *cultural* rights associated, for example, with education and learning, on the one hand, and the pursuit of cultural or recreational activities, on the other. This, I acknowledge, may entail a degree of conceptual conflation, but it is done not least for the sake of brevity and convenience.

REFERENCES

Beattie, R. 2000. Social protection for all: But how? *International Labour Review* 139(2): 129–149.
Bordieu, P. 1997. The forms of capital. In *Education, culture, economy, society*, ed. A. Halsey, H. Lauder, P. Brown, and A. Wells, 46–58. Oxford: Oxford University Press.
Callinicos, A. 2003. *An anti-capitalist manifesto.* Cambridge: Polity.
Chicon, M., Pak, K., Leger, F., and Vergnaud, D. 2003. *A global social trust network: A new tool to combat poverty through social protection.* Geneva: International Labour Organisation.
Clarke, J. 2004. Dissolving the public realm? The logics and limits of neo-liberalism. *Journal of Social Policy* 33(1): 27–48.
Clarke, P. 1996. *Deep citizenship.* London: Pluto.
de Sousa Santos, B. 2006. *The rise of the global left: The world social forum and beyond.* London: Zed Books.
Deacon, B. 2007. *Global social policy and governance.* London: Sage.
Deacon, B., Hulse, M., and Stubbs, P. 1997. *Global social policy.* London: Sage.
Dean, H. 2001. Poverty and citizenship: Moral repertoires and welfare regimes. In *Poverty reduction: What role for the state in today's globalized economy?* ed. F. Wilson, N. Kanji, and E. Braathen, 54–73. London: CROP/Zed Books.
———. 2002. *Welfare rights and social policy.* Harlow: Prentice Hall.
———. 2003. *Discursive repertoires and the negotiation of wellbeing: Reflections on the WeD frameworks* (WeD Working Paper No. 04). Bath: Wellbeing in Developing Countries ESRC Research Group.

———. 2007a. Imagining a eudaimonic ethic of social security. Paper presented to the Foundation for International Studies on Social Security conference, "Social Security, Happiness and Well-being," Sigtuna, Sweden, June 15–17.

———. 2007b. The ethics of welfare-to-work. *Policy and Politics* 35(4): 573–589.

———. 2008. Social policy and human rights: Re-thinking the engagement. *Social Policy and Society* 7(1): 1–12.

Doyal, L., and Gough, I. 1991. *A theory of human need*. Basingstoke, UK: Macmillan.

Dwyer, P. 2004. *Understanding social citizenship*. Bristol: Policy Press.

Eide, A. 2001. Economic, social and cultural rights as human rights. In *Economic, Social and Cultural Rights: A textbook* (2nd ed.), ed. A. Eide, C. Krause, and A. Rosas, 9–28. Dordrecht: Martinus Nijhoff.

Escobar, A. 1995. Imagining a post-development era. In *The power of development*, ed. J. Crush, 211–227. London: Routledge.

Esping-Andersen, G. 1990. *The three worlds of welfare capitalism*. Cambridge: Polity.

Falk, R. 1994. The making of a global citizenship. In *The condition of citizenship*, ed. B. van Steenbergen, 127–140. London: Sage.

Fromm, E. 1976. *To have or to be?* London: Abacus.

Fukuyama, F. 1992. *The end of history and the last man*. New York: Basic Books.

Gilbert, N. 2004. *Transformation of the Welfare State*. Oxford: Oxford University Press.

Gough, I., Wood, G., Barrientos, A., Bevan, P., Davis, P., and Room, G. 2004. *Insecurity and welfare regimes in Asia, Africa and Latin America: Social policy in development contexts*. Cambridge: Cambridge University Press.

Gramsci, A. 1988. *A Gramsci reader*, ed. G. Forgacs. London: Lawrence & Wishart.

Habermas, J. 1987. *The theory of communicative action. Vol. 2: Lifeworld and system*. Cambridge: Polity.

Hardt, M., and Negri, A. 2000. *Empire*. Cambridge, MA: Harvard University Press.

Held, D. 1995. *Democracy and the global order: From the modern state to cosmopolitan governance*. Cambridge: Polity.

Honneth, A. 1995. *The struggle for recognition: The moral grammar of social conflicts*. Cambridge: Polity.

Hunt, P. 1996. *Reclaiming social rights*. Aldershot: Dartmouth/Ashgate.

Ignatieff, M. 1984. *The needs of strangers*. London: Chatto and Windus.

International Labour Organisation (ILO). 2001. *Social security: A new consensus*. Geneva: Author.

———. 2006. *Social security for all: Investing in global social and economic development*. Geneva: Author.

Jordan, B. 2006. *Social policy for the twenty-first century*. Cambridge: Polity.

Kymlicka, W. 1995. *Multicultural citizenship: A liberal theory of minority rights*. Oxford: Clarendon Press.

Mamdani, M. 1996. *Citizen and subject: Contemporary Africa and the legacy of late colonialism*. Princeton, NJ: Princeton University Press.

Marshall, T. H. 1950/1992. Citizenship and social class. In *Citizenship and social class*, ed. T. Marshall and T. Bottomore, 3–51. London: Pluto.

Maslow, A. 1943. A theory of human motivation. *Psychological Review* 50:370–396.

Midgley, J. 1997. *Social welfare in global context*. Sage: London.

Mishra, R. 1999. *Globalisation and the welfare State*. Hemel Hempstead: Harvester Wheatsheaf.

Nussbaum, M. 2000. *Women and human development: The capabilities approach.* Cambridge: Cambridge University Press.

———. 2006. *Frontiers of justice: Disability, nationality, species membership.* Cambridge, MA: Harvard University Press.

Office of the High Commissioner for Human Rights. 2002. *Draft guidelines: A human rights approach to poverty reduction strategies.* Geneva: United Nations.

Perez-Bustillo, C. 2001. The right to have rights: Poverty, ethnicity, multiculturalism and state power. In *Poverty reduction: What role for the state in today's globalised economy?* ed. F. Wilson, N. Kanji, and E. Braathen, 74–94. London: CROP/Zed Books.

Porter, D., and Craig, D. 2004. The third way and the third world: Poverty reduction and social inclusion in the rise of "inclusive" liberalism. *Review of International Political Economy* 11(2): 387–423.

Ramose, M. 2003. Globalisation and ubuntu. In *The African philosophy reader* (2nd ed.), ed. P. Coetzee and A. Roux, 626–648. London: Routledge.

Rawls, J. 1972. *A theory of justice.* Oxford: Oxford University Press.

Rosas, A. 2001. The right to development. In *Economic, social and cultural rights: A textbook* (2nd ed.), ed. A. Eide, C. Krause, and A. Rosas, 119–130. Dordrecht: Nijhoff.

Sen, A. 1985. *Commodities and capabilities.* Amsterdam: Elsevier.

———. 1999. *Development as freedom.* Oxford: Oxford University Press.

Townsend, P. 2002. Poverty, social exclusion and social polarisation: The need to construct an international welfare state. In *World poverty: New policies to defeat an old enemy,* ed. P. Townsend and D. Gordon, 3–24. Bristol: Policy Press.

———. 2007. *The right to social security and national development: Lessons from OECD experience for low-income countries* (Discussion paper 18). Geneva: International Labour Organisation.

Townsend, P., and Gordon, D., eds. 2002. *World poverty: New policies to defeat an old enemy.* Bristol: Policy Press.

United Nations Development Programme (UNDP). 2000. *Human development report 2000.* Oxford: Oxford University Press.

———. 2003. *Human development report 2003: Millennium development goals: A compact among nations to end human poverty.* New York: Oxford University Press.

Williamson, J. 1990. What Washington means by policy reform. Chapter 2 of *Latin American adjustment: How much has happened?* ed. J. Williamson. Washington, D.C.: Institute for International Economics.

Wood, G., and Newton, J. 2005. From welfare to well-being regimes: Engaging new agendas. Arusha Conference: "New Frontiers of Social Policy," World Bank, December 15.

Wronka, J. 1992. *Human rights and social policy in the 21st century.* Lanham, MA: University Press of America.

Yunus, M. 1991. *Grameen Bank: Experiences and reflections.* Dhaka: Grameen Bank.

Part IV
Future of Social Development

11 Toward a New Social Development

Brij Mohan

INTRODUCTION

New social development (NSD) is conceptualized as a postmaterial process of human-societal transformation that seeks to build identities of people, communities and nations. As a field and strategy of social reconstruction, it employs different models and modalities of *social practice* that suit varied situational-ideological imperatives in a given environment. By and large, two models characterized by centralized and decentralized location of power represent only the ends of a spectrum within the developmental process. This chapter is a critique of this duality and an exploration of new horizons suggesting a possible *third way.* An argument is made to rethink top-down and bottom-up models of development in light of new realities of the "post-American world." Postulates of a theory of NSD are proffered for further exploration, discussion and debate.

It is simplistic to theorize about social development within age-old individualistic-collectivist frameworks of analyses. The hazards of such a descriptive approach lead to misconceptions about the developmental process itself. I would argue that evolutionary development leads to theoretical persuasions in harmony with politico-historical situations, and not vice versa. To examine the dynamics of the issues involved, I attempt to use dialectic logic. It is argued that both top-down and bottom-up approaches are fraught with contradictions. We need to rethink these popular but misleading conceptions in a contextually coherent manner that unfolds the archaeology of the hegemonic systems. A counterhegemonic critique unravels the dynamics of coloniality in a "pro-developing" context, which is both logical and humane. I explore the three dimensions of modernity, ideology and postcoloniality in relation to the evolution of certain primary institutions—social, political, economic and cultural—that define and design the evolution and character of society-specific social development. The linearity of models, as currently in academic vogue, is both unsound and unhelpful. To facilitate this discussion, I apply a "comparative-analytic" framework that helps us see multilinearity of outcomes as a freedom–unfreedom paradigm (Mohan 1986, 1–2). The discussion that follows is broadly applied to a simplified systems model involving society, community and individual as three units of analysis: (1) society, countersociety and culture; (2) community and its dissolution; and (3) individual and dehumanization.

THE CONTEXT

Welfare systems are "complexes of complementary policies that [are] most usefully viewed in their entirety" (Haggard and Kaufman 2008, xix). When *social* prefixes work, policy, welfare, security and development, the whole fulcrum of human-social well-being assumes a variegated character. The idea of social development is perhaps innate in the primordial nature of social contract that is the foundation of modern civil society. Human-social evolution, however, did not follow a linear pattern. The history of geopolitical contours of contemporary societies and cultures contains vivid fingerprints of how we have evolved as a human species: similar but unequal; free and unfree; advanced and developing; rich and poor; and rulers and ruled. Developmental paradigms manifest politico-cultural diversities and conflicts. A universal model of social development is a fantasy, a euphemism for neoimperial delusion.

Johan Galtung (1998, vii), the Norwegian scientist, writes in the Foreword to *Ideas of Social Order in the Ancient World* by Vilho Harle (1998),

> We live in a globalizing world. International relations are global relations, not only the foreign policy of a major country or regional relations. How can anyone dare draw upon theory developed in only one region? What kind of provincialism sustains that type of intellectual laziness? (vii)

According to the Community Services Council of Newfoundland and Labrador (2003), "Social Development encompasses a commitment to individual well-being and volunteerism, and the opportunity for citizens to determine their own needs and to influence decisions which affect them. Social development incorporates public concerns in developing social policy and economic initiatives."

Kantian *Perpetual Peace* perhaps encapsulates the essence of Enlightenment dreams that heralded a new age of reason. The ideas, discoveries and innovations that ensued in the following two centuries changed our world forever. As new knowledge and wisdom sprouted through the rugged terrains of old habits of thought and belief, a new transformatory consciousness embraced social evolution of diverse identities and conflicts. Albert Camus famously said, "All modern revolutions have ended in a reinforcement of the power of the State".

The postindustrial society is in a nontraditional transformatory flux. We find confluence and ambiguities that defy any ideologically correct explanation. China and India, for example, represent two top-down and bottom-up models of development. Yet it is hard to generalize. "The real effect of globalization," says Fareed Zakaria (2008), "has been an efflorescence of the local and the modern" (83). How postmodernity will resolve the contradictions of this multilinear development is something about which we can only speculate.

The two approaches, top-down and bottom-up, that are in focus, however, are not symbiotic. They portend to be a compound without any linear explanation. However, what we confront is a Faustian "output" of development in a contrapuntal culture (see Berry 2008). Modernity's triumphalism is not at all a parable of progress. Our advancements are many and genuine, but the irony is that these material strides have all been sources of perennial stress and continued misery. At the cusps of "end of history" (Fukuyama 1989), we witness a societal meltdown. While the state continues to be stable, one may question the validity of the *social contract* that led some governments to save their peoples from themselves. Moreover, while the fall of the Berlin Wall gave us a renewed hope of a globally unified world with states openly interacting with each other in the evolutionary process, the end of the Cold War in reality proved to be an illusion. The post-Iraq reality is a tipping point in a lingering audacity. It is the end of dreams (Kagan 2008).

However, the Platonic paradigm of a utopian republic had begun to crumble long before. Perhaps it never existed. The emergence of rogue states and fundamentalist terrorism, compounded by the contradictions of a unipolar universe, had created new realties that impacted the practice of science and values. This "return of history" is perhaps embedded in the evolution of human nature. Robert Kagan (2008) concludes,

> The great fallacy of our era has been the belief that a liberal international order rests on the triumph of ideas and on the natural unfolding of human progress . . . Our political philosophers imagine a grand historical dialectic, in which the battle of worldviews over the centuries produces, in the end, the correct liberal democratic answer . . . Such illusions are true enough to be dangerous. (102)

Social development as an approach to uplifting societal-human conditions is a result of post-Enlightenment consciousness. Then postcolonial experiences and redemptive awareness further hastened the processes of modernization followed by democratization and globalization. By default and design, social development has evolved as a Western approach to "develop" the so-called Third World referred to as *developing nations*. This conceptualization, and the schools that continue to follow this model, is inherently flawed. Poverty, illiteracy, violence and backwardness are not exclusively the others' (developing world) problems. Developed, industrialized nations, in many ways, are equally victims of the scourges of ignorance and arrogance that breed, incubate and perpetuate these "third world" problems. A sensible transformational approach beyond historical, territorial and ideological trappings warrants a global paradigm. The ideal of global democracy mandates this imperative. Sustainable development cannot sustain when sustainability is in danger.

DIALECTICS AND CONUNDRUMS

Frederik Kaufman argues that the concept of sustainability is in danger of being used to serve the ends of a mass-consumer society, if it promises to allow us to continue our consumerist way of life without the usual environmental damage. He argues that even if we achieve what many supporters of sustainable development envision—namely, modes of production, distribution and consumption that minimize environmental degradation—as a culture, we will be no better off than we are now. Rather than being a mere technological fix that permits us to live more or less as we do now, an enlightened form of sustainable development presupposes a more sophisticated account of the ends that it is intended to serve. Moreover, to the extent that sustainable development ignores past environmental and social harms caused by distorted consumer desires, it fails to acknowledge the demands of justice (Kaufman 2009, 390).

"Output without Development"[1]

"We have a deal in Copenhagen," UN Secretary-General Ban Ki-moon said, adding that "this is just the beginning" of a process to craft a binding pact to reduce emissions. Disputes between rich and poor countries and between the world's biggest carbon polluters—China and the U.S.-dominated the two-week conference in Copenhagen, the largest and most important UN meeting ever on fighting global warming. While Obama labeled the conference outcome an "unprecedented breakthrough", protesters in the streets of Copenhagen demanded "System Change Not Climate Change".[2] The environmental groups called this deal "a triumph of spin over substance".[3] But the accord delivered by the Copenhagen climate talks is hardly far-reaching (*The Economist* 2009d). A conservative presidential hopeful in the U.S., Mike Huckabee, "thinks the climate summit in Copenhagen is a waste of time" (*The Economist* 2009a, 36).

Issues and problems follow a multilinear pattern. Social development is a process of redevelopment and deconstruction that involves a complex dimensionality of time, space and politico-cultural imperatives. At each level, the individual, groups and communities are in interaction with each other. This intrasocietal encounter is not alienated from its own universe. What is happening in Chad and Darfur may seem to be an isolated regional problem in Africa. Its causes and consequences, however, go deep beyond historical and geographical boundaries. An appreciation of this postulate will help understand the dynamics of NSD.

In the postwar era, the developing nations attained their freedom. Why, then, is "the Third World" still a *White Man's Burden* (Easterly 2006)? Development as a process of reconstruction, renewal and regeneration continues its meandering path without achieving transformation. The lingering contradictions and inequalities of nations run counter to the principles of universal democracy and human rights. As a consequence, externally imposed interventions and internally designed models of change have yielded outcomes that are neither desired nor benign. This counterproductivity by way of serendipity is the reason why neither the top-down nor bottom-up approach has ever succeeded. Before we discuss the issues at the three elemental systemic levels identified in the introduction, let us first dissect the anatomy of this dualist formulation.

The top-down model is essentially an elitist structure designed to govern the masses in an authoritarian state. The bottom-up one is posited in the opposites in regard to governmentality, its force, ideology and possible outcomes. In *The Return of History* (2008), Robert Kagan analyses these two forces as "autocracy" and "democracy" (62, 68, 74). One can see that the postulated duality is more abstract than real. It appears that order and freedom are not analogous concepts. Direct democratization solves one problem but creates what is best symbolized by what James Madison called "tyranny of the majority". While its extreme is found in China's one-party rule, its pluralist hypermanifestations are rampant in California. Ronald George, the chief justice of California, recently remarked, "Chickens gained valuable rights on the same day that gay men and lesbians lost them" (*The Economist* 2009c, 47).

The family of nation-states is a metaphorical allusion that underscores the idea and philosophy of global social development. The reality is anything but. The "family of nations" is dysfunctional at best. If nation-states have to be saved from this mega-dysfunctionality, world leaders and citizens

Table 11.1   Elemental Features of the Two Prevalent Models

MODEL	Government	Force	Ideology	Possible Outcomes
Top-Down ▼	Statist design; vertical	Centripetal; centralized	Authoritarianism antidialogical	Dictatorial system, oppression and massive alienation
Bottom-Up ▲	Grassroots democracy: horizontal	Centrifugal; decentralized	Populism; quasi-dialogical	Freedom; lack of order; anomie and chaos

of this new world order will have to think outside the box, both critically and globally. The imminent food crisis and the politics of hunger is a case in point. *The New York Times* editorializes a recent UN food summit when the world's more-developed nations proved, once again, that domestic politics trump both humanitarian concerns and sound strategic calculations:

After 9/11 the world's richest nations saw the link between hunger, alienation and terrorism. They offered a trade deal to eliminate the agricultural subsidies and tariffs that were pushing farmers in developing countries out of the market and further into poverty. Seven years later the tariffs and subsidies are still there. ("Politics and hunger" 2008)

While the state as an institution has survived and government continues to be a viable mechanism, one wonders if the legitimacy of each still holds in a world still mired in primitivistic violence. It is not merely Iraq, Afghanistan and a few other "rogue" and "dangerous" nations that should be on our mind. The governmentality of advanced nations must be laid out for critical investigation in search of enduring prognosis. To illustrate this point, I use a feminist perspective that unravels our collective response to 9/11, a crisis that will continue to haunt Americans for a long time:

The post-9/11 commentaries were riddled with apprehensions that America was lacking in masculine fortitude that the masses of weak-chinned BlackBerry clutchers had left the nation open to attack and wouldn't have the cojones for the confrontations ahead. . . . The bog ruminations of the director of mensaction.net, who was a former military officer himself, was particularly Ripperian. "The phallic symbol of America had been cut off", he wrote of the World Trade Centre, "and at its base was a large smouldering vagina, the true symbol of the American culture, for it is the western culture that represents the feminine materialist principle, and it is at its extreme in America". (Faludi 2007, 8–9)

The perils of progress seem to imperil the future of social development as we would like to see. Sartre famously said, "Success is not progress". Social development, as we find today, is an illusion, a manipulated reality at best. As against top-down and bottom-up, we actually see an "onwards and upwards" trajectory of this developmental process as brilliantly analyzed in a cover story by *The Economist*. The Hungarian Imre Madach's poetic drama, "The Tragedy of Man," published in 1861, "describes how Adam is cast out of the Garden with Eve, renounces God and determines to create Eden through his own efforts" (*The Economist* 2009b, 37). Indeed, the time to rewrite a new Genesis has come. The Hungarian parable brilliantly illustrates the rise and fall of the Enlightenment itself. It is the crisis of modernity that postindustrial society has monumentally failed to overcome. I have extensively elaborated the idea of a new *social contract* as the basis of Enlightenment. To rise *onwards and upwards* beyond the *fallacies of development*—a critique of the contemporary interventionist approach to social development that unravels social development as a paradox of the dissonance of domination (Mohan 2007). Social development has become a myth created by a sense of guilt to compensate for the terrible damage that violence, exploitation, war and terror left behind as the debris of colonialism. The *development delusion* in our globalized culture is a fascinating subject for informed debate (Mohan 2008, 83–88).

The kitsch of "developmentalism" lacks legitimacy and relevance in a "flattening" world. From "nation building" to globalization, there are harsh dualities in a complex neoglobal order that breed certain "de-developmentality". The idea of NSD signifies the symbiosis of human and social development as a mega-project of global-social transformation. The foundation of progress, it may be argued, is rooted in the conviviality of a postideological coexistence. This implies that a second Enlightenment is an imperative of our future—that is to say, a new epoch that promotes counterhegemonic analyses, policies and programs at the expense of age-old myths is in order. But how can we deliver a world from the scourges of poverty, intolerance and war when all around us socio-ethno-economic (and physical) barriers are being built to replace those we thought, for a moment, had crumbled; when terror and counterterror have replaced civility; and when true believers on all sides are caught in a myopic, arrogant delusion? (Mohan 2008, 2007)

The top-down social development activity is not confined to centralized, authoritarian dictatorial regimes wallowing in traditional or modern bureaucracies. Much of International Monetary Fund (IMF), UN and World Bank assistance to developing nations falls prey to the corrupt theocracies of control. A glittering example is a failed strategy of paying $10 billion to Parvez Musharraf's post-9/11 Pakistan to fight terrorism and Al Qaeda insurgency. If probed further, the consequences of *Charlie Wilson's War* reveal disturbing facts, such as that the U.S. did nothing for schools after fighting off the Soviet tanks with Stinger missiles.[4] No wonder that *madrasas* cropped up like mushrooms in the fertile fanatic fields at the end of the Cold War. Social development in the wake of such foreign interventions turns history into a cruel tragedy and farce.

Mass movements from revolutions to Gandhian Sataygrah best exemplify the bottom-up model of development. The Barak Obama phenomenon is an American reality. For the sake of argument, Talibanization may also be viewed as a reactionary grassroots Islamist movement for the attainment of a countersociety. But it is not a person (individual)-focused model. It is quite an anti-individual, anachronistic approach to establishing the fundamentalist Utopia in a digital age. You—the person—"had a great run as Person of the Year 2006". Essayist James Poniewozik concludes (2007–2008): "You're probably just as glad to take off that POY 2006 tiara and go back to dreaming up the future and getting recognized for it, much later, by the rest of us. It's still your world, after all. They just pretend to run it" (174).

In India, a bank for street children has been established. This is another example of a bottom-up program of development. Henry Chu (2008) reports from New Delhi: "Run almost entirely by the youths, a bare-bones bank sponsored by a charity offers a place to stash meager earnings and learn about saving and planning". The history-making rise of Barak Obama as the first African American presidential candidate is also attributable to basic grassroots community-development strategies, which augers well in *the post-American world*.

NEW HORIZONS

Development involves extracting a clear picture. John Williams (1993) reports,

> In a report issued recently in London, the United Nations Children's Fund takes an imaginative new look at the problems of "social development", the catchall euphemism for the evils of poverty, illiteracy, malnutrition, sickness and early death. Entitled "The Progress of Nations," the report ranks national achievement in social development. But it makes clear that the pursuit of development is often an extremely inexact undertaking, rather like blindman's buff. And the blindfold, Unicef says, is a lack of reliable statistics. The report starts with the good news. The minimum needs of most people in the Third World are at last being met. But the lack of accurate statistics is a major obstacle to further progress, Unicef says. In many Third World countries, more is known about VCR imports than about child literacy or maternal mortality.

Modern slavery persists in many forms. Organized sex trafficking of neglected and "thrown away" children is one of the most grievous and offensive crimes. Recently, 345 people were arrested in the U.S. as the Department of Justice concluded five years of its Operation Cross Country. "These kids are victims. This is a 21st Century slavery," says Ernie Allen, president of the National Center for Missing and Exploited Children ("345 Arrested" 2008). On reflection, it is quintessentially a question that the social develomentalist must answer: how, and at what price, do we want to achieve human equality and social justice for all people? Can a faith-based theodicy ever achieve democracy anywhere? Can a civilization that has unleashed a mindless war against mother earth resist the temptation to eschew its own self-destructive trappings?[5]

Social development is intrinsically related to some of the nagging issues that plague our civilization. While our economists and other brands of scientists tend to offer lip service to the vital question of human survival, philosophers, statesmen and world leaders ought to take a serious look at the whole spectrum of issues that connect each one of us on this endangered planet. Poverty of ideas, insanity of war and mindless destruction of ecosystems are intrinsically related issues, which polarity doctrines have failed to answer. A neoideological conflict is underway; it is not the struggle between "the forces of democracy and the forces of autocracy" such as the world confronted in the nineteenth and twentieth century (Kagan 2008, 58). In a postideological context, modern societies are morphing into a postindustrial era where national interests, identities and histories are increasingly playing dominant roles. NSD offers a dynamic view of world realties toward a possible theory and practice: *new global development.*

Despite being the most important and fertile field of knowledge, inquiry, research and interdisciplinary dialogue, social development remains an *incomplete discipline.* While there are a few undergraduate-like textual exercises, no comprehensive system is available to study multifaceted issues and problems in the field of social development, and that seeks to do the following:

1. Explore and attempt to synthesize certain universal commonalities that help define the nature and challenges of social development as a process of social transformation
2. Study local, regional, national and international social issues and problems that call for critical understanding of the dynamics and dimensions of complex developmental processes
3. Achieve a multilinear but unified body of descriptive, historico-analytical zeitgeist that helps unravel social development as a universal project beyond contemporary narcissisms
4. Unravel a fulcrum of identities that build creative systems of development with inclusive coherence and pluralist structures
5. Develop primordial linkages of inter- and intrasocietal networks that humanize technological and scientific advancements and assist in achieving societal progress and human well-being.

I postulate twelve independent but related categories to identify the whole spectrum of social development issues, policies, programs and problems. Table 11.2 is an attempt to unravel the magnitude and scope of social development.

The idea of NSD is an evolution of postmaterial consciousness that seeks social transformation; it employs *social practice* as a unifying modality based on universal values; and it rests on certain postideological postulates that promote peaceful coexistence alongside the diversity of peoples and without inequality and injustice (Mohan 1992). However, new social development, as a specialized field of study and practice, continues to suffer an identity problem because of the overlapping persuasions, interests and missions of its proponents. The poverty of imagination is a U.S.-based professional complexity that impedes the development of NSD (Mohan 2010)

Table 11.2   Social Development: Old and New Paradigms

Core Categories	Social Development Issues, Policies, Programs and Problems (These are not exclusive categories)
I. The Development Paradigm	1. Concepts and constructs; 2. history and evolution; 3. international society; 4. freedom and unfreedom; 5. globalization; democratization
II. The Zeitgeist, Culture of Social Development	1. Ideology, politics of social development; 2. sociology of social development; 3. economics of social development; 4. ethics of social development; 5. philosophy; 6. theory and practice of social development; 7. interdisciplinarity of social development (disciplinarity and interdisciplinarity issues; international social work; comparative social development)
III. The Signature Pedagogies	*Some exemplars:* 1. Bhoodan; 2. Sarvodaya; 3. community development and five-year plans in India; 4. Grameen Bank of Bangladesh; Kibbutz in Israel; 5. other community and locality development innovations
IV. Crossnational Issues and International Problems and Programs	1. Global development; global welfare; global North–South divide; internationalization of social problems; 5. poverty, illiteracy, population, HIV/AIDS; 6. health, education; 7. human trafficking; 8. Third World indebtedness; 9. migration, immigration and related issues; 10. refugees; 11. NGOs' role; 12. organizations: UN, IMF, World Bank; UNESCO, etc.; 13. UN and social development
VI. Environmental Justice	1. Global warming; 2. water crisis; 3. species extinction; 4. environmental (catastrophes; justice; racism)
VII. The World is "Flat"	1. Technology; 2. information revolution: the digital fauna; 3. media, entertainment; 4) globalization and democratization
VIII. Global Conflicts	1. War and development; 2. ethnic cleansing and genocide; 3. terror and terrorism; 4. violence and counterviolence; 5. fundamentalism; 6. blood diamonds; 7. children of war; 8. domestic and interpersonal violence, abuse and terrorism; 9. militarism, nuclearization and social development; 10. water wars; 11. peaceful social development
IX. Regional-Sectoral Issues	1. The rise and fall of the Third World; 2. rural/urban/exurban development; 3. demography of development

Continued

Table 11.2   continued

X. New Social Development (NSD)	1. Challenges to NSD; 2. social movements in the developmental transformation; 3. race, gender, and class, and NSD; 4. Gandhian philosophy and practice; 5. colonialism and social development; 6. postcoloniality and social development; 7. comparative social development; 8. international social work and social development: social work education, practice and research (SW-EPR) in developmental praxis
XI. Aspects and Issues in NSD	1. Social policy and social development; 2. social work and social development; 3. public welfare and social development; 4. public health, HIV/AIDS, nursing and social development; 5. trends and developments in social development; 6. human diversity and social development; 7. human rights and social development; 8. women and social development; 9. youth policy, services and programs; 10. alternative lifestyles and NSD; 11. the state and social development; philanthropy, altruism and social development; 12. NGOs and social development; 13. national development and progress; 14. social development and de-development; paradoxy of development; sectors of social development; 15. corporate responsibility, accountability and criminality; 16. world hunger and social development; 17. community and social development; research in social development; 18. interdisciplinarity of social development; 19. sustainability and social development; 20. international debt and social development; 21. childcare and social development; 22. aging and elderly services; 23. global and social development; 24. September 11 and social development; 25. human-social development; 26. freedom, unfreedom and social development; 27. good government; 28. new social contract and Enlightenment II
XII = I to XI: Counter development	The rise of a countersociety and its varied manifestations and consequences; "poverty of culture" (Mohan 2010).

and its identity (e.g., see the Council on Social Work Education concept of international social work and social development; Estes 2009, 13).

Kenneth Boulding, in his well-known essay on "The Boundaries of Social Policy" (1967) emphasized identity building as the goal of social policy, because economic policies, he argued, are essentially alienating unless public policies are wedded to achieving social justice (see also Mohan 1998). Amrtya Sen (1999) delivered almost the same message at Oxford. Leonard Trelawny Hobhouse's notion of liberty, social change and rationality as the foundation of societies moving toward a world state first set the tone for the construction of social development as a process (1924). The ideals of international citizenship and a global society are based on "rational-humane" considerations. The Enlightenment values that promoted scientific advancements did not, however, go hand in hand with social development. The hiatus that remains is perhaps the greatest challenge that NSD seeks to fulfill, lest the pessimist may finally win. NSD, in sum, involves three elemental postulates as preconditions, agenda and clarificatory substance. These three intertwined constructs are premised on the notion that postindustrial society has failed to reconstruct itself, and its deconstruction, however utopian it may look, rests on reinventing social contract that will synergize global forces towards a second enlightenment: Enlightenment II. This new development synergy is the essence of the new social development that calls for the following:

1. *Global development*: radical human-social transformation (Mohan 1992). Globalization implies the universalization of basic tenets of an international society that is reorganized on the basis of a new social contract among all those nation-states that agree to adhere to peaceful coexistence, implying abandonment of violence and terror as means of social control). This calls for radical human-social transformation (Mohan 1992).
2. *Enlightenment II*: knowledge-based "social practice" (Mohan 2003, 2007). Reason and science have not succeeded in achieving the goals of Enlightenment. A new revolution for global renaissance calls for Enlightenment II—a stage when scientism is enslaved to promote human well-being. This calls for liberating knowledge-based "social practice" that seeks to uplift human conditions (Mohan 2003, 2007).
3. *New social contract*: establishment of communitarian social equality and justice at the expense of "poverty of culture" (Mohan 2010). Contemporary conflict-ridden societies have become sectors of glamour and gloom. The specter is manifested, in a relatively short distance, by Burj Kahilafa (world's tallest building in Dubai) and Yemen's jihadist chaos. On a much larger level, China's economic triumph, on the one hand, and its lip service to human rights, on the other; India's hyped prosperity in the service domain and pervasive poverty in the blighted slums; and America's military prowess and technological advancements, on the one hand, and its failure to internationalize the American creed in a meaningful, rational and humane order, on the other hand—all testify to the paradoxical reality of this civilization's monumental failure to combat the evils of terror, counterterror, poverty and new forms of slavery. I believe it is the "poverty of culture" (Mohan 2010) that thwarts the progress of nations in a communitarian sense of equality and social justice. The nations of Europe and North America have invaded, coerced, conquered and ruled other societies over the last six hundred years. Their reliance on superior

technology did not guarantee success (Headrick 2009). The hegemony of imperialist power over peoples continued until democratic aspirations threatened the age-old trappings of top-down models of governance. NSD lends support to a new social contract for global equality, universal justice and world peace as a unifying theme for the survival of the human family.

"SOCIAL WORK WITH GUNS"[7]: THE RISE OF A COUNTERSOCIETY

Andrew Bacevich depicts a disturbing profile of "the Pax Americana on steroids" that clearly pursues violence and terror as "awe and shock" to maintain the American way of life ("Social Work with Guns" 2009, 7–8). The new strategy reflecting Barak Obama's "change" seems old wine in a new bottle. What Lieutenant General Robert Wagner said in 2004 is a "reset," in McChrystal's words. The belated realization on the part of military professionals is summarized here:

> Rather than a giant computer game, modern wars turned out to be more *like social work with guns*. On the contemporary battlefield, weapons were less important than cultural sensitivity. The real challenge facing US forces was not to kill the enemy but to win over the population. As David Kilcullen, an influential advisor to US commanders in Iraq and Afghanistan, put it, rather than 'assuming that killing insurgents is the key task,' the military needed to focus on 'good governance backed by solid population security and economic development' (8; emphasis added).

One of the puzzling aspects of development theory is its fallacious premise that societal conditions will improve in proportion to the knowledge and resources that we employ to uplift the human condition. On the face of it, it is a positivistic and promising hypothesis. However, human banality defies its logic. This perhaps is the single most important reason why top-down approaches have not delivered as expected.

Let us examine this aspect from the vantage of crime and violence. Why is crime rising in so many American cities? Hanna Rosin (2008) "implicates one of the most celebrated antipoverty programs of recent decades" (40). In a typical functional-positivistic vein, social scientists and policy makers sought to transform the dreaded housing projects with an idea of a middle class, which would eliminate both despair and crime. But this did not happen. Persistent poverty perpetuating dysfunctional behaviors in a hopelessly racist society could not be transformed by the replacement of buildings and blocks. The following case study is instructive:

> Not every project was like Cabrini-Green. Dixie Homes was a complex of two- and three-story brick buildings on grassy plots. It was,

by all accounts, claustrophobic, sometimes badly maintained, and occasionally violent. But to its residents, it was, above all, a community
... Demonizing the high-rises has blinded some city officials to what
was good and necessary about the projects, and what they ultimately
have to find is a way to replace the sense of belonging, the informal
economy, and the easy access to social services. (54)

Social development and community development are symbiotic processes.
Achieving community cohesion in a culture that has destroyed community
as a concept and in practice is a search for the nonexistent reality. The same
is true of *social* development. Debates about trends and patterns only compound conundrums of change. This reality is so vividly descriptive of the
other world, euphemistically called "developing nations," where the multilinear evolution of both society and state is changing the textbook definitions. Colonial and imperial regimes took over nations and rendered them
stateless without any sovereignty. The recent, and perhaps more dangerous,
trend is when societies are transformed into their counterexistence by the
use of violence and counterviolence. Perhaps Iraqification and Afghanista-
nization exemplify this. Pakistan is also nearly at the brink of this psy-
chometamorphosis. Soon after Benazir Bhutto's assassination, Pakistan's
"democratic" People Party leadership was bequeathed to her nineteen-year-
old son, a student in Oxford. Extralegal controls have trumped state prowess in nearly all aspects of life. On the urban front, Karachi's new skyline is
emerging as a haven for Middle Eastern investments and local mafia, both
of which are building luxury and middle-class penthouses and middle-class
apartments for those who can pay, bribe and withstand the uncertainties
of a state in flux.[8] Democracy and development have lost meaning in the
ideological fog of unprincipled politics. "Benazir not only understood that
Pakistan was a chaotic country, she often seemed almost to court chaos
as an ally," Mr. Weisman writes. "I believe that this, in effect, was her
strategy in her current return", writes Patrick Lyons (2007), *The Times'*
former chief correspondent in New Delhi. A new book implicating the
"nation building" strategies of development by Ahmed Rasheed, *Descent
into Chaos*, validates this observation (2008).[9] Pakistan, the most organized postcolonial chaos, teeters on the brink of total collapse as President
Zardari's corrupt leadership is once again under fire. *The Aid Trap*, Glenn
Hubbard and William Duggan (2009) argue, must be revamped as the system of economic development has failed.

The developing world has often been a slate on which the feudal-colonial
forces have dictated the contours of change, which are not always benign.
One must question the premise of transferability of democratic institutions, especially where feudal-tribal-colonial legacies continue to bedevil
society and culture. Pakistan, Afghanistan, Iraq, Iran, Kenya, China and
even Russia will adapt to democratic institutions only in harmony with
their own national traditions. Democracy, therefore, is not a universally

accepted model. "A healthy respect for the enduring power of local political primitivism and a willingness to adapt to it", writes Charles Krauthammer (2008), is a realistic strategy. He concludes,

> Democracy was meant to be the antithesis of feudalism . . . How many decades will it take before we acknowledge that economic liberalization leads to political liberalization may not be axiomatic? . . . In Iraq, that means letting centralized top-down governance give way, at least temporarily, to provincial and tribal autonomy as the best means of producing effective representative institutions . . . For the spread of democracy today, we need to practice our own brand of syncretism and learn not to abandon the field when forced to settle for regional adaptations that fall short of the Jeffersonian ideal. (7B)

Joshua Hammer (2007), who spent six years in Africa as a bureau chief for Newsweek, writes about the African Front: "Kenya's remote north has become a battleground for rising Islamism and its pro-American opponents. Have aggressive post-9/11 policies fomented the very sectarianism they were meant to fight?" Other vignettes of counterdevelopment are in order: "What is creeping into Kenyan psyche is [anger] at American people themselves", Hammer said. "We wonder how they can go on supporting this regime that is brutalizing people like this?" He asked Kimathi if Americans have reason to fear an Islamic awakening in the Kenyan north. "They have reason to fear", he replied: "But their means of combating the awakening is wrong. The hard manner with which they come down on so-called 'radical Islam' does not quell it; it actually propels it higher". In Haiti, "The scrap-wood shanties on a muddy hillside are a poor man's promised land. They have leaky roofs and dirt floors, with no lights or running water. But hundreds of Haitian migrants have risked their lives to come here and work the surrounding fields, and they are part of a global trend: migrants who move to poor countries from even poorer ones", reports Juan Gomez from Dominican Republic.

Congo, Somalia, Yemen and Sudan are other examples of counterdevelopment. When ethnic cleansing becomes state policy and the world watches it with helplessness and impunity, one should not speak of a "family of nations". It is thus abundantly clear that top-down and bottom-up models are not completely exclusive of each other. History and geography impact each other to design the contours of development. The confluence of mitigating forces warrants a *third way* to approach global development from a realistic yet egalitarian point of view.

TOWARD A NEW SOCIAL DEVELOPMENT

An argument for or against the top-down or bottom-up approach is dated. NSD is a postideological outcome of a new reality. Crossnationally, societies and their states are locked into a cobra-mongoose dilemma. The West has failed in its postcolonial nation building. *Afghanistization* represents a meltdown of both the civil society and the state; while Pakistan still endures as a society, as a state, it faces an existential crisis of legitimacy. The two polarities of power—that is, from top and bottom—are locked into a deadlock at each other's expense. This state of counterdevelopment defines *de-developmentality* with far reaching implications for global welfare.

Euphemistically, "stability" is used to underscore the universal need for "order". However, varied versions of *democracy* have not always followed the avowed path of *freedom*. As a consequence, we are *free* in an *unfree* world. Social development itself has become a euphemism for a host of agendas that suit international agencies, foundations, governments and organizations. The target populations are seldom partners in choosing the mode and models of interventions (Mohan 2009). It is the "decider"— whether a president of a country or World Bank or IMF—who decides the contents and contours of developmental planning. The outcome is massive alienation of people in the reconstruction of their destinies. That explains "why the West's efforts to aid the rest have done so much ill and so little good" (Easterly 2006).

No working system can effectively deliver and exist without people's participation, feedback and accountability. The "white man's burden" attitude (see Easterly 2006) has nearly cemented the myth that top-down development is a better, or perhaps the only, strategy. On the other hand, the unfocussed, rudderless, bottom-up modalities are still mired in their cultural inanity and grassroots corruption. Wherever the two approaches are implemented as complementary to each other, bureaucratic morass, political shenanigans and professional arrogance kill the only hope that target groups and populations can have. India's five-year plans, their organization, implementation and outcomes come to mind to exemplify the latter. One finds a skewed, schizophrenic approach to practically every day-to-day issue.

The twenty-first-century world climate is marked with certain distinctive features. It is a multipolar, diverse and complex world of new forces that neither Locke nor Rousseau could foresee; although Hobbes perhaps did. New tribalism, terrorism and technologies have qualitatively changed the way we live, feel and act as members in different groups, organizations and societies. The most notorious caveman somewhere hiding in Pakistan is using Western methods to destroy all that the Western way of life stands for. The emergence of a counterstate as a veritable force has changed the meaning of social development. It is foolish to preach the gospel of dated ideologies in the abysmally dark cultures.

The iron law of social development has not been laid down yet. As a state without *order* leads to *anarchy*, a society without *justice* morphs into *chaos*. Likewise, development without democracy is a farce; democracy without development is hollow. Three elemental formulations will help develop NSD as a concept and reality: (1) "order" and "harmony" must coexist in a civil society; (2) "order" precedes "freedom"; and(3) "social justice" validates both "order" and "freedom." The lack of any of these elements promotes "de-developmentality" (Mohan 2007), which breeds unfreedom.

The top-down–bottom-up duality is a classificatory misnomer. Societies mired in their conundrums incubate de-developmental processes that promote violence and inequality. Hegemonic nation-building models have monumentally failed to uplift human well-being. *Avatar* may be a belated Hollywood fantasy, but it coveys eloquently the perils of territorial imperatives. It is not ignorance (of the blue monkeys fighting for their way of life); it is the arrogance of the corporate-military complex that imperils humankind. Horizons of NSD, though unquantifiable, are enshrined in a *dreamworld*[10] that nurtures only one race, the human race. Universalization of equality and justice, on the one hand, and annihilation of violence, war and disease, on the other hand, will go a long way to ensure NSD's substance, contours and contents. Difficult it may be, but it is not impossible if *rational-humane* considerations are allowed to play out ramifications of the postulated *Enlightenment II*.

NOTES

1. Expression owed to the Chinese historian Philip Huang (quoted by Zakaria 2008, 59)
2. Associate Press photo by Jens Dige in *The Advocate*, Baton Rouge, LA, December 19, 2009: 5A.
3. Ibid.
4. In *Charlie Wilson's War*, a flamboyant congressman's covert dealings in Afghanistan, reveals how politics of assisting rebels in their war with the Soviets have some unforeseen and long-reaching effects. Congressman Charlie Wilson concluded, "These things happened. They were glorious and they changed the world . . . And then we fucked up the endgame."
5. "Without realizing it, we have begun to wage war on the Earth itself. Now, we and the Earth's climate *are* locked in a relationship familiar to war planners: mutually assured destruction." Excerpted from Al Gore's speech accepting the Nobel for Peace.
6. http://www.cswe.org/CentersInitiatives/KAKI/KAKIResources.aspx (retrieved December 22, 2009).
7. The caption is owed to *London Review of Books* review of the same title (2009, 7).
8. NPR report on the development of Karachi as the world's leading urban centers (first week of June, 2008).
9. Aside from crossnational issues, micro-macro intrasocietal systems coalesce in compounding problems of variegated nature and dimensions. Drug abuse and addiction may be such a problem especially in the West. The violence against women in India is another puzzling paradox of a rising democracy. "From womb to grave, Indian women face increasingly violent forms of gender bias," reports India's national magazine, *Frontline* (January 4, 2008).
10. A contextual metaphor.

REFERENCES

345 arrested in child prostitution raids. 2008. *CBS News*. June 25. http://www.cbsnews.com/stories/2008/06/25/national/main4209831.shtml?source=RSSattr=HOME_4209831

Berry, W. 2008. Faustian economic: Hell hath no limits. *Harper's*, May: Vol. 316, No. 1986, pp. 35–42.

Boulding, K. 1967. The boundaries of social policy. *Social Work* 12(1): 3–11.

Chu, H. 2008. Delhi street children count on themselves. *Los Angeles Times*, June 7. http://www.latimes.com/news/nationworld/world/la-fg-bank7-2008-jun07,0,1688072,full.story

Community Services Council of Newfoundland and Labrador. 2003. Social development. http://www.envision.ca/templates/profile.asp?ID=56 (retrieved December 18, 2009).

Easterly, W. 2006. *The white man's burden: Why the West's efforts to aid the rest have done so much ill and so little good*. New York: Penguin.

Economist, The. 2009a. Softly, softly, charming Huckabee. December 12. Available at http://www.economist.com/world/united-states/displaystory.cfm?story_id=15065606

———. 2009b. The idea of progress: Onwards and upwards, 393, 8662. December 17: 37–40.

———. 2009c. The tyranny of the majority. December 17. http://www.economist.com/world/united-states/displaystory.cfm?story_id=15127600

———. 2009d. Better than nothing. December 19. http://www.economist.com/daily/news/displaystory.cfm?story_id=15124802 (retrieved December 23, 2009).

Estes, R. J. 2009. United States-based conceptualization of international social work education. Commission on Global Social Work Education, Alexandria, VA: Council on Social Work Education. 47.

Faludi, S. 2007. *The terror dream: Fear and fantasy in post-9/11 America*. New York: Metropolitan Books.

Fukuyama, F. 1989. The end of history. *National Interest*, Summer: 3–19.

Galtung, J. 1998. Foreword to *Ideas of social order in the ancient world*, by V. Harle. Westport, CT: Greenwood Press.

Gomez, J. 2007. A global trek to poor nations, from poorer ones. *New York Times*, December 27. http://www.nytimes.com/2007/12/27/world/americas/27migration.html?th=&emc=th&pagewanted=print

Haggard, S., and Kaufman, R. R. 2008. *Development, democracy and welfare states: Latin America, East Asia and Eastern Europe*. Princeton, NJ: Princeton University Press.

Hammer, J. 2007. *New York Times*, December 23. http://www.nytimes.com/2007/12/23/magazine/23kenya-t.html

Headrick, D. R. 2009. *Power over peoples: Technology, environments, and Western imperialism, 1400 to the present*. Princeton, NJ: Princeton University Press.

Hobhouse, L. T. 1924. *Social development: Its nature and conditions*. New York: H. Holt and Co.

Kagan, R. 2008. *The return of history and the end of dream*. New York: Alfred A. Knopf.

Kaufman, F. 2009. The end of sustainability. *International Journal of Sustainable Society* 1(4): 383–390.

Krauthammer, C. 2008. Reality limits democratic ideal. *The Advocate*, January 4: 7B.

Lyons, P. J. 2007. Benazir Bhutto and the politics of chaos. *New York Times*, December 28. http://thelede.blogs.nytimes.com/2007/12/27/benazir-bhutto-and-the-politics-of-chaos/index.html?th&emc=th

McClellan, S. 2008. *What happened: Inside the Bush White House and Washington's culture of deception*. New York: Public Affairs Book.

Mohan, Brij, ed. 1986. *Toward comparative social welfare*. Cambridge, MA: Schenkman.

———. 1988. *The logic of social welfare: Conjectures and formulations*. New York: St Martin's.

———. 1992. *Global development: Post-material values and social praxis*. New York: Praeger.

———. 2003. *Practice of hope: Diversity, discontent and discourse*. Philadelphia, PA: Xlibris (Random House).

———. 2005. *Reinventing social work: Reflections on the metaphysics of social practice*. Lewiston, NY: Edwin Mellen Press.

———. 2007. *Fallacies of development: Crises of human and social development*. New Delhi: Atlantic.

———. 2008. The development delusion. *Journal of Comparative Social Welfare* 24(1): 83–88.

———. 2009. Social intervention revisited: Toward a science of change. *Perspectives in Social Work* 24(2): 3–10.

———. *Poverty of culture: Development and delusion* (forthcoming).

New York Times. 2008. Politics and hunger. June 9. http://www.nytimes.com/2008/06/09/opinion/09mon1.html?_r=1&th&emc=th&oref=slogin#

Poniewozik, J. 2007–2008. The year of them. *Time*, December 31–January 7: 174.

Rasheed, A. 2008. *Descent into chaos: The United States and the failure of nation building in Pakistan, Afghanistan, and Central Asia*. New York: Penguin (Viking).

Rosin, H. 2008. American murder mystery. *The Atlantic*, July–August: 40–54.

Sen, A. 1999. *Reason before identity*. New Delhi: Oxford University Press.

Social work with guns: Andrew Bacevich on America's wars. 2009. *London Review of Books* 31(24), December 17: 7–8.

Stengel, R. 2007–2008. Choosing order before freedom. *Time*, December 31–January 7: 44–45.

Williams, J. 1993. Development involves extracting a clear picture. *International Herald Tribune*, October 4. http://www.iht.com/articles/1993/10/04/edjohn.php?page

Zakaria, F. 2008. *The post-American world*. New York: W.W. Norton.

12 Conclusions
Social Development into the Future

Manohar S. Pawar and David R. Cox

INTRODUCTION

In this chapter, we reflect on the content and core ideas presented in this volume and on social development into the future. While we are overall optimistic regarding the future of social development, field realities are often complex and contradictory, and call for the genuine commitment of people and their leaders at all levels. A value-oriented vision and actions are crucial in contemporary societies at local and global levels, and we believe that ideas inherent in social development offer opportunities for bettering lives and promoting universal development.

AN OPTIMISTIC FUTURE FOR SOCIAL DEVELOPMENT?

In the first chapter of this volume, we presented an approach to social development that we see as the emanation of decades of experience, analysis and thought by those committed to this area of practice. Although social development has seldom been presented as one overall comprehensive and integrated approach, which makes sense both conceptually and at the practice level, a careful reading of material—such as the Report on the World Summit on Social Development (UN 1995), where incidentally social development is not even defined; the annual *Human Development Reports* of the UNDP; and a large amount of other material—suggests that most of the points commonly made are, in general terms, consistent with the description of social development contained in Chapter 2. In essence, we present social development as a comprehensive and integrated approach to societal development. It is an approach that is multidimensional (at least economic, social, political, cultural and ecological), multilevel (at least local, national, regional and international) and value based (reflecting the values of equity, equality, social justice and those inherent in a human rights perspective).

For social development to be effective, locally and globally, it should reflect the aforementioned characteristics. Understandably, however, most of the field reality seldom reveals or even permits this comprehensive approach in any complete sense. Moreover, it is sometimes assumed that economic development, based on an economic growth model, is the basic requirement from which all else follows. Alternatively, some have assumed that if a particular model of governance is achieved, that governance system will ensure that all other aspects of development are addressed along appropriate value or ideological lines. Similarly, there are those who place their faith almost exclusively in, for example, national level development, or the establishment of better international structures and systems than have existed to date, or even a focus on people-centered or local community-centered development. Often, such limited emphases are due to an unwillingness to acknowledge, or an apparent inability to envision or address, that wide range of issues, tasks and levels that constitute social development. However, this is not to say that it is impossible to coordinate and build upon all such efforts, provided that the broader vision of social development exists, is understood and is followed.

In Chapters 2 and 3, we have addressed the local, community or grassroots level of social development, not because we place more emphasis on this level than on others, but because we believe that it is far too frequently overlooked in terms of its importance and potential. Experience suggests that even when, and perhaps especially when, other levels of development (especially the national) are floundering, it is often both necessary and possible for people at the local level to be enabled, by carefully devised and implemented policies and programs, to take significant responsibility for their own overall well-being—that is, collective as well as personal. Not only can this approach be beneficial locally; it may also feed into improvements in the social development situation at the national level.

Based on the approaches outlined in Chapters 2 and 3, but even more importantly on the range and depth of experience that underpins this overall approach, we are strongly optimistic that the adoption of social development as the basic overarching development strategy can result in significant and sustainable improvements in universal human well-being. In the 1980s and 1990s, it appeared that many nations and the international community might adopt social development as the guiding light in the struggle for universal improvements in peoples' quality of life. If this no longer appears to be so, we believe that it remains possible to recover this momentum and embrace what is universally, or at least widely, agreed to be the most acceptable paradigm for universal development.

RHETORIC AND ACTION IN THE IMPLEMENTATION OF SOCIAL DEVELOPMENT

While remaining essentially optimistic, we fully appreciate that social development is far from being a clear and straightforward concept or area of endeavor, this no doubt being the reason for its checkered and patchy history since development got under way in the aftermath of World War II. Social development has been questioned at the conceptual and theoretical level, and as a strategy for achieving what are commonly believed to be the goals of development, such as the reduction of levels of poverty, unemployment, illiteracy, infant and maternal mortality and exploitation, and an increase in the freedom to exercise a reasonable control over one's life. Nonetheless, with development often focused on the economic dimension, interpreted largely along Western lines, there has been a strong desire in many quarters to move this focus more toward comprehensive development, incorporating at least the social, legal and political dimensions alongside the economic one. More recently, the widespread awareness of significant ecological challenges has seen this broadly conceived development expanded to include a strong emphasis on the ecological dimension, or sustainable development. However, at the same time, it would seem that most political powers interpret the campaign against global warming, if indeed they accept this is to be happening, as addressing various aspects of economic processes by imposing certain restrictions on such as carbon emissions, instead of considering sustainable development in any overall sense.

The point is that, despite some rhetoric surrounding comprehensive development, the various issues—such as ongoing economic growth (a realistic assumption? [Easterly 2002]), good governance, combating or preventing global warming, promoting democracy, achieving free trade and providing immunizations against certain diseases—became discrete areas of endeavor. In this sense, programmatic development either replaces or sits alongside the project approach common in earlier decades. In this sense, development can become little more than a term embracing the identification of negative aspects of a society or locality and taking consequent action.

Our focus in this volume on local level, grassroots or bottom-up development results from several common conclusions, such as that top-down initiated development is sometimes nonexistent, as in states that have failed or are bordering on failure; that such top-down development as does exist often fails to reach many local areas; that the residents of many, and probably most, local areas have significant ability to engage in their own development, perhaps with a little outside assistance; and that many impoverished local areas are in great need of at least minimal developments to ensure survival and at least a minimal quality of life. However, we cannot afford to be naïve or unrealistic regarding this focus, as there can be many difficulties. For example, a central government, local war lords or a dominant elite may feel threatened by such endeavors; personnel may not be available to facilitate such developments; areas may simply be too impoverished or too remote; or a state may be so unstable that sustainable progress at the local level may stand little chance. Despite the often inherent difficulties, we remain disturbed that governments and development agencies continue, for a range of reasons, to give little emphasis to local level development.

This volume also recognizes the complexity of development as a process, emphasizing that the development process is seldom straightforward but that experience has demonstrated that the possibilities of success are enhanced by the incorporation into that process of certain characteristics. Examples discussed include the need to ensure that the beneficiaries of development are at the same time participants and contributors. Yet, as Chapter 4 points out, it is both easy and common for the initiators of development programs to give little more than lip service to this concept of participation. Truly participatory development will tend to be a slower, more uneven and less predictable process, even as donors and others are demanding conformity to certain accountability and time-line requirements. The idea, for example, that participants need to make mistakes and learn from them, and so experiment as they go, is often difficult for many development agencies to work with.

Alongside the perceived importance of participatory development, it is widely held that sustainable development should promote self-reliance—a concept that remains anathema to those many in authority who derive satisfaction from fostering and managing dependency (see Chapter 5). Similarly, a key aspect of successful development is seen to be capacity building (see Chapter 6). If people and organizations at the local or other levels are to take responsibility for their ongoing development, they may well need to grow in their capacity to do so, however capacity is defined or envisioned.

As a final example from this volume, as international and national agencies engage in development work, it has become common to see success as requiring the encouragement of a partnership approach. However, as Chapter 7 discusses, the term partnership tends to be used loosely to incorporate some very different realities. Generally speaking, it has become quite common for analysts of the development field to identify characteristics that are clearly beneficial in securing positive outcomes, to promote them and find them widely embraced in principle, but then to realize ultimately that they are very loosely or even inappropriately incorporated in practice.

In other words, those providing research-based leadership in the development field have striven to identify those approaches in the field that have produced the best results in developmental terms. Such approaches, however, often failed to conform to what development agencies regarded as best results in organizational terms; while certain levels or types of development aid demonstrated scant concern for processes seen as important in much of the field. This was particularly true, for example, of government-to-government aid, humanitarian and disaster-related aid, and aid directed at such as infrastructure development. It would be naive of us to assume that all development work was primarily concerned with outcomes that revolved around peoples' well-being or enhanced quality of life, at least in any direct sense and particularly at the local level.

The processes of development are varied and complex, perhaps even too varied and complex to be made the subject of any in-principle or even research-based imperatives. While the evidence would seem to suggest that all development should be, for example, participatory—promoting self-reliance, building capacities or partnership based—the diverse reality suggests that no such characteristics will be universal. There are circumstances where such are inappropriate, unrealistic or unacceptable, and we should accept this, while at the same time not negating the importance of incorporating such characteristics as and where circumstances do permit. The evidence shows that they are important characteristics, even if they are often difficult to implement; and it is essential that we get this message across to all engaged in development activities and encourage them to seek to maximize, in a situation-specific manner, the incorporation of these characteristics in their work.

SOME BROADER ISSUES

The processes of development work are clearly important to achieving sustainable outcomes in the field, but some contributors to this volume remind us that it is also important to stand back from the process at times and consider the broader picture. One aspect of the broader picture that is often neglected concerns the overall matter of development and welfare personnel. It is somewhat pointless to identify the needs and potential of remote areas, marginalized populations, female-headed households or persons with disabilities, to take some examples, and to proceed to the formulation of appropriate intervention strategies, as is often done, without ensuring that there are appropriately trained personnel able and willing to engage in such work. As discussed in Chapter 8, we are aware of a widespread shortage of personnel for many areas of social development and social welfare, and across the range of developed and developing countries. So often the media and others focus on such personnel as are in the field and the work they are doing, while ignoring the reality that such workers are few and far between. This applies both to very specific programs, such as community-based rehabilitation, and to broad or comprehensive social development programs within defined areas. Clearly, staffing in much of the very diverse social development and welfare areas is a significant problem in most countries. While overall numbers are generally low, which is the root of the problem, in addition such trained personnel as are available generally prefer to stay urban based, while areas like care of the mentally ill and fragile aged, and work in deprived and remote areas, are relatively unpopular. In reality, much welfare and development work is both challenging and poorly paid, greatly contributing to its unpopularity. So generally speaking, the upwardly mobile sectors avoid the whole field. Beyond this general shortage of personnel, there are issues such as the location and appropriateness of available courses offered by training institutions, especially in the social development area. Without a personnel strategy, our understanding of the development process becomes largely irrelevant if the personnel are simply not there to act on it.

Standing back from the development process even further, Chapter 10, on the ethics of social development, reminds us of the danger of assuming a particular ethical underpinning of development when the reality is much more complex. It is often said that the general aim of development is to enhance peoples' well-being, even though in reality, societal well-being, from various limited perspectives and benefiting only selective population sectors, is what is meant. This aim also assumes, however, that there is a clear and universally endorsed concept of well-being, which is clearly not the case. Much development was initially underpinned by a concept of modernization or Westernization that immediately circumscribed the meaning of well-being. Alternatively, development was aimed at bringing about a certain quality of life, but questions then arise such as was this concept dominated by consumerism in Western terms, or did it include such as social, communal and spiritual components? What is well-being?

Further, was well-being, however understood, a need possessed by people or a right that could be demanded by people? Needs-based and rights-based development have long posed alternative approaches to development in ethical or moral terms. Dean's chapter discusses also the distinction between the hedonic and eudaimonic notions of well-being, the former being concerned with pleasure, and the latter with ontological or spiritual well-being. Once again, the focus on the one understanding rather than the other could result in a significantly different approach to development. Who will make the decision on where to focus—the people, the government, specific institutions or development agencies? Given the potential importance of this and other such ethical distinctions, the question is a significant one, yet seldom addressed. The prevailing reality is, perhaps, that those responsible for program development and implementation simply get on with the task as best they can on a pragmatic level, leaving ethical and moral issues for others to ponder on.

It is possible to envision development that embraces the many dimensions and levels of any society within ideally an integrated approach, that reflects best practice in the field based on over fifty years of experience, and that rests upon an ethical system or set of rights that has formally been universally endorsed. At the same time, we must recognize that implementing such an approach within the diverse realities of the contemporary situation is extremely difficult. Among these realities are not only huge global diversity in many senses, but also professional specializations, the goals of for-profit organizations, the scourge of corruption negating demands for accountability, the common pressure to adopt the most straightforward approach despite often obvious weaknesses, the sheer complexity of the range of levels and structures involved, the range of personal motives and needs at the personnel level, the common shortage of resources, the frequent inadequacies of governmental structures and the common dominance of self-interest within a wide range of contexts. Such realities cannot be ignored, but does this mean that social development is one of those impossible dreams? Is the basic concept of social development inherently flawed, as the penultimate chapter in this volume might seem to suggest?

While Mohan's chapter suggests the need for a new social development model, we do not regard his suggestions as contradicting the approach to social development that we propose. Mohan is clearly right in pointing out that Enlightenment thinking, and the consequent reliance on science and reason, have failed to deliver well-being; that it is difficult to see evidence pointing to the existence of a family of nations working in harmony around universal interests; and that a "new social contract for global equality, universal justice and world peace" is called for if humanity is to survive. Social development, as we envision it, does require major changes to the paradigms that have dominated thinking throughout the modern era, especially in the Western world, and clearly these changes are occurring as some Western systems falter, newly emerging powers with their own cultures and systems present alternative approaches, and the world moves inevitably into a postmodern and more diversified era. Social development can, we believe, not only accommodate these changes but is in many ways based upon an endorsement of them.

GLOBAL AND NATIONAL PRIORITIES AND SOCIAL DEVELOPMENT

Apart from the complexities inherent in implementing social development as it is now widely conceived and accepted, and some broader problems around such as personnel issues and values, there remains the question of the priority given to social development within a context of competing, and potentially competing, priorities. Let us consider a few of these.

Given that the whole thrust of social development is toward achieving peace and security, it is extremely disappointing to witness the increased focus on building up military forces and armaments, the tendency to use war to pursue other goals in such places as Iraq and Afghanistan, the decision to combat terrorism through counterterrorism or a war on terrorism, the seeming inability to broker peace in for example the Israel–Palestine conflict and Somalia, and the largely ineffectual wars on drugs and international crime (Glenny 2008). Internationally, to at least some degree, and more often nationally in many cases, the priority seems to be to rely on military or military-like force to combat threats to national security or national interests, as if this were a demonstrably appropriate way of responding, thus leaving a number of nations with both limited resources and limited credibility for embarking on social development either at home or abroad. A recent media report that focused on the U.S. conveys some illustrations of the general problem being reflected.

Just before Christmas [Dec. 2009], US President Barack Obama signed into law one of his country's biggest aid pledges of the year. It was bound not for Africa or any of the many struggling countries on the World Bank list. It was a 10 year deal for US$2.77 billion to go to Israel in 2010 and a total of US$30 billion over the next decade, mainly to be spent on US military hardware.

According to work done by the Congressional Research Service, the US spent 17 per cent of the US total aid budget—or US$5.1 billion—on military aid in 2008, of which US$4.7 billion was grants to enable governments to receive military equipment from the US.

Between 2003 and 2009, a massive US$49 billion was poured into Iraq through the Iraq Relief and Reconstruction Fund and the defence budget. The Afghanistan program over the same period consists of US$11 billion in traditional foreign aid and another US$15 billion in defence funds.

Under the Obama Administration, the 2010 aid budget has been increased by 10 per cent to nearly US$50 billion to support his counter-terrorism strategy. The big increase is in assistance to Pakistan, which was recently given an additional US$1.5 billion a year for the next five years, tripling its aid. But it has been alleged that Pakistan has diverted elsewhere 70 per cent of the US$9 billion in military assistance paid since 2001. (Davies 2010)

Another priority in recent times, which culminated globally in the December 2009 summit in Copenhagen, was the strong possibility of a looming ecological crisis. The widely accepted phenomenon of global warming and its implications—such as widespread extreme weather events, along with the local and global impact of such as deforestation levels, the excessive exploitation or habitat destruction of many species to the point of extinction in some cases, and the high levels of pollution affecting health levels in many parts of the globe—are all examples of unsustainable and potentially disastrous abuse of our natural environment. The importance of the ecological dimension within social development has long been recognized. Within our integrated approach to social development, the emphasis is on, for example, the interaction of economic growth and ecological realities; the interaction of the size and location of urban centers and the ecology; the economic and social pursuits of people and the health of rivers, seas, wetlands, woodlands, and so on; and the development of transport systems in terms of their ecological impact. By contrast, the recent focus on global warming has been largely on limiting carbon emissions and promoting less polluting forms of energy. It is as if some modification of productivity systems, as distinct from lifestyle patterns and the organization of society (urban–rural balance, urban dimensions, transport systems, recreational patterns, etc.), would be a sufficient response to emerging ecological realities. This response seems to reflect the common emphasis on economic development, and the perceived importance of economic growth and technological solutions, in that, when economic, but also other aspects of, development threatens the ecology, the only obvious answer is to modify economic development by using economic mechanisms such as carbon trading or rebalancing technology by switching to alternative forms of energy supply. When such limited approaches to serious ecological issues are used, and pursued within a party political context nationally and a national interest context internationally, in contrast to a broader more objective social development approach nationally and globally, it is difficult to be optimistic about the outcomes.

One specific consequence of the ecological crisis in the near future is likely to be a food crisis. The ecological deterioration of significant areas of the land and seas has already resulted in the depletion of certain food supplies, while more frequent extreme weather conditions—droughts, floods, cyclones and extreme temperature days—are further reducing food supplies and undermining the viability of many primary producers. Despite widespread poverty and malnutrition levels, and the inflationary effects of food shortages and their implications, there remains little commitment in most quarters to confronting an almost certain pending food crisis. It would seem that an internationally organized and sanctioned system of food production and distribution—an essential aspect of social development globally—will be an essential component of universal food security if widespread suffering is to be avoided. A state-based, or even region-based, competition for scarce food-producing resources (land and water, etc.) and food products could have disastrous consequences for many people.

A further matter, related to both the general ecological situation and food supplies more specifically, is that of global population growth and distribution, allied inevitably to aspirations regarding standards of living and lifestyle. It seems inevitable that population growth from here on will exert significant pressures on a deteriorating environment, dwindling food supplies in many areas, and pressures to migrate, legally and illegally, to places perceived as more prosperous. If population growth rates and distribution patterns are to be left largely to natural processes, meaning that the fastest rates of growth will be in the poorest areas, then a focus on comprehensive social development will become ever more important. The alternative will be increasing inequalities in peoples' quality of life, as competition for essential but increasingly scarce resources, such as food, water and a healthy and secure environment increases, probably leading ultimately to a fight for survival between competing population groups.

These last two examples of food supplies and population growth are not so much a question of adopting an inappropriate priority as of giving insufficient direct attention to an essential aspect of overall social development, to the point where the consequences may become unacceptable and almost perhaps irreversible. Many see this as having occurred in regard to the impact of human activity on the environment, resulting in climate change and other ecological changes, and it may be happening in relation to food supplies and population growth.

In a way, the adoption of priorities with only limited consideration of the broader context, or the ignoring of an aspect of social development requiring some priority, while often understandable, are ultimately detrimental to overall social development. In some cases, this is because the priority itself detracts from social development. This is so, for example, with a focus on large military forces, enormous armament stockpiles and the pursuit of the resolution of national or group interests through conflict. In other cases, it is because it results in biased development. This is a consequence of, for example, a focus on urban development at the expense of rural development, or on excessive consumerism resulting in either the unnecessary and unsustainable exploitation of scarce resources or an unnecessary and deleterious impact on the environment—or both. In most cases, however, it is simply because social development, to be successful, requires a planned and integrated approach that balances the many interacting elements of, and factors pertaining to, the development process. Since priorities will probably always exist, ultimately it is a matter of pursuing those seen as essential on a short-term basis and then restoring equilibrium to the situation. This, however, requires a significant degree of objectivity and commitment on the part of those assuming leadership in the management of the development process, and some no doubt will regard this as unattainable.

REMAINING OPTIMISTIC ABOUT SOCIAL DEVELOPMENT

It will be clear by now to readers that social development, however conceptualized and presented, is not a blueprint for development at any level. Nor will its pursuit ever be easy in the face of complex realities, especially the form of comprehensive social development seen as necessary in Chapter 2. Human nature and power politics at all levels will probably result in an uneven development path, while prevailing and changing circumstances will regularly present major challenges. Nonetheless, if communities, societies and the international community have no vision, or only a vague one, of acceptable and effective goals and processes for development, then development will be largely determined by the outcome at any point of the struggle or conflict between competing interests and power groups, with little regard for the environment within which this takes place or for the best interests of outside and less powerful groups.

Despite this significant caveat, we remain convinced that social development, as it has evolved in recent times and as we have presented it in Chapter 2, provides an appropriate and essential paradigm for development, albeit one that will require regular monitoring and reinforcement (see also Cox and Pawar 2006). Some communities, nations and areas of international activity will always be open to implementing social development as depicted, while others will, for a variety of reasons, be experiencing difficulties that will need to be overcome to at least some degree before normal social development can proceed in any complete sense. Even then, however, recognition of the nature of social development may well guide the process of addressing presenting difficulties, at least in some quarters.

We need to move beyond continuing tendencies to distinguish between economic development, social welfare provision and social development, and to paying minimal respect to the need for sustainable approaches in each area of activity. Integrated comprehensive development along sustainable lines would seem to present the only viable pathway ahead, and we are optimistic that adherence to this goal is achievable and that an enhancement of human well-being will follow. Social development does not, however, envision the creation of utopias. It is inevitable, for example, that a degree of inequality will always exist, and that developmental responses to changing realities will tend to lag behind those changing circumstances, even in societies committed to social development, and that commitment will of course vary considerably, simply because neither systems of governance and structures for development, nor the people who staff them at any level, will be perfect. A degree of bias, corruption, inefficiency and inherent systemic limitations may temper social development outcomes in some contexts, and we must accept this as an aspect of the human condition.

At the same time, however, good outcomes in social development and in well-being terms call for vision, commitment and the best possible approaches to ongoing development. We believe that social development, as it has evolved and is buttressed by the human-rights regime and other commitments that are in place, provides this vision, although it needs to be more strenuously promoted and implemented. Moreover, over fifty years of development experience and the regular analysis and evaluation of much of this have provided us with models of, and approaches to, social development that are widely believed to have inherent within them a high possibility of success in terms of internationally endorsed objectives, such as the Millennium Development Goals. What is demonstrably still required is the necessary degree of commitment—commitment at all levels, including at least the local, national, regional and international. In this regard, we can already look to significant progress in a range of contexts, but not as yet sufficient to ensure widespread achievement of social development goals. Hopefully, however, that reality will characterize a new era ahead.

REFERENCES

Cox, D., and Pawar, M. 2006. *International social work: Issues, strategies and programs.* Thousand Oaks, CA: Sage

Davies, A. 2010. Record US aid goes on armaments: Billions to Israel, Egypt and Pakistan. *The Age*, January 1–2, 13.

Easterly, W. 2002. The elusive quest for growth: Economists adventures in the tropics. Cambridge: MIT Press.

Glenny, M. 2008. *McMafia: Crime without frontiers*. London: The Bodley Head, Random House

United Nations. 1995. *World summit for social development report*. New York: Author.

Contributors

Rufus Akindola is an honorary Research Fellow in the School of Philosophy, Anthropology and Social Inquiry at the University of Melbourne, Australia. Rufus graduated in journalism and worked briefly in Nigeria as a journalist before migrating to Australia. He also holds a PhD in International Development from the University of Melbourne; a bachelor's and a master's in social work from La Trobe University; and a graduate diploma in journalism from RMIT University, Australia. His research interests include poverty reduction, gender and development, governance, globalization, project management, monitoring and evaluation. Email: rufusba@unimelb.edu.au

Dr. Ingrid Burkett is vice president and Oceania representative on the board of the International Association for Community Development. Ingrid is also social innovations manager at Foresters Community Finance, Australia's only community development finance institution, where she manages the research and education program. Ingrid has researched and written extensively in the areas of community development, community economic development, community development finance, microfinance, social enterprise and social innovation. She has designed education and training programs for many local and international organizations, including Oxfam Australia. Ingrid also manages a community enterprise, Upatree Arts Co-operative, which is focused on community cultural development.

Dr. David R. Cox received his initial university education in arts and social work at the University of Melbourne, and his PhD at La Trobe University in the field of the sociology of migration. He worked in the refugee, migration and international social work areas for twenty years full-time, before beginning to teach in these fields in schools of social work in Melbourne, becoming professor of social work at La Trobe University in 1988, where he remained until 2001. During his teaching career, he carried out extensive fieldwork, largely with the UN/ESCAP and various NGOs. He has published two books in social work with immigrants, and over sixty monographs, research reports, book chapters and journal articles in his selected areas. Dr. Cox is married with two children, both currently working in the international field.

Marsela Dauti, MA, MSW, is a doctoral student at the George Warren Brown School of Social Work, Washington University in St. Louis. Marsela graduated from the State University of Tirana in 2003 with a BSW. She received her MA from Central European University and her MSW from Washington University. Marsela's research focuses on institutions, institutional processes and local development. Despite her prime interest on local development in central and eastern Europe, Marsela's work expands to Mongolia, China and India. Her research is supported by the Open Society Institute, Fulbright Program, and Center for New Institutional Social Sciences.

Hartley Dean is reader in social policy at the London School of Economics and Political Science. He began his career as a welfare-rights worker in Brixton, a deprived multiethnic inner-London neighborhood, before moving into teaching and academic research. His principal interests are social welfare and social rights, poverty and exclusion, and the survival strategies of marginalized social groups. His publications include *Social Security and Social Control* (Routledge, 1991); *Dependency Culture: The Explosion of a Myth,* with Peter Taylor-Gooby (Harvester Wheatsheaf, 1992); *Welfare, Law and Citizenship* (Prentice-Hall, 1996); *Poverty, Riches and Social Citizenship* (Macmillan, 1999); *Begging Questions: Street-level Economic Activity and Social Policy Failure* (ed.) (Policy Press, 1999); *Welfare Rights and Social Policy* (Prentice-Hall, 2002); *The Ethics of Welfare: Human Rights, Dependency and Responsibility* (ed.) (Policy Press, 2004); *Social Policy* (Polity, 2006); and *Understanding Human Need* (Policy Press, 2010). He is currently coeditor of the *Journal of Social Policy.*

Madhavappallil Thomas received his master's and PhD in social work. He has practiced the social work profession in the area of teaching, research and practice in various cultural contexts including India, Canada and the U.S. Currently, he works as an associate professor of social work at the Department of Social Work, California State University, Bakersfield. He teaches social welfare policy, research and practice courses for graduate students. His research interests include risk and resiliency in children, acculturative stress and social support, comparative social work education and social development themes. He has published on a variety of topics that have national and international reach and readership. He is very active in the professional and academic community in various capacities. Email:mthomas5@csub.edu

Brij Mohan is author, most recently, of *Fallacies of Development: Crises of Human and Social Development* (2007), *Reinventing Social Work* (2005) and *Unification of Social Work* (1999). Having served at Louisiana State University as a dean (1981–1986) and professor (1976–2009), he lately retired as professor emeritus. Dr. Mohan's original contributions to critical social theory have enhanced the development of social practice in many a field inclusive of social philosophy, mental health, comparative social development and international social work. *Journal of Comparative Social Welfare*, which he founded in 1981, is releasing a special volume to honor his fifty years in social work education (2010). Recently, the Mahatma Gandhi Kashi University, Varanasi, honored him with an honorary degree of Doctor of Letters (DLitt) for his outstanding achievements. NASW-LA Ch. awarded him a special Presidential Life Time Achievement Award, which has been given only once prior to his recognition. His forthcoming book, *The Poverty of Culture: Development and Delusion*, is due out shortly. Email: dialog@cox.net, swmoha@lsu.edu

Manohar S. Pawar is a professor of social work at the School of Humanities and Social Sciences, Charles Sturt University (CSU), Wagga Wagga, NSW, Australia. He is also an active research member of the Institute for Land, Water and Society, CSU. In addition, he is the president of the Asia-Pacific branch of the International Consortium for Social Development. He has over twenty-five years of experience in social work education, research and practice in Australia and India. Professor Pawar has received a number of awards, including the recent citation award for outstanding contributions to student learning (2008), from the Australian Learning and Teaching Council; he also received a Quality of Life Award (2001) from the Association of Commonwealth Universities. His current areas of interest include international social development, social work and social policy, social aspects of climate change and water, social work education, informal care and ageing, NGOs and community development. His recent publications, including co-authored works, include *Community Development in Asia and the Pacific* (Routledge, 2010); *International Social Work: Issues, Strategies and Programs* (Sage, 2006); *Data Collecting Methods and Experiences* (ed.) (New Dawn Press, 2004); and *Communities' Informal Care and Welfare Systems: A Training Manual* (CRSR, 2004).

Kwaku Osei-Hwedie is a professor of social work at the University of Botswana, Gaborone. He received his BA Summa Cum Laude with highest honors in sociology, and PhD in social welfare from Brandeis University, Waltham, MA; and postgraduate diploma in international law from the University of Zambia, Lusaka. He has taught at Brandeis

University; Virginia State University, Petersburg; St Paul's College, Lawrenceville, VA; and Makerere University, Kampala Uganda. He has held the position of deputy director of the Commonwealth Youth Development Programme, Africa Regional Centre in Lusaka. He has authored and coedited several academic works in the areas of social and community development; culture, indigenization and social work; youth development; and HIV and AIDS, among others.

Bertha Z. Osei-Hwedie is associate professor of international politics and chairperson of the Centre for Culture and Peace Studies at the University of Botswana, Gaborone. She received her undergraduate degree from the University of Zambia; master's in political science from Carleton University, Canada; and doctorate in politics from Brandeis University. She has also taught at St. Paul's College, Lawrenceville, VA, and the University of Zambia. Her research interests include state and development, Africa–Asia relations, developed–developing countries, regional cooperation and integration, democratization, HIV and AIDS, and culture and peace.

Mr. Alex Ruhunda is the director of Kabarole Research and Resource Centre (KRC); chairperson, Rwenzori Association of NGOs and Networks; chairperson, Uganda Governance Monitoring Platform; and current president of the International Association for Community Development (IACD). Mr. Ruhunda holds a bachelor's degree in social sciences and a master's in gender studies from Makerere University, Uganda. He also sits on a number of boards of charitable organizations, including Rotary International, where he serves as an assistant district governor, and the Deepening Democracy Program in Uganda, as an eminent Ugandan.

Gautam N. Yadama is an associate professor and director of international programs at the George Warren Brown School of Social Work at Washington University in St. Louis. A significant thrust of his work is concerned with understanding how natural resource dependent communities engage in the governance of resources and the conditions under which they are successful. As a Fulbright Professor in Nepal, he studied 150 urban neighborhoods in Katmandu and levels of collective action in the supply and maintenance of neighborhood quasi-public goods. He was a lead team member for the *Nepal Human Development Report* (2001), which won an award from the UN for its contributions to advancing Millennium Development Goals. In China, he is studying microinstitutional mechanisms for managing quasi-public goods. His current research in collaboration with Foundation for Ecological Security is applying system dynamics modeling to examine the dynamic complexity between human and natural resource systems in dry-land regions of India.

Index

Page numbers in **bold** refer to tables or figures; page numbers followed by n refer to notes.